JESUS LAND

JESUS LAND

STORIES FROM THE UPSIDE DOWN
WORLD OF CHRISTIAN POP CULTURE

JOELLE KIDD

Copyright © Joelle Kidd, 2025

Published by ECW Press
665 Gerrard Street East
Toronto, Ontario, Canada M4M 1Y2
416-694-3348 / info@ecwpress.com

All rights reserved. No part of this publication may be reproduced, stored in a retrieval system, or transmitted in any form by any process — electronic, mechanical, photocopying, recording, or otherwise — without the prior written permission of the copyright owners and ECW Press. The scanning, uploading, and distribution of this book via the internet or via any other means without the permission of the publisher is illegal and punishable by law. This book may not be used for text and data mining, AI training, and similar technologies. Please purchase only authorized electronic editions, and do not participate in or encourage electronic piracy of copyrighted materials. Your support of the author's rights is appreciated.

Editor for the Press: Jen Sookfong Lee
Copy editor: Kenna Barnes
Cover design: Caroline Suzuki

LIBRARY AND ARCHIVES CANADA CATALOGUING IN PUBLICATION

Title: Jesusland : stories from the upside down world of Christian pop culture / Joelle Kidd.

Names: Kidd, Joelle, author.

Description: Includes bibliographical references.

Identifiers: Canadiana (print) 20250140438 | Canadiana (ebook) 20250140950

ISBN 978-1-77041-779-3 (softcover)
ISBN 978-1-77852-392-2 (ePub)
ISBN 978-1-77852-393-9 (PDF)

Subjects: LCSH: Popular culture—Religious aspects—Christianity. | LCSH: Christianity in mass media.

Classification: LCC BR115.C8 K53 2025 | DDC 261—dc23

This book is funded in part by the Government of Canada. *Ce livre est financé en partie par le gouvernement du Canada.* We acknowledge the support of the Canada Council for the Arts. *Nous remercions le Conseil des arts du Canada de son soutien.* We would like to acknowledge the funding support of the Ontario Arts Council (OAC) and the Government of Ontario for their support. We also acknowledge the support of the Government of Ontario through the Ontario Book Publishing Tax Credit, and through Ontario Creates.

PRINTED AND BOUND IN CANADA   PRINTING: MARQUIS   5 4 3 2 1

Purchase the print edition and receive the ebook free.
For details, go to ecwpress.com/ebook.

For Jon,
My life with you is heaven on earth.

CONTENTS

INTRODUCTION 9

CHAPTER ONE	Wow, Not What I'd Call Music	17
CHAPTER TWO	Boy's Bible, Girl's Bible	31
CHAPTER THREE	Jesus at the Box Office	66
CHAPTER FOUR	Pledges and Purity Rings	102
CHAPTER FIVE	Declarations of War	140
CHAPTER SIX	First There Was Nothing, and Then It Exploded	172
CHAPTER SEVEN	The Root of All Evil	210
CHAPTER EIGHT	Clean Comedy	244
CHAPTER NINE	Armageddon Outta Here	277

SOURCES 317

ACKNOWLEDGEMENTS 341

INTRODUCTION

It's strange the responses you garner when you tell strangers, friends, and new acquaintances that you're writing a book about "evangelical Christian pop culture of the 2000s." Some people will stare at you blankly or ask what that means. Some people will express bafflement that there exists even such a thing as "Christian music" (oh sweet, secular friends). Memorably, I terrorized my entire masters program workshop with the musical impressions of Chris Rice (see chapter one). And at least one person—okay, my dad—responded with, "No offense, but is anyone going to read that?"

Admittedly, it is a niche topic—but not as niche as one might think. Because just as often, when I reveal the topic of my book, the other person's eyes go wide. They know exactly what I'm talking about. They, too, can still remember every lyric to their favourite Relient K song, had a subscription to *Brio*, or rocked a rubber Livestrong bracelet that read *Jesus Is King* or *Live for Him*. Like anyone with experience of a niche subculture, finding a fellow former peer is a weird kind of homecoming. I can't explain to you the ecstatic feeling of singing about talking to tomatoes and having a new friend chime in with the next line. If you know, you know.

My entry into the world of Christian pop culture came along when I started at a Christian school in 1999. As the millennium rounded the corner, I was learning not about Britney and Justin, or stars of reality TV and the then-nascent internet, but about pop groups who sang about Jesus, books that spun "inspirational" fiction out of Christian lives, and movies that splashed stories from the Bible onto the screen.

At the time, these products and media were simply another thing to get used to in my new school, in my new life. At times they seemed corny, at times fun. But like many in my age bracket in Canada and the United States who grew up in evangelical culture, my worldview and politics came to radically clash with those of this faith subculture I was raised within. Today, when I look back on the 2000s pop culture of evangelical Christianity, I see something dangerous: The subtle (or at times, very loud) messages of shame and hatred that were carried under a sugary-sweet coating. I can't help but see the interweaving of that pop culture with the politics of the time—leaders using evangelical beliefs and culture to promote warmongering, homophobia, and Islamophobia—just as I can't help but trace that legacy to the conservative political movements in North America today that are currently clawing back women's healthcare, denying the effects of COVID-19, and attacking 2SLGBTQIA+ rights.

This, for me, was the impetus of this project: to return to and reappraise the pop culture that shaped the way I saw my own faith, the way I learned to believe (or not) what it seemed I was meant to.

WHO ARE EVANGELICALS?

Throughout this book, I use the term "evangelical" to categorize the kind of Christianity that I'm talking about—namely, the kind that makes these pop culture products.

Christianity is a big tent; a religion segmented into hundreds of sects over thousands of years. At the same time, it's a nebulous title: Everyone who calls themself a Christian has some belief that their version of Christianity is the truest way to believe.

Evangelicalism, however, is a particularly North American subculture born originally out of the Great Awakening in 18th century colonial America. A 2016 study by Wheaton College estimates that 30 to 35 percent of the U.S. population (90 to 100 million people) consider themselves to be evangelical, and nearly half of Americans consider themselves Protestant Christians. This population is present in Canada as well. According to the 2021 census, 53.3 percent of Canadians consider themselves to be Christians, with 12.3 percent of the population identifying as part of different Protestant denominations.

Part of the difficulty of quantifying evangelical Christians is that this term is not strictly defined, nor is it a centralized denomination with a single governing body. What is clear is that those churches, denominations, and organizations that identify themselves as evangelical share a foundational belief in the importance of evangelizing, that is, converting others to Christianity. The necessity of this project is drawn from Jesus's Great Commission in Matthew 28 to "go and make disciples of all nations." The "mission" of evangelism is what perhaps makes evangelicalism so suited to the creation of popular culture, as the media created is used as a tool to "win souls" or "share the Gospel." Since the motivation is to missionize, it stands to reason that Christian media would mimic popular culture, maybe even try to break into that mainstream, in an effort to get as many eyes and ears as possible on the "good news."

In his book *Evangelicals Incorporated*, religious historian Daniel Vaca argues that commodification is not something that has *happened* to evangelical Christianity, but it is inherent to it on a foundational level as a religion structured along the lines of a capitalist enterprise. For evangelicalism, the closest thing to the kinds of governing bodies at play in other sects of Christianity is the National Association of Evangelicals in the U.S., which was founded in 1942, an interdenominational body that aims to cultivate "common purpose" among this loosely defined group—even this organization, Vaca says, operates more like a trade association than a form of church governance.

"Despite evangelicals' frequent claims that the Bible is the source of their social and political commitments, evangelicalism must be seen as a cultural and political movement rather than as a community defined chiefly by its theology," scholar Kristin Kobes Du Mez argues in her book *Jesus and John Wayne*. Writer Daniel Radosh agrees, pointing out in his book *Rapture Ready!* that the evangelical framework offers no distinction between culture and theology in practice:

> While I would make a distinction between a ritual object and a consumer one, in the evangelical mind, the blending of religion and pop culture is itself a form of religious practice. The biblical foundation of evangelicalism is the Great Commission.... By definition, evangelicals engage with the culture at large. Paraphrasing John, evangelicals often protect their faith by sealing themselves off from society not tailoring their faith to society's rules. That's the philosophy at least. In practice, almost all do a little of both.

While the bounds of evangelicalism are somewhat nebulously defined, its politics are easy to see: These are the socially conservative, nationalist, and reactionary beliefs exemplified by figures like Jerry Falwell, Pat Robertson, and James Dobson. The political activism led by these and other prominent evangelical figures became central to Christian pop culture, creating young Christians whose faith was served to them entangled with issues like abortion, abstinence-only education, creationism, and "homosexuality." This is not to say that individual churches that identify as evangelical can't also be politically progressive. There are plenty of individual queer-affirming evangelical congregations in North America (for instance, the Metropolitan Community Church denomination which has been running since the 1970s),[*] and Christians who identify as evangelical hold a wide range of individual views. Likewise, there are plenty of mainline or non-evangelical churches that hold conservative political views—they just tend not to make and market mass media products.

Similarly, the consumer-marketing machine that creates Christian pop culture also bred a subculture deeply lacking in racial diversity. Both Vaca and Radosh have noted this, with Radosh calling Christian pop culture "an almost exclusively white affair." This held true in my experience of 2000s Christian pop culture, as well as the 2000s Christian church. For me growing up, Christianity was overwhelmingly white—not because only white people are Christian (in fact, then as now, the most quickly growing segments of Christianity were communities of colour) but because Martin Luther King Jr.'s oft-quoted observation of Sunday morning as "the most segregated hour in America" seems to have held true well into the 2000s, if not still to this day.

Y2K FOR JESUS

The first decade of the 2000s comprised almost exactly my time at Christian school, and therefore it was my most in-depth interaction with the world of Christian pop culture. Accordingly, in this book, I've elected to discuss mainly media produced between 2000 and 2009.

I've come to see this era as a particularly interesting one for Christian pop culture. The 2000s represent the peak of Christian

---

[*] Linda Kay Klein, *Pure*, p. 282.

retailing, just before the internet heralded the decline of brick-and-mortar and related industries, like music and publishing. This was a decade of peak profitability for Christian corporations, when the production of this media had been refined into a seamless machine.

It was also a time when Christianity broke through to the mainstream. Writing in 2008, Radosh notes that "not long ago, virtually the only places to buy Christian books, music, and gifts were Christian bookstores . . . These days, roughly half of all Christian goods are bought at stores like Wal-Mart, Barnes & Noble, and Amazon.com. With the attention from mainstream retailers, sales of Christian products jumped 28 percent between 2002 and 2005." Culturally, it was a decade of cross-over hits, from bands like Switchfoot and Jars of Clay making it onto the secular charts to teen stars like Jessica Simpson and the Jonas brothers spreading their Christian message on MTV and the Disney Channel. It was the decade when a Jesus movie, *The Passion of the Christ*, became a global blockbuster, and a family from a niche, right-wing evangelical sect, the Duggars, became reality stars.

It was also a decade that I so often see reflected in what's happening right now. It was the decade when an anti-abortion stance was elevated as a tentpole evangelical issue; when a U.S. president was seemingly elected on the strength of the evangelical vote; when the foundations were laid for a push toward Christian nationalism in the U.S. and Canada; when Christianity waged a reactionary war against advancing 2SLGBTQIA+ rights; when there was a spike in legal challenges to evolution in science curricula and the start of an upward trend in homeschooling. So often in my research, when I expected to uncover relics of the past, I instead found material that felt all too prescient. Just like the comeback of spaghetti straps and low-rise jeans, the 2020s seem to be cycling back into the same political territory.

MINING THE PAST

I conducted several different forms of research in writing this book. In the notes and citations for each chapter, you'll see research material around historical and factual claims and primary sources for the pop culture I've revisited throughout. I also drew on my personal history and memories in places. Here, I have done my best to accurately relay events as they happened, allowing for the slippages of memory and time that we all are prone to. Names and identifying characteristics of friends and family members have been changed in the interest of privacy. I also conducted a number of interviews for the chapter "Pledges and Purity Rings"; respondents' names and identifying characteristics have been removed to anonymize those accounts.

As someone who spent a long time steeped in this culture and has always practiced some version of faith, I have tried to be attentive in these pages both to the honest and profound depth of belief that one's religion represents as well as my questions, doubts, and concerns about how Christianity, in its own pop culture, is practiced and played out in today's wider political landscape.

I've read many books in the course of my research by "outsiders" to the subculture who attempt to put aside the question of faith when discussing Christian pop culture. But in my view, those two things can never really be separated. When I am critiquing the cultural output of this religion, yes, I am to some degree critiquing the religion as well because if you're going to organize your life around something, do you really want that something to be a way for rich mega-pastors to sell Bible-verse-laced diet books, or for multinational corporations to hawk cheaply made Jesus tchotchkes?

I'm sure there are times when my balancing act in this regard might tip a little too far in either direction, but I hope readers will understand my attempt to address such a large and strange topic with both empathy and levity.

While I hope these essays uncover some of the more uncomfortable truths about Christian pop culture, looking back now, I still see something "pure" in these things—not in the moral sense, but in the strange human way common to most subcultures. The way that people build castles in the air—and pretty elaborate ones at that—based on their shared systems of community and belief, an act that carries joy for the people involved. The enjoyment I took in some of these songs, movies, books, and more as a child was real, even if it had an asterisk next to it.

Growing up, I was taught by pastors and teachers that the role of a Christian was to be "in the world, but not of it," which meant to participate in society, to live amongst others, but not to be swayed by "earthly" things. However, this didn't square with the evangelical culture I saw around me, which seemed to replicate the world almost precisely while being strangely removed from it: retaining all the trappings of capitalism, popular aesthetic trends, and the forces of patriarchy and racism, but delivering it all with a Christian twist.

In the Bible, Jesus calls heaven an "upside-down kingdom" where all power structures are inverted, and the social order is the opposite of what one might expect after a lifetime of living on Earth. Christian school couldn't quite achieve that. It was more like a funhouse mirror—regular secular culture, but a little distorted. Similarly, the self I look back on is one I don't quite recognize, one who was stretched and pulled out of shape for a little while. But eventually, you get to leave the carnival. These essays are my attempt to relive those cultural touchstones with the clarity of time.

CHAPTER ONE

WOW, NOT WHAT I'D CALL MUSIC

THE STRANGE MIRROR WORLD OF CHRISTIAN POP

I was seven years old when my family moved back to Canada. We'd only been away for three years, my dad filling out a term with an international accounting firm. But at the time, that was half my life—most of what I'd experienced of how the world worked had occurred an ocean away, in Bratislava, Slovakia.

I came back in a daze of mild culture shock. It was a strange thrill to wander through the mall and be able to understand the conversations around me, to read all the signs in English. We slept on mattresses on the living room floor in the townhouse my parents had rented, waiting for our transatlantic-shipped furniture to catch up with us. In the mornings, I excitedly flipped through the unfamiliar channels of Canadian TV.

On a family member's recommendation, my parents enrolled my brother and me in a Christian private school located in a rich neighbourhood at the edge of Winnipeg's south-end suburbs. It was small, hadn't been around for very long, and was recommended as being full of nice families and caring teachers. When I asked as an adult why they chose a Christian school, my parents said they wanted their kids to have "good influences." They were worried, probably because I was a quiet, shy sort of kid, that I'd be bullied or easily peer-pressured in public school, and as religious people themselves, they thought a Christian school seemed a more trustworthy place to turn their child over to for seven hours a day.

We got a tour of the school, and I had an interview with the principal. She was a sweet, plump woman with fluffy blond hair. She led us through the halls, which smelled of floor wax and citrus cleaner. Salmon-pink walls were set with rows of cubby holes and coat hooks, bulletin boards crowded with elementary-student artwork. She showed us through a hallway draped with construction tarps where we could peek into a building expansion—the school was getting a fancy new gym where the high schoolers could play basketball and volleyball.

The school was inside a Baptist church, and the building was a kind of Frankensteined half church, half school. I'd never seen a church so big, or so shiny and corporate-looking. The back half, where we'd entered, had a playground and a flagpole, wide doors and an office; a stark contrast to my previous school, a blocky concrete building with bars on the windows. The church half had a big cross and, out front, one of those sign boards where you can move the letters, advertising the church's sermon series. The floors in that front half were carpeted, and there was a big lobby and a main auditorium, lined with cushioned pews facing toward a stage. I was overwhelmed by how wide and spacious everything felt, moving from a European scale to a Canadian one. My family had always gone to church, so the markers of Christianity were familiar, but I'd never seen them appear this way: Bible verses on colourful printed posters or Jesus fish clamped to the bumpers of the cars in the parking lot.

♥ † ♥

The culture shock continued when school started. I was self-conscious that I was a year younger than everyone else, having started in the British school system in my international school, which skipped kindergarten. Where we'd all found a secluded corner of the classroom to change before gym class at my old school, I learned that boys and girls were separated in this new school, crowded into the church's washrooms. I discovered that Canadian kids had learned to visualize math with little tiles and squares, and I had learned some archaic British method of stacking numbers. And then there was the confusing stuff that had nothing to do with school.

I hadn't been totally cut off from pop culture while living in a different country—in fact, since one of the only English-language channels we got on our television was MTV, my family was weirdly up to date on music. I'd seen the popular animated movies aimed at my age group—sometimes dubbed into Slovak, but still—and was still mourning the collection of Disney tapes I'd sadly had to relinquish since they wouldn't work in a Canadian VCR. Hell, the Mary-Kate and Ashley fan club even delivered to Eastern Europe.

But none of this was preparation enough to fit in with my new social set. There was an entirely distinct world to which I'd not been privy: evangelical pop culture. And its greatest ambassador was Christian music.

I observed a strange phenomenon in my new school: Whenever someone mentioned a musician, artist, or band, the first response would be, "Are they Christian?" I decided I needed to learn who was Christian and who wasn't. This was apparently an important part of knowing about famous people.

When my family lived in Slovakia, we attended a Lutheran church. It was less than a decade after the Velvet Revolution turned over control from the religiously restrictive Communist Party. I'm guessing that was why the church was accessed by a tiny door in a back alley. Walking through that alley felt somber, automatically reverent. Inside was a hushed, ornate sanctuary with a pulpit set high in the wall. I never really understood what was happening or what the sermons were about, but I still remember the peaceful feeling I had in that sanctuary, where music bounced back in echoes and grown-ups sat in straight-backed lines on wooden pews; where Advent candles quivered in the darkness; where, for Christmas, the pastor gifted me a delicate corn-husk doll in the shape of an angel, complete with a tiny wooden flute and a twist of jute in a halo around its head.

Later, back in Canada, we attended a small neighbourhood Mennonite church where every hymn was sung in four-part harmony and every get-together was a potluck. The atmosphere was different, but it felt comfortable, homey. There was a simple, backlit wooden cross at the front and rows of mismatched pews. The building smelled like old wood and new paint. Again, I had trouble focusing on the sermons, but I understood the important rituals—like Coffee Time, when the adults stood around laughing loudly and the kids raced each other through the basement. I was proud when it was my turn to take on a job that rotated between kids in the church: standing next to the overhead projector during Worship Time and switching out the transparencies that held the lyrics to the songs everyone was singing.

These expressions of Christianity seemed to convey the only two elements of the faith that still hold any remaining sway over me: The first, an ancient, sacred solemnity; the second, a down-to-earth sense of community. As I've grown, through all the shifts and transformations in my personal sense of "faith" (and what that even means to my life), I've never failed to see at least some sense of value in those two elements of religion. On the one hand is the reminder of something larger than yourself, something that stretches thousands of years into history; on the other is the opportunity to connect tangibly in the here and now to the place and people in which you are situated. Both of those things feel spiritual to me, and Christianity, though not the only way in, was the first time I experienced either feeling.

Oddly, though, it was the trappings of evangelicalism that, despite slick attempts to imitate secular coolness, always threw me into existential dread. Christian pop is like the uncanny valley of music—almost, but unsettlingly not quite. It's a passable, or even quality, imitation, but it's closeness to that thing actually makes it stranger. For me, the dread came into play when I began to question the larger meaning—when I thought about an omnipotent God looking down from on high and seeing Himself reflected in these small, much too human ways.

In the car on the way to school, my mom had started listening to CHVN 95.1, the local Christian radio station. Their logo had a halo hovering over the C. There was a strange song playing constantly that year called, "Cartoons." In retrospect, this might have been the perfect introduction to both the world of Christian music and to the evangelical sense of humour that I would have to learn to navigate. I'm not sure how to describe this song other than to say the premise is simply three straight minutes of impressions of different cartoon characters saying the word "Hallelujah," (*yabba-dabba-loo-yah . . . Scooby-dooby-doo-yah . . .*) kind of jammed into a melody.

In my recollection, my mom chuckled at this song the first few times she heard it, but after weeks of the onslaught, she'd groan at the opening chords and flip to another channel.

I accepted CHVN as a fact of our new life in Canada, the way you do in childhood, often accepting what happens around you to be some rule of nature—in Canada, everyone listens to the Christian station. At some point in our first year back in the country, I remember overhearing my mom telling a friend she'd been listening to Christian radio. "It's kind of weird," she had said. "It's like every song is a Christian version of a normal pop song."

I was confused by her lack of allegiance to Christian radio. I'd thought it was always on in the car because she was a fan, but it seemed she had been listening to CHVN for my benefit. She wanted to shelter her kids from secular pop, which she often complained was "all about sex." Maybe she thought my young ears were safer sticking with *yabba-dabba-loo-yah*.

Her eccentric CD collection was mostly crooning female singer-songwriters, Tracy Chapman and Dolores O'Riordan of The Cranberries. She would put them on in the car or load them into the rotating six-disc slot of our home stereo system to play while she went about her day, humming quietly along. In Slovakia, my parents didn't own Christian music, other than a compilation of Slovak Christmas carols my mom had bought at Tesco. Even though my parents read me Bible stories and took me to church every week, I hadn't necessarily thought of faith as fundamentally intrinsic to my family's identity but simply as one element of who we were. Christian school disabused me of this notion: Being a Christian, I learned, was supposed to be *your whole life*. What's more, there were *Good Christians* and *Bad Christians*, and you could know one or the other by how they dressed, how they spoke, if they swore, if they drank, how good they were at praying out loud—and what music they listened to.

♥ † ♥

I found myself a best friend on my first day at Christian school, and I didn't even have to do anything. The teacher stood me and the other new kid up at the front of the class and asked for two volunteers, one for each of us, to show us around.

A little girl in a white turtleneck shot her hand up to volunteer to be my friend, and there we were. I was fascinated by her turtleneck which had tiny pink flowers all over it, and her teal corduroy pants, which matched her little round glasses. I'll call her Angela.

Angela was my access into Christian Land and my first instructor in Christian Music Appreciation. Her family not only listened to CHVN, but they also bought CDs of Christian music from the Christian bookstore. And she somehow knew all about the musicians themselves. On the playground, in the classroom, on the soft carpeted floor of her bedroom, she'd tell me all about them. She'd learned some makeup tips from Point of Grace. "Always use lip liner before you put on lipstick," she instructed me, despite the fact that we were both too young to have ever worn lipstick. Too many questions flooded my brain—what's lip liner? How did she get this information? Did she subscribe to a magazine? Was there a lip liner club, like the Mary-Kate and Ashley fan club? Who was Point of Grace? I couldn't decide which to ask so I just nodded, absorbing this information as best I could.

I was an eager student but not a very good one. My mom bought a Point of Grace CD, and I tried listening to it, but the songs all blurred together in a wash of gospel-influenced harmonies and smooth, easy-listening backing tracks. I paged through the liner notes; they all kind of looked like my mom and her friends, with layered haircuts framing their faces and comfy button-up shirts in different blue tones. I stared at their lips, trying to figure out if they were "lined."

Confronted with so much newness, I became unwilling to ask questions, worried that I'd betray my lack of knowledge and look stupid. I thought I could just blunder my way through, observe what everyone else was doing and try to copy it, like a newbie at a dance class where everyone else had been studying the choreography for years.

Maybe that's why, even though I know, intellectually, that I spoke a lot in those first years back in Canada, my voice isn't contained in my memories. I was a quiet kid but not as quiet as I remember. I remember conversations with my classmates where I can almost hear their little voices still imprinted on my brain, but my half is blank—I know I must have said something, but that piece of the tape is empty. I remember the sensation of feeling detached from my body—not outside myself exactly but *too far in*, as though I were a very small version of myself, sitting far back inside my own head, piloting my body. Was it because I was merely parroting back what they said, or trying to figure out what they wanted to hear? I had no idea how I felt about anything that was happening to or around me; I was only preoccupied with figuring out how I was supposed to react. Maybe that's why I can't remember anything I said—I wasn't really saying anything at all.

♥ † ♥

Music was one of the only things that really made me feel Christian. Not the hits on Christian radio, but church music. As a kid, I spent most of church playing tic-tac-toe on the Sunday bulletin with my brother, but I always loved the musical part of the service. Standing and unleashing your voice, part of an amateur chorus of warbling harmonies, felt good. I liked trying to sight-read along with the hymnal and choruses where the worship leader divided the church into sections and made us sing in a round.

All my fond memories of church involved music. I was always bored by the recitation of Bible passages in odd, formal language, and the drone of a sermon rarely held my attention no matter how hard I tried to listen closely. But at every church I attended, I loved the singing: Somber organ songs, old-school hymns, or cheesy choruses were all fine by me. Even as a toddler, I perched happily on various laps in my grandparents' vaguely hippie-ish house church. My memories are a blur of shaggy beards and acoustic guitars, but the songs—the one comparing love to a magic penny, the one about being a joyful servant—remain lodged in my brain.

At school, the music wasn't as good. At our elementary school services, which opened the school day three times a week, Worship Time consisted of a gym teacher placing a boom box on the stage in front of us and pressing Play. We sang along to the canned music, songs like "Our God Is an Awesome God," and "(The Bible Is the) L-I-G-H-T," all of which had elaborate ASL-inspired actions choreographed along with them.

Still, the kind of Christianity I was encountering at Christian school, I assumed, must be *real* Christianity, the kind of faith that made you a Good Christian. I worried about how little I felt, emotionally, during these assemblies; chastised myself for letting my mind wander, for being bored. When music was good,

I thought it felt the way religion was supposed to feel: like ecstasy, like the world was cracking open to reveal some grander meaning, some outsized, omniscient truth.

I wanted to be a good Christian, and I certainly didn't want to go to hell. But I was confused about why holiness didn't seem to be coming as easily to me as to others. A few years into my Christian school experience, in Grade 6, I acutely remember the drudgery of a particular 45 minutes spent sitting on the band room floor, listening to a guest speaker drone through a sermon, the subject of which I had somehow forgotten before the talk was even over. My mind drifted the entire time. I was planning future craft projects, mentally finishing my homework, wondering what was for dinner that night. In the service the next morning, another student got up to share how affected she'd been by the brilliant, powerful sermon the day before. She stood at the front of the room, holding the mic and explaining to us all how she'd seen two angels in the room, hovering over the speaker's head. Beaming almost beatifically, she pointed to the corners of the band room where the angels had been: "There and there," she said, breathlessly.

I was baffled and ashamed. I'd been in that same room, sitting a few feet away from her! But not only had I not seen the angels, I'd been so unmoved by the sermon that I hadn't retained a single word. Was I so obtuse that all sorts of mystical things were simply passing me by? Perhaps I should have been suspicious of the girl's vision, could have questioned whether there had really been angels, whether she thought she saw them or had just made it up, or even why she was the only one who could see anything out of the ordinary. But at the time, that would have felt like a betrayal. To me, my obliviousness could only be construed as failure to be a Good Christian.

♥ † ♥

Perhaps that was why I fixated on understanding Christian music. Throughout elementary school, I dutifully applied myself to try and find Christian music I liked, though I didn't have much luck. My friends were into the Christian versions of boy bands and girl groups. There were Christian sound-alikes of Britney and Christina, and then there were those Hanson boys, who were secretly Christian but played on the normal radio. Stacie Orrico, Jaci Velasquez, Rebecca St. James—it all blended together.

Angela loved a band called Superchick. In a nostalgic mood, I recently visited SongMeanings.com to remind myself of the (to me, entirely befuddling) lyrics of their song "Barlow Girls." As a kid, I'd been confused by a line in the song that references boys finding girls attractive . . . if they resemble their mothers. Online, none of the commenters—the most recent of which made their contribution in 2006—seem to have the same hang-ups I do about dating a boy who says you remind him of his mom. "It's good that some artists are making songs about NOT having sex," one commenter muses. Another wrote in 2002, "When i first hear [sic] this i phreaked out!! I was like OMiGOSH!! thats me!!!! this is an awesome song." I was struck by a sudden memory of typing "OMiGOSH" into an MSN Messenger window, carefully making sure to emphasize that I was not taking the Lord's name in vain through a sinful "OMG." Feeling overwhelmed by the cringeworthy nature of this memory, I decided to leave the site.

In a video now available on YouTube of the 2003 Dove Awards (an annual awards program by the Gospel Music Association of America), Superchick performs this song live. The video looks like something I'd make up to explain how weird Christian music is, almost a parody of itself: squeaky-clean rockers bouncing around on stage, layering their pop-punk guitar riffs with lyrics about abstinence. The singer's blond hair is elaborately gelled into a spiky faux-hawk, she has a thick choker necklace, and she's wearing a skirt over leather bell-bottom pants. She's gorgeous, with big eyes and scarlet-red lips. But something about her looks too

... nice. She has no piercings, and she won't let her smiling face collapse into a snarl or a frown, even as she sings. And her studded, bedazzled tank top, where some punk message might be printed, reads only: ROCK.

♥ † ♥

Angela also introduced me to the band Jump5, a pop group of five squeaky-voiced, blond Christian kids. She particularly loved the song "Spinnin' Around," which was ostensibly about God but just sounded like a love song and could therefore be easily applied to whatever blond, squeaky-voiced Christian kid in our class she had developed a crush on.

Jump5's music videos, available heavily pixelated on YouTube, are pretty standard preteen fare. The five of them bop around in brightly coloured outfits, the camera toggling between framing elaborate choreography and individual shots of quirky, cutesy action—picking the petals off a flower, riding a carousel or bumper cars, climbing over jungle gyms. The style couldn't be more early 2000s—tiny round coloured glasses! Frosted tips! Skinny scarves! Skirts over jeans!—but they are also clearly putting out a more chaste version of pop stardom. Their choreography is unsexy to the point of being almost robotic, nary a body roll in sight. They give the camera big, goofy smiles instead of pouty looks, and the girls are permitted only a little bit of shoulder-baring.

They do have one Unique Selling Proposition, as a marketing exec might put it, which is that they can do backflips. In most videos, some or all of them—it's hard to keep track with the grainy quality—particularly the boys, are flying around like circus acrobats, flipping and wheeling through the air with abandon.

I remember Angela conscripting me and several other girls into making up a choreographed dance to this song during "indoor recess" (a Winnipeg winter phenomenon when the temperature dipped below −25 degrees Celsius, and we couldn't go outside for our 30-minute break for fear of bodily harm). We twisted our lanky little bodies around in fits of giggles. A lot of spinning and pointing was involved.

I could get into this Jump5 band, I thought.

I asked my mom to buy me a CD entitled WOW HITS 2003 from the local Christian bookstore. WOW HITS were compilation CDs that came out annually—the Christian Contemporary Music version of *Now That's What I Call Music* or *Big Shiny Tunes*. This edition had a Jump5 track, which I already knew I liked. I would study the rest of it, I thought—it was like a CliffsNotes guide to becoming the kind of person who was up on current Christian music.

I was determined to find something I liked on the WOW HITS compilation. It was a two-disc affair, and I deemed at least half the songs skippable. I tried to listen to the whole thing at first, but I soon had a routine. I'd slide the disc into the blue-and-silver boom box I'd received for Christmas and press the Forward button until I reached "All I Can Do" by Jump5. And then I'd twirl around my tiny room, slipping on the baby blue area rug, dive-bombing my bed, imagining I could be one of those kids twirling backflips through the air, filled with the light of Jesus.

The strange thing about Christian music as a genre is that it carries an additional purpose—it's not simply entertainment but a conversion tool, or a teaching tool, or a message to God. There's a clip that went viral in 2011 (according to Know Your Meme), of a boy who came to be known as Nu Thang Kid. The video, under a slick of '90s video grain, features a ten-year-old in lilac Zubaz pants and a matching purple T-shirt that reads *Jesus Is Lord*. Microphone in hand and a look of supreme concentration on his face, he earnestly performs—for 2 minutes and 50 seconds—the Christian pop song "Nu Thang," in a spirited arrangement that attempts, with one voice, to include the main and background vocals, rapping, and a dance breakdown.

There's something particularly endearing to me about this clip, an earnest, full-throttle commitment I recognize from my own childhood. Kids will always throw themselves into what they're doing, but the addition of religion creates some kind of strange alchemy. It's the same combination that makes it so difficult to listen to Christian pop. It's the introduction of the sacred to the commercial, with a dash of the utterly mundane. You watch a boy in his patterned pants trying to moonwalk and think, *He's doing this for the benefit of an omniscient, all-powerful being who controls the universe?* This inherent tension is what I found so disconcerting and hard to navigate at Christian school: Everything was wrapped around these giant concepts of sin and salvation, damnation, eternity, and purpose but expressed through slogans and kitsch, "wholesome" pop bands and *Jesus Is My Homeboy* T-shirts. That's, I think, what makes it absurd. Surely, the divine is meant to bring you outside yourself, to make you understand your smallness in the universe in a way too profound to be commercialized. It's one thing to embody your faith in the everyday, but to sell it and sloganize it?

When we look backward, it's hard to see clearly the things that happened to us, the things we thought and felt and believed through the distortions of not only the years but the layers of meaning we assign to our lives, the ways we narrativize and reframe and understand ourselves. As a teen, I wanted to reinvent myself, forget who I was as a child. As a young adult, I wanted to correct all the ways my younger self had been wrong or wronged—to write myself out of the aspects of Christianity that had hurt me back then, or the ones I was ashamed of and blithely participated in. Now I search the internet for 2000s Christian pop, looking for a time-machine view, an ability to remember what I felt then.

Perhaps the reason Jump5 resonated with me, while the other treacly hits on my *WOW HITS* CD did not, was that their songs contained few, if any, direct references to Christianity. They were love songs, de-sexed enough that they could be aimed at other preteens just as easily as they could be aimed at Jesus. And because they were not singing about morality, or the fate of one's eternal soul, or a God I wasn't entirely sure actually existed or made any sense, I could just sing and jump along. It was sugar-free candy; not bad for you, not particularly good, either.

But maybe that's the point of creating a Christian version of something, other than as a niche marketing maneuver. Perhaps the intent is to create enough of a positive association to an artifact that the good feelings also become linked, in one's mind, to the religion itself. If I set certain search parameters on my memory, I can zoom through a montage of moments from my childhood and adolescence: singing along ironically to Christian pop with youth-group friends; turning up Relient K in my friend's car to belt out our best nasally-faux-punk harmonies; swaying with eyes closed to some corny Switchfoot song, delirious in the hunger pangs of a fast to raise money for charity; dancing to Jump5 on a classroom rug, falling into my friends and collapsing in laughter. It felt good to belong for a moment—for music to stretch the bridge between body and mind, between self and others. It felt good to be in the warm glow of a crowd moving in unison, whether raising your "praise hands" in the dim light of a church sanctuary or swivelling your little kid hips on the playground.

A lot of who I was as a kid didn't feel *authentic*, but it did feel *good*. The music itself may not have been authentic either, may have been a mere marketing ploy for the religion I was having trouble connecting to. But it was good for me, too, at least for a while.

CHAPTER TWO

BOY'S BIBLE, GIRL'S BIBLE

GENDER, PURITY CULTURE, AND THE "NEW LOOK FOR TEEN BIBLE PUBLISHING"

"In focus groups, online polling, and one-on-one discussion, Transit Books has found that the number one reason teens don't read the Bible is that it is too big and freaky looking," says the publishing copy. "This fashion-magazine format for the New Testament is the perfect solution to that problem ... *Revolve* is the new look for teen Bible publishing!"

I don't remember thinking the Bible was "freaky looking" when I was a teen, but I do remember *Revolve*. First published in 2003, this "Biblezine" sandwiched an accessible translation of the Bible's New Testament between soft, glossy covers printed with the bright pink, blue, and orange hues of the early 2000s. On the cover were three laughing girls, their faces partially obscured by fashion-mag-style headlines:

"Are you dating a Godly guy?" and other Quizzes

BEAUTY SECRETS you've never heard before!

How To Get Along With Your Mom and Other Relationship Notes

I remember being 12 or 13, lying on my friend's bed, deep in a fit of giggles, paging through this Bible's glossy magazine-stock pages to find quizzes that would tell us whether our (non-existent) boyfriends were "Godly," whether we were introverted or extroverted, and a million other small quirks of personality. We flipped through to find every "Guys Speak Out" feature, which were sidebars scattered throughout the scripture text that featured Q&As with unnamed guys. These guys were represented by stock photos of men dunking basketballs and leaning against trees. We'd compete to find our favourite guy, arguing over which of them were cute.

Our enjoyment was half ironic, half sincere. We were, technically, spending our Saturday night sleepover reading the Bible, evidently, the way the publisher intended, the way we would read a "real" teen magazine. There just happened to be a bunch of ancient religious text in there that we were flipping past, too.

Twenty years after it was published, I flip through again, this time without the tactile sensation of the magazine pages. After frustrated attempts to buy a used copy from someone in the southern U.S., I have to settle for scrolling digitally through this relic of my preteen years. The Y2K-era fonts and illustrations, and the cheesy photos of laughing teens, light up some nostalgic centre in my brain. In a "Beauty Tip" sidebar, this Bible suggests that I pray every time I apply my sunscreen so as to condition myself to pray more. (The biggest problem with this is that I am very bad at remembering to apply sunscreen.) Another sidebar gives me ultimately quite sound advice about what to do in the aftermath of a sexual assault, though this is accompanied by a terrifying stock image of a crying girl with thick lines of mascara running down her face. A calendar page for January 2003 suggests that, on January 3, I should "Pray for a person of influence; Today is Mel Gibson's birthday." A cutesy-looking Q&A section entitled "Blab" offers this exchange:

> **Q:** The Bible says I'm supposed to be loving my enemies. Does this mean I'm supposed to love Satan?
>
> **A:** The answer is no, we are not to love Satan. Satan is the enemy of God. He is more than a foe to us; he is evil itself and as children of light we cannot love darkness or have any part in it.

So, no, there's no way you could confuse this for a regular teen magazine. But in many ways, it offered the same thrills: Something to giggle about with your friends, and the possibility lurking that you might read some advice, some "tip," that would change your life, transform you from an awkward teen girl to a stylishly confident and competent adult.

Revolve was far from the first evangelical product to adopt the form of popular media as housing for its religious messaging. For me and my friends, it was just one of the many that surrounded us. There were Christian girl groups and boy bands (as discussed in chapter one), a Christian girls' magazine (*Brio*), and apparel—graphic tees, jewelry, scarves, and more—printed with Christian messages. *Revolve*'s publisher, Thomas Nelson, had identified teens' issues with the Bible not as substantive or ideological but as a problem of form—*too big and freaky looking*—and decided to simply repackage religion for a new generation using one of the more popular media of the time, teen magazines. Other than the fact that *Revolve* and its ilk were available at the Christian bookstore instead of the mall, and our mothers and grandmothers seemed much more eager to buy them for us, these products seemed like just another drop in the sea of pink glitter being constantly marketed to us at the turn of the millennium.

But these Christian versions of teen media tended to carry another layer of presumed meaning, representing not only another option but an alternative. As researcher Sara Moslener (PhD) puts it, evangelical pop culture "simultaneously valorizes and critiques popular media, asking its audience to reject the meaning of popular culture without rejecting the 'meaning-making devices' that form that culture in the first place." They both displaced and depended on those other products. Secular teen magazines, like *Seventeen* and *J-14*, were meant to be unholy, immoral in a myriad of ways. But stick the Bible in there and make some of the beauty tips reference Jesus, and it becomes a good thing. I wasn't supposed to reject teen magazines outright; I was supposed to only buy *Christian* teen magazines. The culture we consumed was cobbled together from the evangelical-produced and the fringes of acceptable non-Christian media—never wholly Jesus and never really wholly secular, either.

It makes sense that evangelical publishers would want to capitalize on this market. If you are, like me, old enough to remember the era before the internet dominated all of our lives, you probably recall how big a *thing* magazines were to teenagers. For teen girls in particular, magazines were an authoritative resource to help those feeling adrift in the anxious, hormone-soaked years of being a teenager. Their pages spoke with the confident voice of grown-up women writers and editors who had made it through to the other side, become adults, and were now kindly reaching back to offer help to those still struggling through. Much of the format for teen magazines took on this advisory tone: There were endless "tips," advice columns, quizzes, and guides—the kinds of writing that suggest the reader is in search of answers.

While secular teens turned to *Sassy*, *Seventeen*, and *Teen Vogue*, Christian readers had the aforementioned *Brio* and the *Revolve* Bible. For the publishers behind them, they were the perfect proven medium to deliver Christian instruction to teen girls.

As I scrolled in a nostalgic rush through the "Guys Speak Out" features, and colourful calendars, the question I now wanted to ask was: How innocent was this instruction? Evangelical media "for girls" was meant to reinforce the message of Christianity, of course, but it's hard to ignore the other messages they carried, messages spelled out in iridescent glitter: This is what girlhood means. What else would I think when even the scriptures were filled with beauty tips, when *Brio* promoted books like *Secret Keeper: The Delicate Power of Modesty* or asked, in an article about building good habits, if your habits would one day make you "a blushing bride or a Miss Piggy"? Ideas about gender were being marketed alongside, and becoming entangled with, religion. Every pink Bible and *God's Precious Daughter* T-shirt was also selling a script, and every glossy issue dropped in a millennial teen's mailbox had lots to say—about purity, modesty, and gender compliancy.

♥ † ♥

In 2003, the year *Revolve* was published, my fellow Grade 6 classmates and I would be led into the school library for a class simply called *Library*. During this period, we were meant to browse the shelves and find books to read, which we would check out by adding our names to the lined index card tucked in the pocket at the front of the book. Our teachers clearly hoped the mere proximity to books would enrich our little minds somehow; if not, we could also be bribed with a coupon for a Pizza Hut Personal Pan Pizza doled out to the kids who read the largest number of tomes each month.

Along with speed-reading installments of *The Baby-Sitters Club*, one of my favourite Library activities was looking through issues of *Brio*, to which my school had a subscription.

What I didn't know while flipping the glossy pages in the school library was that *Brio* was a publication of evangelical media giant Focus on the Family.

Founded by family psychologist Dr. James Dobson in the 1970s, the Christian publishing and media "ministry" ballooned over the following decades into a multi-million-dollar empire headquartered in Colorado Springs. Focus on the Family was responsible for some of the most widely read and listened-to Christian media and resources, including parenting manuals, the popular kids' radio show *Adventures in Odyssey*, *Brio* and its for-boys counterpart *Breakaway*, and Dr. Dobson's daily advice radio show, which was excerpted into a short segment called "Dr. James Dobson's Family Minute" and played on Winnipeg's Christian radio station every morning as my mom drove me to school. His reach was immense. By the mid-2000s, Dobson's show was carried on more than two thousand American radio stations, with six to ten million listeners weekly; his books had sold upwards of ten million copies; and, as journalist Dan Gilgoff reported in his 2007 book *The Jesus Machine*, Focus on the Family regularly received so much fan mail that it required its own zip code.

Dobson formally stepped down from heading the then-$130 million, 1,300-employee organization in 2003 to form a fundraising action committee that could focus on exerting influence in American politics without the pesky IRS rules imposed on Focus on the Family due to its status as a nonprofit. Despite his relatively low profile outside Christian circles, Dobson's influence was huge—enough to reach from suburban Colorado to a small city in the middle of the Canadian prairies. Dobson has been compared to celebrity evangelist Billy Graham in his reach and has been called "the most influential evangelical leader in America."*

Back in Library class, I was surely slipping the latest copy of *Brio* off the metal magazine rack and scanning its table of contents for something that promised even mild titillation. I'd take anything: a single makeup tip, a way to make my hair less frizzy, a mildly amusing quiz. I don't think, in retrospect, I really liked *Brio*. I kept reading it because it was *something*. Other than the aforementioned *Baby-Sitters Club*, the school library didn't have

---

* Gilgoff, pp. 2, 7, 14

much media for girls that held the interest of my less-holy preferences, like the Spice Girls or the *Princess Diaries* books. Most pop culture aimed at girls was deemed too sexy, too adult, too frivolous, or simply not Jesus-y enough. The evangelical world, it seemed to me, was mostly a serious, masculine place. Faith was about being a warrior, and about being rigorously intellectual so that you could shut down any argument an Evil Atheist might throw at you. Feminine things, by contrast, were at best unserious, and at worst straight-up sinful. There was no room for girl power, for Barbie and her many plastic shoes, for makeup and earrings that adorned your body but not your soul.

Brio was "decidedly boring, written more for the parents who paid for a subscription than for the teen girls who might read the magazine," wrote blogger Stassa Edwards in 2016. Writer Lyz Lenz has also called the magazine "deeply uncool," even for her, a "homeschooled evangelical teen." The publication boasted bland interviews with Christian celebrities (Candace Cameron Bure and the like), lists of wholesome fun activities to keep teens occupied so they wouldn't be tempted to drink or have sex, and features deconstructing the supposed sinful messages in contemporary secular pop culture (a scan of a particularly enjoyable article on the evils of *Twilight* is available on Reddit). Very little of what I read in the school library made a lasting impression on me, and nothing struck me as enjoyable enough that I would consider getting my own subscription. It was bland fun, a way to pass the time before the bell rang.

The occasion of Edwards's article was the 2016 relaunch of the magazine. Current issues are not available online, but the aesthetic vibe of the 2020s version of *Brio* seems less centred around violently green flowers and pink hearts than I remember, and much more pumpkin-spice-Instagram-girl: thin, invariably white teens photographed mid-laugh, dressed in oversized flannel blanket scarves, tastefully dark-wash skinny jeans, and wide-brimmed hats. Writing at the time of its launch, Edwards noted:

Politics were implicit to *Brio*, particularly amid the early '90s evangelical effort to resist the lure of secular culture and build a subculture of their own, but never articulated. All magazines for teen girls are didactic, but some less obvious than others. They offer up a narrative of what girls should be, implicitly assuming their interests. What teen magazines share is the assumption that the teen years are particularly difficult for girls, vulnerable as they are during that long stretch towards becoming a woman.

Brio offered a way to be serious about your Christian faith but still girly. It also offered a rigid definition of what being a girl meant and looked like. Returning to the magazine 20 years later, I thought I would recapture that sense of mild fun. Instead, I was confronted with very unsubtle messaging about the intractability of the gender binary and iron-clad walls defining the boundaries of those binary options. Every article rested on the presumption that everyone can be categorized as either a man or a woman (or, in the parlance of *Brio*, a "girl" or a "guy") and that those categories are stable. Girls are sweet, fun, nice, emotional, and meant to support their friends and romantic partners. Guys are visual, logical, action-oriented, and meant to be leaders. "God had Adam in mind when he fashioned Eve," one 2006 article attests. "God designed her to please him. When God woke Adam and presented Eve, Adam's response was, in a sense, 'Woah!' 'Man!' 'Wo-man!' He liked what he saw."

Reading the articles now, I see messaging about gender was not incidental, it was the main message. The magazine was entirely a vehicle for promoting purity culture and regressive gender roles. Those politics Edwards identifies are never articulated but nonetheless extremely stark, perhaps nowhere more so than when discussing the topic of modesty.

Purity culture has become somewhat of a buzzword in recent years, referring to the near-universal evangelical adoption of so-called sexual purity as a central tenet of the faith. This shift rose throughout the '70s and '80s but peaked in the '90s and 2000s, in the boom years of the abstinence movement, Kristin Kobes Du Mez writes in *Jesus and John Wayne*. Sexual purity, though, was not just about not having sex before marriage; it was about remaining pure in every way, in thought and deed. Depending on your individual denomination or church's teaching, anything from kissing or holding hands down to masturbating or simply *thinking* about sex could be considered an impure and therefore sinful action worthy of repentance.

As a cis girl growing up steeped in this culture, *modesty* was a word I heard a lot—not in the sense of humility but in the sense of modest dress.

"If you've read *Brio* for long, this won't be a new idea to you. But even if you're reading it for the 100th time, it's worth reading again," a 2004 article entitled "Modelling Modesty" attests. "The type of clothes a girl wears can instantly distract a guy from what he has on his mind to thoughts bordering on or diving in to lust."

The article bills itself as a handy guide to finding modest clothes to wear, the kinds of clothes that won't "distract" the boys around you or instantly project lustful thoughts into their heads. The author is aware that the average Christian girl's day might have to involve some movement. But she is eager to let the reader know that, no matter the context, they should nonetheless feel ashamed.

> Have you noticed that when you raise your hands in the air, your shirt goes up, too? Whether you're worshiping God or signing for the hearing-impaired, a cropped top is going to be on the move when you raise your hands above your head. Do you really want

to expose your tummy and back to other Christians while they're worshiping? Why distract people from the Lord?

According to the article, deciding what clothes to buy is an intense moral weight. "With one look, people can guess whether you're showing off personality or sexuality, whether you're living for the Lord or living for the world and whether you're trying to get a guy's attention with your body." Along with helpful tips like "buy sleeveless shirts that have smaller armholes," choose shorts with at least a seven-inch inseam, and "don't even consider low-rider pants," the article suggests doing a number of physical moves inside a clothing store fitting room that will help determine whether the selected item of clothing might ever accidentally slip out of place in the course of your regular day-to-day signing for the hearing impaired. For instance:

> While wearing a new shirt, bend over in front of a mirror. Can you see into the shirt through the neck hole? Lift your hands above your head. Does the shirt rise so that your tummy is visible? Take a side view of yourself with your arms slightly raised. Can you easily see into your shirt through the arm hole? Is your bra visible in any way? . . . With a pair of shorts, is your underwear visible in the back when you bend over? When you sit on the floor in front of a mirror and spread your legs apart as if you're stretching, can you see your underwear or see into your shorts? (If so, they're not a good buy.)

Suddenly, I remember that during my entire teen years, every morning when I put on a shirt before school, I would bend over in front of my mirror and squint down the front of my own shirt, trying to make sure I couldn't glimpse any bra—or worse, see into my bra—down the neckhole. I'd entirely forgotten this strange ritual. But like muscle memory, the feeling comes flooding back.

♥ † ♥

When I started kindergarten, it was at a British-run international school that mandated uniforms. In my closet was a little row of black pinafores and crisp white collared blouses, each with a name tag that my mom had painstakingly hand-stitched in. I've always loved clothes and always had a slightly chaotic sense of style, so when we moved back to Canada, I was happy to be able to wear my own clothes at my new school—particularly as my new peers introduced me to the wonders of the mall: glitter-and-cartoon-covered tees from Northern Getaway, tracksuits from La Senza Girl, puffy newsboy caps in baby pink and blue, arm hair–pinching charm bracelets. But just because there were no uniforms at Christian school didn't mean we were free. There was still the Dress Code.

Among the outlawed items were strapless or spaghetti-strap tops, anything that showed cleavage or midriff, underwear that showed above your pants, and anything with "inappropriate" slogans or images. (The latter is the only rule I personally heard of applied to a male student, when my cousin was reprimanded for wearing a T-shirt with the Molson Canadian logo on it.) Our shirts had to be long enough to meet the tops of our low-rise jeans, the dominant style of jeans then available at the mall. Tank top straps had to be no thinner than the width of three fingers pressed together. Skirts and shorts had to fall past the tips of our fingers when our arms were at our sides. Many of us became experts at subtly stacking our fingers on top of each other, at pushing our shoulders low and tugging our hemlines down, just enough.

It was around this same time, in 2004, that the three-piece Christian pop-punk band BarlowGirl released the song "Clothes," on their self-titled album. There may be no more perfect distillation of the attitude that an evangelical Christian girl in the 2000s was meant to have about fashion, clothing, and her own body.

The two-and-a-half-minute song rails against clothes that "don't fit," are "too small" as if made for a doll, and are meant to "flaunt" girls' bodies. The message is that clothes used to be modest but are now skimpy and sinful. The song then culminates in a chorus encouraging girls to cover up in clothes "that fit," an encouragement for girls to cover up.

Mind you, this song also seems to present a world in which we girls are being frog-marched into baring our midriffs. The lyrics repeatedly reference an unexplained "they," I guess standing in for society, secular culture writ large, which demands girls unquestioningly follow fashion trends for the aim of getting attention.

Of course, in 2004, I understood this feeling on some level. The first decade of this millennium was notorious for its representation of the female body as white, hyperfeminized, and extremely thin, as well as for subjecting anything else outside that narrow norm to harsh ridicule. Cultural historian Heather Radke calls the 2000s "a period of extreme fat anxiety within the popular media," recalling the overinsistence on retouching and airbrushing fashion photography, the rise of cosmetic procedures like liposuction, the fashion industry's glorification of extremely thin bodies, and a celebrity media that ridiculed stars like Alicia Silverstone, Drew Barrymore, Jessica Simpson, and Beyoncé for being fat. Meanwhile, mainstream feminism struggled to articulate a coherent position on these issues, attempting to reconcile increased choice with cultural coercion, and the decade was mired in a complicated conversation about whether wielding cis-heteronormative female sexuality was self-empowering or a self-entrapping capitulation to the male gaze.

So BarlowGirl doesn't exactly seem wrong to question the pressures they feel. And yet, the tone of their song rings familiar in a different way. The lines referencing an autocratic culture that demands girls wear certain things, that they obey, don't speak to the pressures I felt from fashion trends; instead, they trip the wire that floods me with the feelings I had at Christian school. The ultimate message of the song is not to promote self-expression or self-love, or a wider acceptance of others, but to encourage a rigid conception of modesty that boils down to not showing certain parts of the body. It collapses girls' choices around clothing into a simple dichotomy: showing skin bad, modesty good.

That's why the constant companion of modesty in the evangelical world is the phrase "Do not cause your brother to stumble." The origin of this language is biblical, but its spread is so diffuse that it's unclear how it entered the popular Christian vernacular and solidified a meaning synonymous with what women choose to wear on their bodies.

Here's how it works: The basic premise is that men are "visual creatures." Seeing something attractive sparks sexual arousal for a man. But in the framework of abstinence- and purity-based sexuality, even sexual arousal can be construed as sinful, leading as it does to sexual thoughts and feelings. Men are not simply able to *stop* feeling sexually aroused by women's body parts, the thinking goes, so it's much easier to cut things off at the source. Women should dress in a way in which there is no possibility that men will think sexual thoughts about them, and then everyone will be holy and happy.

Advocates of this way of thinking would probably ascribe some measure of responsibility to the man—after all, he's constantly bombarded with sexed-up images in advertising and music videos. He can't possibly insulate himself from all the heathen women walking around the world in crop tops and low-cut shirts, so he must have to rally his own defenses. In fact, *Every Young Man's Battle*, a popular book about purity in the 2000s for teen boys, instructed young men to "bounce [their] eyes" away from women to keep from taking in arousing sights.

But that doesn't stop the pressure that's placed on Christian girls. As you can probably guess, this line of thinking tips very quickly into victim-blaming of the worst kind. If your outfit can *cause* a sinful sexual reaction in someone else, it's barely a push farther to say that his arousal is your sin, too.

There is no hard-clad scientific evidence that men are, in fact, "visual creatures" any more than women are. This was not purely a creation of evangelicalism: In 2004, the *New York Times* proclaimed that "In Sex, Brain Studies Show, 'La Difference' Still Holds." Relatively new (at the time) MRI and brain scan studies of men and women's amygdalae in response to arousing stimuli were touted as proof of a sex difference in visual stimulation—though, despite the headline, the *Times* piece goes on to note that the study showed little difference in amygdala response between the sexes. Researchers' theories about the supposed evolutionary basis for men choosing mates based on visual cues and women choosing mates based on emotional fulfillment were, even then, contested. By 2019, however, *Scientific American* was fully puncturing the myth, pointing to a research group that analyzed brain imaging findings from 61 relevant studies and found no difference in men's and women's responses to visual stimuli when social scripts and researchers' own biases are stripped away.

Of course, none of that was particularly relevant to evangelical Christians who are not exactly known for their unwavering respect for science. That old chestnut *don't cause your brother to stumble* is still right there in the Good Book.

Actually, the verse this language draws from reads in full: "Therefore let us stop passing judgment on one another. Instead, make up your mind not to put any stumbling block or obstacle in the way of a brother or sister."

In my experience, the not-passing-judgment part is largely ignored.

This language pulled from Paul's Epistle to the Romans is actually about food. Paul continues, telling the readers not to worry so much about which foods are "clean" and "unclean" and to "act in love" if anyone is "distressed by what you eat," catering to their preferences. Writing to a mix of Gentiles and Jewish people who had recently converted to this new religion, the writer seems to be saying that old purity laws are less important than a functioning community that acts out of love.

Aside from the fact that none of this is about low-rise jeans, this is a very different message than the one pushed by the modesty police.

Writer Linda Kay Klein points this out in her book *Pure*: "In the Bible, the term *stumbling block* is used to reference a variety of obstructions that can be placed before a Christian. The concept is used in reference to sexuality just once," she notes. This is in Jesus's Sermon on the Mount, in which he says:

> You have heard that it was said, "You shall not commit adultery"; but I say to you that everyone who looks at a woman with lust for her has already committed adultery with her in his heart. If your right eye makes you stumble, tear it out and throw it from you; for it is better for you to lose one of the parts of your body, than for your whole body to be thrown into hell.

As a kid, I often heard the first part of this—the equation of a "lustful look" with adultery—referenced, but much rarer was it to hear anyone suggest the teen boys in my class gouge out their own eyes. Klein agrees, writing:

> In the years I spent as an evangelical Christian, I never once heard anyone use the term [*stumbling block*] the way it's used here—in reference to the onlooker's lustful eye. Instead, I heard it used time and time again to describe girls and women who somehow "elicit" men's lust. As I have heard it said, sometimes our interpretations of the Bible say more about us than they do about the Bible itself.

To be clear, I am not suggesting that all religious expressions of modesty come from the same place. While it's impossible to disentangle patriarchy and misogyny from religion (like many other facets of society), I do recognize that there are expressions of modesty that are freely chosen, rooted in a less gendered and judgmental framework, that do not necessarily conform to these same patterns of victim-blaming and shaming.

There's also nothing wrong with dressing in whichever way makes one feel comfortable. But having to view your clothes like a fortress, with the goal of protecting a million anonymous men from your dangerous and therefore sinful body, with the sense that anything you wear could be your or someone else's downfall—that's a lot of pressure. And that pressure creates a lot of shame.

Swimming in these shame-based waters of purity can have powerfully traumatic effects on young women and men. Ultimately, as Klein notes, the term "stumbling block" has the effect of dehumanizing a woman and removing all sense of agency.

"The implication that my friends and I were nothing more than things over which men and boys could trip was not lost on me," she writes. "By the time I was in high school and had my first boyfriend, I had been 'talked to' about how I dressed and acted so many times that my annoyance was beginning to turn into anxiety. It began to feel like it didn't matter what I did or wore; it was me that was bad."

I was called to the principal's office on a warm fall day in high school. For a quiet "good kid" who rarely got in trouble, the summons caused a sweaty-palmed spike of anxiety. A range of possible tragedies flooded my mind as I walked to the little office at the back of the school building, tucked next to the kindergarten hallway with its rows of tiny shoe–filled cubbies. Was my brother

sick? Were my parents in a terrible car accident? Was someone I loved dead? It didn't occur to me that I was being called in for punishment. I rarely did anything wrong—certainly nothing I wasn't sure I could get away with.

But when I arrived at the office, the kind receptionist handed me a piece of paper that read: DRESS CODE VIOLATION.

"Your skirt is a little short," she said, tucking her head apologetically to the side. Her blond hair swooshed over her shoulder. "It's just a warning for now. You don't have to go home and change." The punishment for repeat offenders. If their parents wouldn't come get them, they might have to wear a pair of sweatpants dug out of the lost-and-found.

"Oh," I said. And then, "Sorry," because I didn't know what else to say.

"I know how it is!" she said in a chipper voice. "You're so tall. It must be hard to find things that are long enough."

I looked down at my long, spindly legs. It was true. I'd never owned a pair of pants with a hem below my ankle. I also didn't try very hard to find things that were "long enough." I liked my long legs, liked the way short skirts made my proportions look, the way they transformed what I perceived as an awkward, sticklike body.

Then the receptionist said: "The principal noticed your shorts were too short on the first day of school, too. He didn't want to say anything on the first day."

The image of our principal, who also happened to be my friend's father, scoping out my legs was extremely unsettling. "Okay," I replied, still not knowing what to say.

I'd worn the offending shorts on the first day of school for that reason and never re-worn them. I figured the dress code wouldn't be too strictly enforced on the first day, which was mostly about going from class to class and collecting syllabi. I loved those shorts. They were high-waisted, which had just recently become cool to my great celebration. They had an extra thick band with three vertical buttons. I'd worn them with my favourite vintage T-shirt tucked into the front.

I left the office after signing some kind of acknowledgment that I'd received a talking-to about my skirt. I hadn't even thought about the dress code when I'd gotten dressed that morning. I'd picked a tiered, ruffly dress out of my closet that I'd bought on a family vacation. I usually felt so good in that dress, except for that day. Trying not to think about it, I caught myself tugging at the hem.

♥ † ♥

In a 2001 *Brio* article entitled "Straight from a Guy," writer Rory Partin breaks down the male Christian evangelical mindset with the aid of a food-based metaphor and an anecdote about seeing lions while on safari "in Africa" (ellipses not added):

> This is crazy . . . but hey, that's the kind of guy I am . . . so use your imagination here . . . okay? What if I had gotten out of the van to get a good picture of the lions? What if I'd tried to pet one? What if I had hung fresh raw steaks around my neck? Yeah, I know what you're saying: "Uh, Rory . . . it doesn't take a rocket scientist to say that you would have ended up on their breakfast menu!" [. . .] Can I be honest? I mean . . . really, really honest? Like from a guy-to-a-girl honest? Don't get mad, OK? I'm gonna give it to you straight. Here goes! Just as a lion would be tempted to attack someone wearing sausages, it's the same to guys when girls wear things designed to arouse certain instincts and attentions in males. (OK, go ahead and get mad. I know you want to! But you said I could be honest, remember?)

I most certainly did not, Rory, and I don't appreciate through-the-page gaslighting. Anyway, Rory explains himself:

> So often girls wear clothing that's tight, low-necked, or short-skirted and expect guys not to react the way God designed them. Listen, *Brio* Sisses, when you wear revealing clothes that show a little extra this or a little extra that, it brings one thing and one thing only to a guy's mind. Sex. That's how God wired us.
>
> That's not to say we don't have a responsibility to live self-controlled, pure lives. But a lion is a lion, and a guy is a guy; I don't care who he is.

As a woman, I certainly don't love having my fashion choices compared to slinging sausages around my neck, and I don't quite understand the metaphor of the lion, as it seems to equate a man's sexual attraction to a woman as something dangerously violent (although, maybe . . .). It's dehumanizing, of course.

But reading it now, I was upset to realize that, despite my best intentions, this too had seeped into my subconscious. All the times I'd been told, *be afraid of men, be afraid of the boys around you—all they think about is sex—they don't see you as human, only as a potential sex object* . . . It wasn't really fair to them and surely shaped not only my relationship to my own body but my relationship toward men. What does it do to someone to have that message broadcast to them constantly?

Listening to "Clothes" on BarlowGirl's YouTube channel, I recognized a certain spirit of rebellion. In fitting with the pop-punk aesthetic, the song presents the Christian worldview as one that's rebellious against the mainstream. The average secular person would probably assume that the rebellious choice would be to take clothes *off*. Sexual freedom, personal choice, and liberation were supposed to be a rebellion against the kinds of aesthetics that Christian modesty promotes. How interesting to turn the tables that way, to make the Christian choice the rebellious one.

♥ † ♥

In addition to male-authored articles like the one by Rory, most issues of *Brio* had an "Ask a Guy" feature, in which some unnamed guy would give a male perspective on different topics, which were mostly the same two topics: abstinence and dressing modestly. But I was surprised when rereading the magazine at how often a regular article, bylined by a woman, would quickly switch voices to give a "man's perspective," with the writer inviting their husband or a male friend to comment and back them up on the point they were making.

Take, for example, an article from 2002 entitled "What Advertisers Know About Your Body!" It starts with the story of an "embarrassing moment" that happened to the writer, Dannah Gresh, on the way to her "high-paying, high-profile, fast-paced advertising job"—namely, she bent over to get something from her car, and the man in the car next to her saw up her skirt. The piece then abruptly transitions to teaching girls why they should avoid revealing clothing based on principles the writer has learned in her advertising job. Despite her pedigree in this high-powered position, she soon turns the article over to her husband, introduced only as "Bob" (no job credentials), who assures the reader that God created women "to complete and finish man" (double entendre probably not intended) and claims that skimpy clothing is actually *even worse* than nudity.

"It's much more tempting for a guy to see a girl dressed in today's skimpy fashion than it would be to see her naked," Bob writes. "Does that astound you? It's true. A Christian couple I know recently flew to France for vacation. At one point, this pair unwittingly stayed in a hotel next to a nude beach. It wasn't tempting at all. In fact, my friend was rather grossed out."

The real danger is when something is left to the imagination, since men's assumptions about what women's vulvas look like are apparently far more enticing than actual real vulvas that are right in front of their eyes. "If a guy sees a girl walking around in tight clothes, a miniskirt or short shorts, you might as well hang a noose around the neck of his spiritual life. To us, this is not 'just fashion.' It's a constant source of spiritual failure. Have some mercy!"

Mercy indeed. Dannah, the actual writer of the piece, swoops in after this to confess that her embarrassing moment from the top of the article was actually *her own fault* for wearing a short, tight skirt to work. Also, she gives us a primer on the Gestalt theory, I guess to prove Bob's analogy about the nude beach somehow: "The Gestalt Theory teaches a graphic designer to control a viewer's time by forcing him or her to mentally complete a visual image. . . . How do you think this theory works when a girl walks down the street in front of a guy wearing a tight shirt with her belly bared? *Yikes!*"

In a magazine written for girls, helmed and edited and written by women, why is there such an overbearing need for the male perspective?

I suspect the answer lies in the theological positioning of *Brio*'s publisher, Focus on the Family, and more specifically in a not-so-little idea called *complementarianism*.

In her book *Jesus and John Wayne*, historian Kristin Kobes Du Mez notes that "two parallel movements" were rising within evangelical Christianity around the turn of the millennium, two movements which would play key roles in shaping evangelical conceptions of gender: purity culture and complementarian theology.

Championed by the Council on Biblical Manhood and Womanhood (CBMW), an evangelical organization founded for this cause in the late 1980s, complementarianism boiled down to the idea that men and women are not equal but rather different in complementary ways. As a way of structuring marital and familial relationships, it hinges on a belief in "male headship," with the husband as patriarch of the family.

In conservative evangelical circles, this belief was often cast as traditional and drawn directly from the Bible. Certain passages are generally offered up as foundation, including the 31st chapter of Proverbs, which details the characteristics of a "wife of noble character,"* or 1 Peter 3:2, which tells wives to "submit" to their husbands. Of course, in reality, the complementarian ideal of the single nuclear family unit only became prominent in North America in the 1950s, and these specific interpretations of those scriptures were on a slow boil only through the last half century: percolating through the '50s, bubbling up in the backlash to women's liberation in the '60s and '70s, and concentrating through the '80s and '90s panic over working mothers and latchkey kids.

By 2000, the movement had taken hold and the CBMW held a conference in Dallas, documented by Baptist Press. Attended by more than eight hundred evangelical pastors and leaders, the meeting cemented the complementarian stance. It was becoming more than a matter of theological interpretation, Du Mez writes; it was becoming a belief that was fundamental to Christianity itself. "Among complementarians, other doctrinal commitments seemed to pale in comparison to beliefs about gender, and ideas about male authority and the subordination of women." Among other Christians, she notes, "true evangelicals" were those who shared these regressive gender definitions rather than those who held the same beliefs about, say, baptism, or communion, or whether Jesus was fully God or not, or any number of other theological or doctrinal positions.

---

* Among the noble wife's many qualities are that she is industrious, brings "good, not harm" to her husband, takes care of her household, is charitable to the poor and needy, and is wise, strong, and dignified. Oddly, for all its use in complementarian circles, much of the passage is devoted to the wife's work outside the home, making her own money, and making land purchases herself.

That men should have dominion over women, that women shouldn't be allowed to be pastors or even work outside the home, or that God's purpose for all Christians was to get married and procreate were not necessarily positions held by the teachers, principals, or administrators at my Christian school. Yet these ideas were carried in, smuggled inside the pages of *Brio* and *Revolve* and their ilk, products of ultra-conservative American publishers that no one thought to question.

In the aisles of the Christian bookstore of my childhood, it was impossible to miss the intense emphasis on gender essentialism in the evangelical worldview. The division between pink and blue was almost as stark as in the toy aisles at department stores. I remember wandering the aisles and seeing piles of books with soft covers in soft colours offering devotionals for women, parenting advice, and *Chicken Soup for the Mother's Soul* interspersed with tea cozies and embroidered cloth Bible cases. When the books were meant for men, titles sounded like Old Spice deodorant scents, liberally sprinkled with words like *warrior, adventure, fight,* and *power*. The men's books were faux-leather-bound, implying theological rigor, whether or not it was actually present. While my mom read a Women's Devotional Bible with a watercolour flower–printed cover, my dad had an unadorned navy hardcover edition of the New International Version (NIV) by his bedside table.

And while my friends and I were reading our magazine-styled "Bible for Girls," my brother had the "Boys Bible," a full NIV (Old and New Testament) decked out with a gunmetal treadplate cover. Along with pre-highlighted verses "worth memorizing" and "interesting and funny facts about Bible times," the printed marginalia included sidebars called "Grossology": "Gross and gory stuff you never knew was in the Bible."

I recall once, as a preteen, paging through my brother's copy, wondering how the other half lived, and seeing these gross-out fun facts. The one I remember was appended to Proverbs 26:11:

"As a dog returns to its vomit, so fools repeat their folly." The sidebar helpfully explained that dogs commonly eat their own vomit, which, it's true, I did find to be gross.

♥ † ♥

A huge number of books were penned around this time telling good Christian women and men what roles they should be inhabiting, in the home and in society. Had it not been the 2000s, perhaps these ideas would not have spread very widely. Like earlier movements, they might have filtered through select sets and sects and settled as part of the subcultural fringe rather than becoming identified so strongly with mainstream Christianity. But by the 2000s, Du Mez notes, there was already a "mature market for resources on Christian masculinity," with distribution channels—from the Christian bookstore, then at the peak of its profitability, to established radio programs and, looming on the horizon, podcasts—already in place.

Christianity had a long history with militant masculinity, ranging as far back as the Victorian era, as Du Mez traces in her book. As this aggressive version of masculinity ebbed and flowed over the years, in the 1990s, Christian masculinity was manifest in movements like Promise Keepers, a Christian group centred around teaching men to be better husbands and fathers. While the messaging was similarly essentialist, the version of masculinity presented was softer, the archetype Du Mez identifies as "tender warrior" after a book of the same name by Pastor Stu Weber.

But in 2001, John Eldredge released his book *Wild at Heart: Discovering the Secret of a Man's Soul*, which would eventually sell more than four million copies in the U.S. alone. This was a clear departure from previous men's ministry teachings like Promise Keepers. Rejecting tenderness and doubling down on aggression, Eldredge presented a militant, warrior conception of masculinity. "Spawning dozens of copycat books that borrowed copiously from Eldredge's formula, it would frame evangelical explorations of masculinity for years to come," Du Mez writes. In Eldredge's world, men wanted to fight battles and women wanted to be saved and protected. And there was nothing worse than an emasculated man—probably the fault of "clingy mothers" and public schools. His book was liberally sprinkled with secular pop culture references to Mel Gibson heroes, Indiana Jones, *Die Hard*, and James Bond—pinnacles of ideal masculinity.

Another relic of the time was James Dobson's *Bringing Up Boys*, also released in 2001. "In his book about boys, Dobson found occasion to denounce Hillary Clinton, 'bra burners,' political correctness, and the 'small but noisy band of feminists' who attacked 'the very essence of masculinity,'" Du Mez writes. "He praised Phyllis Schlafly and recommended homeschooling as 'a means of coping with a hostile culture.' He advised girls not to call boys on the telephone . . . and encouraged fathers to engage in rough-and-tumble games with their sons." The book sold more than two million copies.

Du Mez makes the connection that both of these books—as well as a very dumb entry called *Future Men: Raising Boys to Fight Giants* by Douglas Wilson—were published in the months before September 11, 2001. They reached a public primed to dive headlong into aggressive, militant ideas about what ideal masculinity should look like—and then, mere months later, a real battle for Americans to fight presented itself. Masculinity wasn't the only thing in crisis; the crisis was coming for America itself.

In a 2001 sermon, Pastor Mark Driscoll stood in front of his Seattle-area megachurch, Mars Hill, and said:

> There is an intense femininity that has crept into Christianity. Islam is a masculine religion. That's why

> they run an airplane into the World Trade Center, and we meet in Central Park in New York, and we get men like Elton John to play the piano and cry. That's our response as a nation: gay men with wigs, cry. Because mean men with facial hair beat us.

When he spoke these words, Driscoll was already head of one of the U.S.'s largest religious gatherings, part of a new wave of megachurches where thousands met weekly to hear the words of celebrity-like pastors, who paced the stage with headset mics and broadcast their messages to satellite locations, or via TV or radio. While Driscoll's personality was abrasive and his message often outright hostile, he would grow over the course of the 2000s to be one of evangelical Christianity's most popular speakers, particularly among young men—a harbinger of a new kind of Christian masculinity that emphasized male strength and painted manhood as a noble calling of protection over women and children.

Of course, when I say *new*, that's not exactly accurate. "There is nothing new under the sun," as King Solomon says. The kind of masculinity Driscoll preached had its roots in a movement called *muscular Christianity* that swept England and America in the late 19th century. As historian Sara Moslener writes, muscular Christianity was exactly what it sounds like: It "fused athleticism, patriotism, and religion and emphasized the importance of training the body for the purposes of protecting the weak and furthering righteous causes." Ironically, in the Alanis Morissette kind of way, these dudes bulking up for Jesus were reacting to the 19th century's own purity movement, one driven largely by feminists whose biologically essentialist view of gender was used as a tool to weaponize female purity in pursuit of empowerment and greater rights for women.

The more women gained political and religious influence, the more men fled to muscular Christianity to "restore their dominance," Moslener writes.

Muscular Christians were propelled by fear and disdain for what they saw as effeminate Christology, clergy, and hymnody characterizing mainline Protestantism. As a reaction against women's religious leadership and a response to the influx of immigrants, Protestant men saw themselves as men of action and aggression who, unlike the feminized Victorian gentleman, could stand up to the challenges of modernity in the same way that Christ stood up to the challenges of the Roman Empire.

They followed four ideals: manliness, morality, health, and patriotism.
    Sounds familiar. *"An intense femininity has crept into Christianity. We get gay men with wigs to sing and cry because mean men with facial hair beat us."* The resurgence, led by Driscoll and others like him, was muscular Christianity again. He talked about growing up working class in a tough neighbourhood and beating up other kids. He told the men in his church he was going to kick their asses in a way that would make them better people. He explicitly linked masculinity with patriotism and nationalism. He railed against "effeminate" envisionings of Jesus and reimagined him as a militant commander-in-chief. He declared America a "pussified" nation. He equated entering other churches with "walking into Victoria's Secret," criticizing their feminine decor, emotional "love songs to Jesus," and crying, effeminate pastors.
    Mars Hill started in 1996 when Driscoll was only 25 years old. According to the *Christianity Today* podcast *The Rise and Fall of Mars Hill*, at its height, the church had 15 locations in five states, with Driscoll preaching five services each Sunday. Its podcast and online stream had more than 260,000 views every week, and Driscoll's books made the *New York Times* bestsellers list. In 2006, the church claimed more than $31 million in assets, a sprawling conservative evangelical beacon in the midst of liberal Seattle, Washington.

The empire came crashing down, as most do, in 2014, when Driscoll was plagued by a series of scandals. First, he was accused of plagiarizing sections of his books from other writers and failing to cite their research. Then it was uncovered that Mars Hill church had paid $210,000 to get Driscoll's books on the Best Sellers list. Former congregants and pastors from the church began to come out of the woodwork, telling stories about Driscoll's quick temper, verbally abusive leadership style, and harsh, cut-them-loose approach to management. Finally, someone leaked posts from a church message board in 2000 from a poster screen-named "William Wallace II"—an alias, it turned out, for Pastor Mark Driscoll, made so that he could anonymously post such gems as: "I love to fight. It's good to fight. Fighting is what we used to do before we all became pussified."

When these posts came to light, Christian media seemed to treat the scandal as a shocking revelation. But reading through William Wallace II's posts, they don't seem far off from the opinions (and even the language) used in Driscoll's "official" teachings.

Throughout the 2000s, Mars Hill made use of new technology to spread those teachings far and wide. They were among the first churches to capitalize on the burgeoning technology of podcasts, they had internal message boards as early as the late 1990s, and as they grew, they created a cutting-edge website and hired their own camera crews and media team. The use of these mediums made it easier to reach Driscoll's core audience: young conservative Christian men.

The raucous preacher's style appealed to them. One young man recalled loading five to six Driscoll sermons onto his iPod to listen to at his landscaping job, enjoying the "stand-up comedy style" of the preaching.*

Years later, young men would find the same appeal when listening to podcasts by Joe Rogan and Ben Shapiro, or lectures

---

* Du Mez, p. 198.

by Jordan Peterson. Like these figures, Driscoll was also adept at walking a tonal line between irony and dead seriousness. He invited young men in with jokes and then sold them on his version of masculinity—a version he made seem not only appealing but crucial to individual happiness, national flourishing, and the survival of society and the human race.

Driscoll himself had identified his mission as primarily to speak to young men. Under the complementarian framework of his views, he believed that "reaching the men" would be a gateway to putting the domestic sphere in order and, eventually, all of society. In 2001, on the same message board unearthed in 2014, Driscoll and William Wallace II both posted notices to the men of the church that there would be a special meeting. "Only men are welcome. At 10 am the door will be locked and all late men will be sent away. . . . We will not be charging, though we may take a payment out of your hide. Bring a Bible, paper, and a pen. Anyone who brings a Promise Keepers book should also bring a cup and some headgear."

The meeting "would not have any food. We will not have any heat. We will not have any band. We do not have any name. We do not have any T-shirts. We do not have any bracelets. We do not have any psychologists. If you are late, we may only let you in after a cavity search, and force you to wear a dress."

Under threat of emasculation, many men of the church attended. According to former pastor and elder at the church Jeff Bettger, who spoke on *The Rise and Fall of Mars Hill* podcast, the meeting consisted of Driscoll "yell[ing] at them for two hours." He demanded that if the men of the church didn't entirely buy into the church's message, they should leave "because you can't charge the gates of hell with your pants around your ankles, a bottle of lotion in one hand and Kleenex in the other."

William Wallace II had referred to this meeting on the boards as a "manly fight club." Podcast host Mike Cosper notes that *Fight Club* was a favourite movie for Mars Hill members, that it fit with the general militant language of the church. Cosper explains:

> Men were to be warriors for God, so they attended theological fight clubs . . . The ministries of the church were described as "air war" and "ground war." They didn't go away to "men's retreats" because real men don't retreat from battle. They went away to "men's advances." They had a sense that they were giving their lives away to a war worth fighting, and they were going to be tested in the process.

The podcast draws parallels between Driscoll and Tyler Durden, the split personality of the depressed, disenfranchised *Fight Club* narrator. William Wallace II was Brad Pitt to Mark Driscoll's Edward Norton, an "over-the-top agent of chaos, stirring up trouble and provoking" the church's young men online.

I think Christian men missed the point of *Fight Club*. They certainly didn't understand the nihilism of the film's final scene, where Edward Norton's and Helena Bonham Carter's characters calmly watch the destruction of their entire city before their eyes. The Chuck Palahniuk novel that served as the film's source material imagined a world where corporate consumerist neoliberal culture turned slighted, fragile men into terrorists. Christian dudes saw the movie and thought, *Hey, cool—that looks pretty good. Except the illegal stuff.* Maybe they all stopped watching after the scene in which Edward Norton's character forces his boss to bend to his will by making it look like his boss has struck him violently. Maybe the Christian boys watched Ed Norton breaking his nose with his own fist, throwing himself into a plate of glass in a shower of blood, and thought, *That's all I have to do—beat myself up.*

♥ † ♥

All of this testosterone and rage was meant, ultimately, to serve the protection of women. At least, that's how Driscoll presented it. In 2009, a video clip from Driscoll's sermon on "Marriage and Men" went viral in the Christian community, though I would only encounter it a couple of years later as male friends at the Christian missions organization I volunteered with argued over the merits of Driscoll's aggressive masculinity. In the clip, which comes from the end of an over 70-minute sermon, he begins screaming.

> Some of you guys . . . you just, it's so frustrating. Some of you guys have been coming here for years—you still have your hands all over your girlfriend. Some of you guys, you've been coming here for years—you're still not praying with your wife. . . . Some of you have already whispered in her ear, "I'm sorry, I'll do better, trust me, let's just move on real quickly." HOW DARE YOU? WHO IN THE HELL DO YOU THINK YOU ARE? Abusing a woman? Neglecting a woman? Being a coward, a fool! Being like your father, Adam! WHO DO YOU THINK YOU ARE? YOU ARE NOT GOD! YOU'RE JUST A MAN! AND NOT AN IMPRESSIVE MAN!

While reporting the story on *Christianity Today*'s podcast, Cosper confirmed that, despite Driscoll's assertions in various interviews that this speech was made off the cuff, the pastor gave the exact same performance five times that day for the five different church services Mars Hill offered on Sundays. It was also followed immediately by an invitation to give money to the church and a passing of the offering plate.

Claiming a passion for "protecting" women, Driscoll would get intensely fired up when preaching about men's responsibility to keep women from abuse and mistreatment. But his anger and militancy seem to me just as dangerous. The church explicitly forbade married women from working outside the home, linking it directly with destroying the institution of family, communities, and the nation. He preached that Mars Hill families "should buy houses, grow deep roots in the community, and that they should have lots of kids if they can,'" and men in the church could be disqualified from leadership positions if their wives worked. Church leaders were overly involved in parishioners' lives, including their friendships, families, and sexual relationships—sometimes elders did such things as "separating husbands and wives for a season, intervening in psychiatric care, demanding written confessions of histories of sinful behavior, or requiring strict shunning of former staff members or friends."

Driscoll made a name for himself as the pastor who was unafraid to talk about sex—or, to put it less generously, the pastor who was obsessed with sex. But his sermons on sexuality were also based around these rigid conceptions of gender. To him, men were dangerous animals that needed to be shamed into submission, and women were mere desirable objects.

The author of the book *Biblical Porn*, Jessica Johnson details Driscoll's teaching that wives were meant to "please their husbands sexually whenever and however they wanted, otherwise the men would clearly go outside of marriage for sex." In a sermon on the Song of Songs (a book of erotic poetry in the Bible), Driscoll told a story about a woman who convinced her non-Christian husband to go to church by—on Driscoll's explicit direction—plying him with oral sex. He criticized "aggressive," "brazen and dirty" women who "dress provocatively" and claimed he'd been propositioned while serving communion in the church. He told women that the Song of Songs advocates they must strip

---

* The echoes of white supremacy and the need to perpetuate whiteness through childbearing are a little chilling here. It seems to me that Mars Hill's theology was very similar to an idea which is often reflected in fundamentalist Christian communities: If you want more Christians, simply make them yourself by having many children.

for their husbands and have sex with the lights on; otherwise, "he is not getting the full joy that he desires and, maritally, deserves."

Men were warriors, and women were sexual servants.

♥ † ♥

By comparison, the song "Clothes" doesn't seem so bad. Being told to wear clothes that fit is a much nicer takeaway than "men deserve sex from you at all times." But every expression of conservative gender roles from the 2000s shares a strange commonality—this counterculturalmentality that positions itself as an underdog to mainstream culture, even while amassing more and more power. Despite growing out of so-called traditional family values, ideas about gender and modesty were sold as a rebellion against mainstream society.

When I was a teen, there was a common slogan on Christian merch, the kind you could get in the pink aisle of the Christian bookstore: *Modest Is Hottest*. Even in my teenage years, this phrase bothered me with its continual reliance on the idea that what mattered was being "hottest." Presenting modesty and purity as a countercultural force for self-expression, rather than an oppressive obligation of one's religion, made it easier to swallow and more familiar to a generation growing up on empowerment feminism. As Moslener notes, the movement even adopted some of the language of queer activism, such as in cases when abstinence spokespeople referred to "coming out of the closet" as a virgin, presenting abstinence as a culturally marginalized sexual identity. But ultimately, this amounts to co-opting feminist language for one's own subjugation. Men played into oppressive gender roles as well, burying their real personalities under camped-up performances of aggressive, militant masculinity, ignoring their own humanity as much as the humanity of the women around them.

In high school, our health classes were divided by gender. While the boys got yelled at about not doing drugs or masturbating, we girls were subjected to endless dating and abstinence talks, lectures on body image and modesty. One memorable guest speaker, a former student who had graduated a few years previously, came prepared with a PowerPoint presentation full of images of magazine spreads. She was speaking about how damaging this kind of media was to our body image and self-esteem, how it had affected her as an impressionable teen. I remember feeling conflicted throughout the presentation, wondering what was missing. In a way, I could see her point: the lean, photoshopped bodies of pale white starlets splashed across every page, ad after ad featuring models of all the same impossible body proportions. But I couldn't understand what she was offering instead. *God thinks you're beautiful* was just not enough, in my opinion. From the long view, I can see what was missing: *God loves you* left little space for you to love yourself; it was meant to naturally follow, but how could it? Especially when God's love seemed so tenuous, so tied to careful adherence to the dress code, the gender norms, the rules about kissing and holding hands and heavy petting that we were being bombarded with every week. The thing about self-esteem is that it *can't* "come from God," as so many teachers told me it would. It essentially has to be an outgrowth of the self. A self that evangelicalism was always trying to diminish. *More of you and less of me*, a common prayer went.

On that day in health class, the guest speaker asked if anyone had a teen magazine. My friend, Taylor, tentatively put up her hand.

"Let me see it," the speaker said, striding over to her desk.

She pulled a thin stack of glossy paper out of her backpack— *Teen People*, maybe, or *Tiger Beat*, or one of those lost to time like *J-14*. The speaker held out her hand, and my friend placed the magazines in her outstretched palm.

"You don't need these!" she said. She lifted them up for all of us to see. I don't remember her exact words anymore. "You are all beautiful. Don't let these images tell you what you should be." Something like that.

And then she defiantly stomped to my health teacher's desk and deposited them triumphantly in the trash can.

Later, when everyone had filed out of the classroom, we snuck back in so that Taylor could fish the magazines out of the garbage.

It's a foggy memory, but I think I can still remember the look on her face: a little upset, her mouth in a line, shoving them back in her bag. She rolled her eyes as if it didn't matter, but I could feel it wafting off her, that familiar whiff of shame.

CHAPTER THREE

JESUS AT THE BOX OFFICE

THE WORLD OF FAITH-BASED FILMS

In the fall of 2003, the hot pop culture gossip from my friends in the lunchroom was not about celebrity couples or wild pop stars. It was that God was trying to smite someone.

At the time, Mel Gibson was making a Jesus movie, *The Passion of the Christ*. This was big news. We'd watched *The Jesus Film*, a 1970s biopic of Our Lord and Saviour—featuring a glossy-haired brunette white Jesus*—in elementary school, but that production was dated, and it certainly wasn't financed by the action star famous for *Lethal Weapon* and *Braveheart*.** No, this was a Big Deal; this was a movie star putting his faith on the big screen—and it was a dramatization of the death of Christ, not the life of Christ. A big bloody blockbuster that might make Christianity cool again.

Or maybe not because maybe God was displeased with it. The rumour, as I remember it, was that the actor playing Jesus had been struck by lightning while on the cross. A friend at school

---

* Upsettingly, Wikipedia attests that the actor was chosen for his "ethnically correct" complexion (he was a slightly tan British man) and wore a prosthetic nose to give him a "Mediterranean look."

** In fact, *The Jesus Film* was financed by Campus Crusade for Christ and distributed by Warner Brothers.

told me this in a conspiratorial whisper. It's a sign, she said, that God doesn't want the movie to be made.

That kind of made sense, I thought. The God in the Bible was not so keen on graven images, after all, so would he want a filmic representation of his death to be beamed out to every movie theatre in the world? Though of all the people God might choose to smite—all the people in this world doing evil things—an actor trying to get a paycheque seemed like pretty small potatoes. I wasn't sure what to make of it.

This rumour revealed a kind of anxious question that I silently asked about any representation of Christianity in wider pop culture: *Are they going to make us look stupid?* Evangelicals were invested heavily in their faith: It was their entire life. So it collectively stung when we saw ourselves portrayed as fuddy-duddy milquetoast Ned Flanders on *The Simpsons* or as backward bumbling idiots on *South Park*. No one really knew how to feel about *Jesus Christ Superstar*, which was getting the message out there but seemed suspiciously gay.

That tension I felt about how Christians were portrayed in the movies and shows that I watched seems kind of silly now. Or at least seems insignificant compared to the sometimes-frightening ways other Christian groups put themselves out into the world: The fictional Christians on *The Simpsons* were goofy, sure, but the footage of Westboro Baptist Church protesting on the news was much worse—and it was real. Especially in comparison, the sitcom jokes weren't even that mean.

According to the *Entertainment Weekly* archives, actor Jim Caviezel really *was* struck by lightning during filming, though it was while carrying an umbrella around set, not while hoisted up on the cross. One of the film's assistant directors was also struck two different times. (The publication chose the headline "Charged Performance," which seems a little rude, honestly.) The real story is not quite as dramatic and doesn't have the same flavour of potential deific displeasure, but with a little tweaking, it was made to suit the evangelical rumour mill.

For evangelical institutions closer to the centre of power, Gibson was pretty effective at cutting off any potential criticism at the pass—they didn't seem to have the same worries that my Canadian middle school world did. "Christian leaders and conservative pundits who've attended invitation-only screenings have called the movie a masterpiece and praised its fidelity to the Gospels," that same *EW* story reports, "while such Jewish organizations as the Anti-Defamation League have expressed fears that the movie blames the Jews for Christ's execution and will spark anti-Semitic [sic] violence." Those fears never made their way to my lunchroom gossip. The myopia of evangelicalism, it seemed, made us hyper aware of our own perception, yet completely disengaged with any other community.

Biblical epics are, of course, nothing new: There was *The Ten Commandments* in Hollywood's Bible-story heyday, and the biopic that dubbed the life of Jesus *The Greatest Story Ever Told*. The story of Jesus's life, death, and resurrection was incorporated by comparative mythology writer Joseph Campbell into his idea of the hero's journey, the cross-cultural "monomyth" that could be used to structure any story—which became a popular influence with Hollywood screenwriters. By 2003, Jesus had amassed biopics, multiple musicals, and fantasy tales about his life. So really, it should have been no surprise that a big-budget movie star—especially one whose father was a Holocaust denier and member of an extreme orthodox Catholic group, though I didn't know that at the time— would be capitalizing on the classic tale.

Strangely, while talking about Christian movies with my dad, he recalled one of his "born-again"* cousins visiting their farm when he was growing up. It was around the time when *Jesus Christ Superstar* was being filmed. My dad's cousin reported that the production had gone through four different actors to play Jesus and was now on its fifth. Why? They kept getting struck by lightning and dying. God clearly didn't want the movie to happen, he said.

"I didn't have Google," my dad reminded me. "So, I just believed him. I kept thinking, *Why would that fifth guy take the part?*"

Funny how we heard the same rumours nearly three decades apart.**

What fascinates me is the fear of, and concern with, the representation in these mainstream Christian movies, which is really at the root of these kinds of rumours. As soon as *The Passion of the Christ* was released in theatres—with the endorsements of famous U.S. evangelical Christian leaders and organizations—and began to pull in money at the box office, suddenly the people around me at Christian school didn't seem so concerned. The movie was a success; therefore, it must follow, God approved. From that year on, in our Easter assembly, a teacher would cue up a clip from the *Passion* on the overhead DVD projector, and we would watch a bloodied Jim Caviezel be brutally tortured and murdered for our sins. (Actually, I wouldn't "watch" per se, unless you count staring at my shoes or palms—I've always been pretty squeamish about movie gore.)

It was the same motivation, I think, that made a church leader in 2005 round my entire youth group up into minivans to go see

---

* Born-again Christians are evangelical, usually from a "charismatic" tradition like Pentecostalism, that incorporates the more supernatural elements of Christian belief (faith healing, speaking in tongues, et cetera). The nomenclature comes from the idea of being "reborn" as a Christian with a personal relationship with Christ and arose out of the hippie-inflected "Jesus People" movement of the 1960s and '70s.

** Since I do now have access to Google, I've fact-checked my father's cousin's claim, and it seems there was no lightning or any other smiting happening on the set. In fact, *Superstar*'s Jesus seems to have had a much nicer time filming than Caviezel or the star of *The Jesus Film*, who was taken out by pneumonia while filming; per Wikipedia, the cast of *Jesus Christ Superstar* apparently spent their time on set reading Levi H. Dowling's *The Aquarian Gospel* and playing volleyball on teams named "Jesus" and "Judas."

The Nativity Story—a dramatization of Jesus's birth featuring a young Oscar Isaac as Joseph—on opening weekend, to help contribute to the box-office take. We had to show secular culture that there was a market for Christian movies, that we were an economically valuable subculture to, well, pander to. Our money was validation.

Perhaps the example most indicative of this mindset is the story of the Kendrick Brothers and Sherwood Pictures.

The story, as told in a Christian Broadcasting Network profile, is that Alex and Stephen Kendrick grew up in Georgia, the sons of a preacher father and teacher mother. They loved movies and used to make stop motion animations together using an 8mm film camera before progressing to a 1980s video camera in their teens. It seems they were always interested in filmmaking, but their early work was limited to a couple of Chick-fil-A training videos.

As adults, the pair were hired as associate pastors by Sherwood Baptist Church in Albany, Georgia, a megachurch in the Southern Baptist Convention that identifies itself as having "traditional values." After spending a few years making internal videos for the church, the brothers decided to launch their dream of making a feature-length Christian movie. According to the church's website, Alex Kendrick "approached Senior Pastor Michael Catt with an idea to make a low-budget, full-length movie as an outreach to the community" in 2002.

"Alex and Stephen had written a simple script about a dishonest car salesman (played by Alex) who turned his life around after re-committing himself to God," *Time* magazine reported in a 2011 profile of the brothers. "With $20,000 raised from church members, Alex bought a digital camera, a boom mike [sic] and some lights from Home Depot; the cast and crew, made up of 60 church volunteers, filmed in the evenings on donated sets and built dolly tracks out of PVC piping." The resulting film, *Flywheel*, opened at a single cinema but extended its run and expanded to more regional theatres when audience response proved larger than anticipated. "Within months it had sold around 100,000 copies on DVD."

From there, the "ministry" of Sherwood Pictures grew. The next film, *Facing the Giants*—this time about a struggling *football coach* who turns his life around after re-committing himself to God—was made for $100,000 (again raised from the Sherwood Baptist Church congregation) and pulled in $10 million at the box office with help from Sony-owned distributor Provident Films, which won the movie a nationwide release. *Fireproof*, the brothers' third movie, was the one to really break through. Following a struggling *firefighter* with a crumbling marriage who turns his life around after re-committing himself to God (and following a 40-day marriage-saving challenge called The Love Dare), it earned $33 million on its $500,000 budget, making it the highest-grossing independent film released in the U.S. in 2008. (It was also the first Sherwood Pictures film to star someone other than Alex Kendrick, with Christian actor Kirk Cameron taking on the leading role.)

In media coverage at the time—Christian and secular—the Kendrick brothers are painted as an unlikely success story, a scrappy David coming up against the Hollywood Goliath through sheer audacity.

"None of these Christian-themed movies is up to Hollywood production standards, though by one metric—box office compared to budget—they're some of the most profitable films in modern history," the *Hollywood Reporter* marvelled, noting that *Facing the Giants* and *Fireproof* took in 102 times and 67 times their budgets, respectively, in contrast to big-budget flicks like *Iron Man 2* and *Thor*, which earned three times their production budgets. *Giants* played in 441 theatres, with $4 million USD in marketing behind it, and *Fireproof* in 905 theatres with a marketing budget of $7.5 million USD. "You can almost picture the Hollywood studio execs scratching their heads," said ABC News in an article that calls the Kendricks the "Christian Coen

Brothers." "A film that was made for $500,000, relied more on word of mouth than television and print ads, and is headlined by an actor best known for a 1980s television show, opens at No. 4 in the country and rakes in $6.8 million in ticket sales."

"Our goal is to use movies to change culture," Alex Kendrick told *Time*. "How many sermons would we have to preach to reach five million people?"

I kept my distance from Sherwood Pictures while at Christian school. I have a vague memory of hearing about *Facing the Giants*, but *Fireproof*—released in 2008, when I was just entering Grade 12—centred around saving a marriage and wasn't really youth-group material. I'd also reached the age where I had firmly separated Christianity from Christian culture: I didn't want to watch a poorly made movie about God or listen to cheesy Christian pop. I wanted to moon over *500 Days of Summer* and Broken Social Scene.

It was a few years later when I encountered the Kendrick Brothers, after the release of their next film, *Courageous*—this one, rather than firefighters trying to be good husbands, focused on police officers trying to be good fathers. I watched it on a missions trip, in a small American-founded evangelical church in Italy, amid my own growing doubts about the kind of faith American Christianity was attempting to export around the world. I remember watching the movie on a folding chair in a dimly lit church sanctuary, surrounded by Milanese churchgoers—or perhaps unsuspecting friends of churchgoers—who'd come to the free church movie night our hosts were putting on, and thinking, *I hope no one here speaks English well enough to understand this movie.*

I was expecting *Facing the Giants* to be a feel-good sports movie with God tacked on, but it's actually a God movie with sports tacked on. Director Alex Kendrick stars as a high school football coach of a Christian team that can't seem to win any of its games, so he goes on a journey from sad sack to success by deciding one day to . . . pray more? Believe in God harder? It's a little unclear, though it comes after a soul-searching scene in which he takes a Bible out into a softly sunlit field and commits himself to Jesus. Pretty standard fare: The first half of the movie sets up a host of problems, and in the second half, God solves them. The football team keeps losing; they turn the season around, make it to the playoffs and win. Money's tight at the coach's household; he gets a raise, and the community donates to him a brand-new truck to replace his clunker of a car. The kids at the school seem unmotivated; the kids on the football team start a "revival" and the whole school spends the day praying on the football field. After years of trying to have a child, the coach finally gets his sperm tested and learns he's infertile; at the end, his wife finds out she's pregnant. Oh, and my favourite—every scene that takes place in the coach's house starts with him or his wife loudly complaining that it stinks in there; during a happy montage, they pull a dead rat from the air duct. After recommitting to God, everyone is happy, pregnant, and living in nice, odour-free homes.

In a *Christianity Today* interview after the movie's release, interviewer Mark Moring asks Alex Kendrick about this miraculous turnabout:

> [Interviewer:] My main quibble with the film is after Grant gets serious about his faith, everything goes right. It doesn't usually work that way in real life.
>
> Kendrick: That's always the first negative comment we get after our test screenings. I'm not a name-it-and-claim-it guy; I think God does allow us to struggle. . . . We ended up with our story for two reasons: Number one, we had seen it happen around us. And number two, it's a movie and we wanted

people to leave inspired and encouraged. . . . While we were making this movie, every single prayer that we begged God for was answered. Every single one—a state-of-the-art camera, a professional crew, the $100,000 budget, the editing equipment, the school to shoot in, even the theatrical distribution. . . . We tried to make the point in the movie where Grant says to God that no matter what, I'll praise you. The wife says that whether or not she gets pregnant, "God, I will still love you." The coach tells the team whether we win or lose, we praise him. . . . That's the point of the movie, not that everything works out. I am stunned that people don't see that.

As usual, Christians want to have their cake and eat it, too. The whole point of the movie, it seems, is that Christians *should* be ready to love God, "praise him," win or lose. The football team pledges to play hard and give it their all, whether they're winning or losing, and be proud either way. Seems like an okay lesson, until the metaphor is extended to the coach and his wife: When the wife mistakenly receives a negative pregnancy test at the doctor's office, she goes to the parking lot, leans on the hood of her car, and through tears promises God that she loves him anyway, whether he grants her a baby or not. And then, of course, the nurse rushes out to correct the mistake; now that she's proved her fidelity, she can be rewarded with what she really wants.

This kind of depiction of prayer is simplistic enough to render the whole thing pointless (Why pray if doesn't matter? And if it does, how to explain an unanswered prayer?) but also neatly shows off the kinds of mind games I was taught to play with God. Taught implicitly, of course, through media just like this. If you want something, pray for it; if you don't get it, pretend you never really wanted it in the first place, or that you're happy without it. And then God will give it to you.

In the movie, the team's kicker, *David*, kicks the winning field goal against the opposing team, the *Giants* (get it??), and his father, who uses a wheelchair, stands to watch him. This isn't quite a miracle moment (thankfully), as the movie establishes previously that the character is able to stand up for short periods of time. But it does serve as a good allegory for the kind of empty "inspirational" motivation at play. The action really means nothing.

But there comes that box-office haul. Was the movie's message true? This was the little scrappy team unexpectedly punching way above its weight class, facing off against big Hollywood pictures and coming out strong.

2008 was when this narrative really solidified, thanks to *Fireproof*. Instead of Alex Kendrick playing the lead role, this time they had bona fide Real Actor Kirk Cameron of *Growing Pains* fame. The film follows Caleb (played by Cameron), a firefighter trying to prevent his wife from divorcing him. It's not entirely clear what their relationship problems are. Most of them are laid out in a scene in the couple's kitchen where they fling accusations at each other: She doesn't do his laundry enough, she doesn't "respect him," he wants to use their savings to buy a boat while she wants to make minor renovations to the house, and he keeps wasting time on the internet (which, it turns out, is code for looking at pornography). Caleb gets nose-to-nose with his wife and screams at her in a way that needs a trigger warning, and then goes outside to beat up a rubber trash bin with a baseball bat.

On it goes, with Cat (the wife) flirting with a doctor at her job, and Caleb repeatedly visiting his father to complain about his disintegrating marriage while making petulant teenage remarks to his mom. Things turn around when his father gives him a handwritten book called *The Love Dare*, which contains 40 days of small acts he can do to save his marriage, and subsequently converts him, praying with him in front of a large wooden cross in a sun-dappled field that looks suspiciously similar to the one in *Facing the Giants*. After being converted by his own father—and subjected to a strange marriage metaphor that includes gluing salt and pepper shakers together by an upstanding Christian firefighter colleague—Caleb proves himself by extending a modicum of human decency to his wife (calling to ask how her day was, caring for her while she's sick, et cetera), donating his boat money to buy a wheelchair for her mother, and most importantly, struggling not to click a porn pop-up[*] on his computer, smashing *that* with a baseball bat, and replacing the computer with a vase of roses.

At the end, the couple renews their vows in front of God, a crowd of witnesses, and a wedding cake with salt and pepper shaker bride-and-groom toppers.

There's also a couple of action scenes—a fire and a car accident—and some boys being boys joshing around at the fire station, which really have no bearing on the plot. There's an attempt to marry (no pun intended) the two pieces together with some analogy about "never leaving your partner behind," but it doesn't really make sense, even in the context of the movie, since Caleb does all his marriage-fixing activities on his own without even informing his wife, and in the fire scene he is literally split up from his partner and has to save a small girl alone. But I digress.

The book Caleb follows, *The Love Dare*[**], was released as a companion to the movie and sold "600,000 copies within weeks, reaching number one on the *New York Times* list of best-selling paperback advice books," according to *Christianity Today*.

---

[*] It's a Christian movie, so this is depicted as a picture of a smiling woman's face that says, "Want to see more?" underneath it.

[**] In the end, it's revealed that it was not Caleb's dad but his *mom* that wrote *The Love Dare*, and that Caleb's dad only wrote it in his handwriting because Caleb wouldn't have listened if he knew it was coming from his mother. This makes Caleb tearfully apologize to his mother for . . . hating her for no reason, I guess? Alas, the film does not go as far as acknowledging Caleb's unfounded simmering misogyny toward every woman he encounters.

In profiles and interviews, the Kendrick brothers stress that their process is led by prayer* and that the willing volunteer labour and supply they are given must prove God's approval over their film projects. From a profile in *Christianity Today*:

> When they asked a fire chief for permission to use his reserve trucks, he offered them the free use of some brand-new vehicles that hadn't even been used by any of the fire crews yet. ("We had trucks as nice as a $200 million Hollywood movie," says Stephen [Kendrick]. "Oh yeah, nicer than *Backdraft*," Alex concurs.) And when they asked if they could shoot some scenes in a hospital, they were given free rein of a wing that was about to be remodelled and was thus free of patients and hospital staff.
>
> "Does it make sense that everybody rolls over and says, 'Here's our best stuff, for free. What can we do to help you?' Does that make any sense?" asks Alex. "We didn't pay a dime for any of that. So we saw the favour of the Lord go before us in every aspect."

What seems to go unquestioned in these interviews, even the ones from secular sources, are the ethics of using donations and volunteer labour to make a movie, and then profiting from it.

"*Fireproof* has made millions, but it's split multiple ways," a 2008 Baptist Press headline declares, a little defensively. According to the article, roughly half of the film's total gross went to the theatres, with the remaining portion split between Sony Pictures, Goldwyn Films, Provident Films, Carmel Entertainment, and finally, the church. Sherwood's executive pastor and executive

---

* Their current day website (KendrickBrothers.com) has an FAQ page that offers tips to aspiring Christian filmmakers. The first one reads: "PRAY FIRST: Filmmaking is very influential, and you will be held accountable by God for the influence of your films. It is very important to prayerfully consider the cost before aspiring to become a filmmaker."

producer, Jim McBride, is quoted in the article, declining to reveal the amount the church brought in through theatrical release and DVD sales and noting that all proceeds "have gone to the church's 'Generations' campaign—a fundraising campaign to pay for a new $5 million sanctuary and build an 82-acre, $4 million sports park."

McBride adds, "We commonly say at the church that with one of these movies we've felt like the little boy with five loaves and two fish who gave what little he had to Jesus and stood back in awe at what God did."

The *Time* profile of the brothers takes a slightly different tone, calling the films "a windfall" for the church. "The ministry has constructed a two-story prayer tower where volunteers pray for the movie studio and the region 24 hours a day. For the city of Albany [Georgia] (one of the poorest cities of its size in the country, with a per capita income of just $21,3000), the church has constructed an 82-acre sports park complete with an equestrian centre." The article adds that the church also "stocks food shelters throughout southwestern Georgia, supports a local drug and alcohol treatment facility and is launching new churches nationwide, including two in Baltimore and one in San Francisco."

Unlike the films, which split their profit between marketing and distribution and bring money back into the church coffers, *Fireproof*'s companion book, *The Love Dare*, was a product of the Kendrick brothers, not their church ministry—which seems to suggest that the authors, rather than the church, directly profited from the royalties.

Is it morally objectionable for a religious organization to profit off media creation? Framing the production company as a ministry has the dual purpose of positioning it as a fundraising arm—like a church bake sale taken to the nth degree—as well as a tool of outreach; while the films' audience is arguably entirely made up of other Christians, the Kendrick brothers clearly see their movies as evangelism tools, a product meant to convert nonbelievers to a Christian way of life.* Clearly, the Kendricks' community is won over by this framing, as the movies collected their shoestring budgets from parishioner donations of money and free labour. Even Kirk Cameron worked "for free"; *Christianity Today* reported that the actor asked that his salary for starring in the movie be donated to his nonprofit venture, Camp Firefly.

But as someone who spent many years of my life involved in churches and now works in a creative field, I can't help but see this as insidious. The cast and crew of *Fireproof* may not have been professionals, but they were doing the jobs of professionals. Shouldn't they be compensated? Shouldn't the church be transparent about its profits? And what about the distribution companies and theatres profiting from the film—Samuel Goldwyn Pictures wasn't building a community sports complex. Should churchgoers donating their time be lining a distributor's pockets?

The use of volunteers rather than professional actors has another benefit for the Kendricks that I didn't consider until reading the 2008 profile of the brothers in *Christianity Today*: It acts as an under-the-table morality clause. By casting only Christians from their specific church community, the Kendricks avoid any of the "controversies" (as the *CT* writer frames it) that have plagued more professional Christian productions in the past. The two referenced in the piece, top of mind in the 2000s, were the Christian films *End of the Spear* (2005) and *The Nativity Story* (2006)—the former was criticized for hiring a gay man to play the lead role of a martyred missionary, while the latter caught heat because the 16-year-old actor who played Mary, coincidentally, announced a pregnancy immediately prior to the film's release.

---

* "We've had 50 screenings of the movie all over the nation, and people are saying something to the effect of, 'This made me want to draw closer to the Lord,' or 'This made me want to give this area of my life to God, because I realize this is a giant in my life,'" Alex Kendrick told *Christianity Today* about *Facing the Giants*.

"Although we would like every aspect of our movie to be excellent, the number one priority for us is the ministry... The most important message we could ever share with the world is the message of the gospel. For us, we do not want to put somebody in front of the camera who proclaims it in the movie and doesn't believe it themselves," Kendrick told the magazine, casting some extra shade at the talent of his volunteer actors.

The Kendrick brothers' success continued beyond the 2000s, as Sherwood Pictures morphed from scrappy upstart into a full-scale film production company that just happened to be anchored to a church. By 2014, it seems the brothers outgrew Sherwood; they left to start their own company, simply called Kendrick Brothers. According to an article in the *Tennessean*, striking out on their own was "necessary for them to grow as filmmakers and recruit actors and crew nationwide." While not explicit, the article implies that the Kendricks no longer use volunteer labour, and some internet searching yields casting calls that go through a formal casting agency. There's also a reference to the brothers bringing in "about 20 interns from different universities" to work on one of their films—no word on whether those internships were paid.

"They're also giving back," the article notes. "The brothers are using the fruits of their success to help up-and-coming filmmakers with projects, as well as mentor a younger generation of hopefuls."

♥ † ♥

Sherwood Pictures' success kicked off a spate of copycat churches-turned-production-companies and pastors determined to wade into Christian filmmaking in the 2000s. Whether this was artistic inspiration, or the lure of bringing in millions at the box office to finance church projects, I can only speculate.

In a 2011 *Christianity Today* article, optometrist David Evans—a parishioner at Calvary Church of the Nazarene in Cordova, Tennessee, who had written and directed the church's annual

Easter passion play for 15 years—shares the story of being inspired by the Kendrick brothers' film. "After watching *Fireproof*, he came away believing Calvary should make a film too," the article reports.

"I realized that God had been preparing us for the last 15 years to do something far greater than we could ever imagine, and that's what set off the course of actions for me to begin writing the basic story of *The Grace Card*,' he said."

Yep, it's true: *Fireproof* bears direct responsibility for the 2010 film *The Grace Card* being born into this world. And yes, that title is a pun on the phrase "playing the race card," and no, it's not metaphorical—there is an actual "grace card" in the film. Evans took from the Kendricks' playbook, quite literally. "I got my hands on every word they had spoken on filmmaking . . . Casting call sheets, shooting schedules—everything they used I was able to use," Evans told *Time*. Made for $460,000, the movie took in $2.4 million at the box office.

Edgier than *Facing the Giants* or *Fireproof*, the film seems determined to take on *real issues*, most notably, racism. It does this, however, in the form of a buddy cop drama wherein Mac (Michael Joiner), a racist white police officer, is paired with a Black partner, Sam (Mike Higgenbottom), and slowly sees the error of his ways. The movie is hard to watch, especially scenes that visually echo horrific examples of police violence against Black victims.* The film hinges on deeply troubling, racist messages that foreground respectability politics and place a heavy emphasis on grace and forgiveness: Louis Gossett Jr.—the big actor "get" in this movie—plays Sam's grandfather, and tells him a story of his formerly enslaved ancestor who loved and forgave his slaveholder. This scene alone is enough to give this movie the Kirk Cameron baseball-bat-to-the-computer treatment, though that would

---

* Though obviously drawing on a longstanding cultural memory of police racism, both high-profile and everyday, the film was released before the police killings of Michael Brown, Philando Castile, George Floyd, and many more were heavily circulated on social media, so it's possible that these visual reminders are more visceral to the viewer today than they would have been in 2010. But perhaps that's extending too much benefit of the doubt.

mean missing the climactic moment in which Mac accidentally shoots his own son while investigating a break-in,* kickstarting a contrived series of events that ends with Sam donating his own kidney to save the boy's life. This ultimate act of grace wins Mac over to the point where he can forgive the Black man who accidentally killed his older son while driving away from a police chase. This backstory seems to imply Mac's racism was *caused* by this accident and also offers the film an opportunity to present a Black character being reformed by the prison system (the dangerous driver finds God in prison and ultimately becomes a missionary in Kenya).

Despite, ostensibly, a lifetime of lived experience inside American systems that are provably, stunningly racist—policing and the justice system—none of the Black characters in the film seem to consider racism as anything other than individual disagreements between singular, prejudiced people. The film equates any examples of individual "judgment" to racism, categorizing both as sins in the eyes of God. Racism can be solved, the film posits, by the victims of racism simply overextending and sacrificing themselves, being both so upstanding and so deferential that racists are simply forced through this goodwill to recognize their humanity.

This is obviously a deeply disturbing message, but therein lies the problem with these sorts of Christian independent films. "Media pastors" striking out on their own seemed to be portrayed in the press at the time as Davids going up against Hollywood Goliaths, spreading their message with the tenacity and elbow grease of an auteur on a shoestring budget, and then raking in the cash when the hordes of Christian viewers showed up to be inspired and edified by their message. But what *of* that message? With no oversight, churches are free to pump out movies full of

---

* While it's probably not "inspirational" in the sense it was attempting, this movie is, in fact, an extremely compelling argument for abolishing policing.

problematic tropes and sketchy theology, chalking any quibbles up to artistic licence.

Inspiration is the common thread in most Christian movies that don't follow a biblical story—so much so that it is the generic code for religious storytelling. You'll find Christian movies under the "Inspirational" tab of most streaming services. But when a story is fictional, what's so inspiring about it? I reflected on this watching the characters in *Facing the Giants* rejoice over their answered prayers. The audience is meant to be inspired by the idea that something like this *could* happen to them—almost like comforting oneself by reading stories about lottery winners.

Similarly, the film *October Baby*, released in 2011, uses a loose connection to real experiences to push an "inspiring" anti-abortion message. The movie is "inspired by" the life of anti-abortion activist Gianna Jessen, who was born during a failed late-term abortion. This link to a true story seems meant to validate the film's message, though the character in the movie diverges drastically from Jessen's story. Jessen was born in the late 1970s during an installation abortion, a rarely-used method of late-term pregnancy termination; the film's main character, Hannah (Rachel Hendrix), was born in 1991 when the usage of this procedure had fallen to a rate of less than 1 percent of all abortion procedures in the United States.* Jessen claims that health challenges plague her as a result of the unsuccessful abortion attempt, which the movie takes up but changes the actual ailments; while Jessen has cerebral palsy, Hannah has epilepsy, asthma, and depression (conditions which seem to disappear halfway through the movie, just there, one supposes, to provide an inciting incident). Doubling down

---

* Installation abortion accounted for 1.7 percent of U.S. abortions in 1985 and 0.8 percent in 2002. Wikipedia also notes there are only two documented cases of unsuccessful installation abortion attempts that resulted in live births, of which Jessen is one.

on the "true story" angle, the movie's credits are quickly taken over by an interview segment in which the directors and actor Shari Wiedmann, who played Hannah's birth mother in the film, explain the movie's relevance to her experience:

> Jon [Erwin, one of the directors] emailed me the script and, of course, I was so excited, I think I sat down that very night [to read it]. I got to the point of the birth mother, and I was overwhelmed, I started crying over it because the story actually had been, truly, written for me. And Jon and Andy [Erwin] didn't even know my backstory at all.

The actress had had an abortion 20 years prior, a fact which, oddly, Jon Erwin shares in the intercut interviews rather than Wiedmann herself. The other director, Andrew Erwin, appears onscreen to explain the benefit to the film:

> For the post-abortive mother [sic], it was very important to be very sensitive to that and to have this be a healing movie for them. So having Shari's voice and having her play the role was just phenomenal, to make sure that came across very authentic and very sensitive.

While filming the scene, "I just knew that the Lord was with me," Wiedmann says. "I slide down that door [in the filmed scene], and I'm crying—that wasn't acting. That was my moment with God, to hear Him say, 'It's okay, it's over, and you've been forgiven.'"

Just as a Christian film's box-office take seems to validate its quality or purpose, its ability to "inspire" evidently proves it worthy of existing. And while the film's profit acts as a marker of external approval, on the inside of the evangelical subculture, filmmakers always seem to be pointing toward a thumbs up approval from

On High, whether an answer to prayer while filming or a God Moment like the one Wiedmann describes. Here is positive proof that the film was *inspirational*, even to its actors—therefore it must be good and God-approved.

The duo behind the movie—Jon and Andrew Erwin, another brother team—had a stronger professional pedigree than writing church passion plays, as they had been working on Christian music videos and documentaries for years. But it was, again, an encounter with the Kendrick brothers that inspired them to make their own Christian feature films. Jon Erwin was directing the second unit on the Kendrick brothers' film *Courageous* when Alex Kendrick asked him, "What's your purpose?"

"I didn't know the answer because up until that point, my purpose was to get paid," Erwin told *Christianity Today* in 2012. "It convicted me that I needed to step out,* and that Andy and I needed to use our gifts for the Lord in a greater capacity." As the brothers tell it, it was this conversation that directly led them to make *October Baby*.

Despite the source of their inspiration, as they tell it, the goal was never to copy the Kendrick brothers. "We want variety in a Christian space," said Jon Erwin. "Comparing us to what the Kendricks are doing is like Peter and Paul in the Bible—they both had the same calling, but they had totally different jurisdictions and they were sent to different audiences."

♥ † ♥

October Baby also features a comic relief character, Truman, to break through the endless soul-searching and treacly messaging. This character is played by James Austin Johnson, who today is

---

* In case you don't speak Christianese, this is a shortened form of the phrase "step out in faith," meaning to take a risk with the confidence that God will provide whatever support you need. Also, to be *convicted* is to feel conscience-stricken, though this is generally spoken of as a positive thing and as coming from the Holy Spirit.

a cast member on *Saturday Night Live*, famous for his Donald Trump impression. In a 2021 podcast interview[*] about growing up evangelical and working in the Christian film industry, Johnson describes how Christian film evolved between the 2000s and the 2010s, explaining that movies in the early 2000s were aimed more at converting secular audiences, but over the next decade and beyond became more focused on viewers who are already Christian, essentially "preaching to the choir."

While Christian media has always catered to its subculture, the rise of the Kendrick Brothers model of filmmaking seemed to me like a sign of things to come, when Christian movies would mainly shore up a base, not try winning new people to the fold. The intervening years have seen the rise of the *God's Not Dead* series of movies—culture-war fantasies wherein an upstanding Christian *proves* the existence of God to a hard-headed atheist.[**] The Kendricks' most recent film, *Lifemark*, saw them reunite with Kirk Cameron to tell an anti-abortion story, and in 2023, the "Christian thriller" *Sound of Freedom* became one of the highest-grossing independent films of all time, pulling in $250 million, and featuring former Jesus Jim Caviezel as the founder of an anti-sex trafficking organization in a plot that critics have accused of stoking QAnon conspiracy theories.[***]

It continues to be possible to live a hermetically sealed Christian life, consuming only the evangelical propaganda that fits with one's worldview. This became clear to me when I signed up for a free trial of Pure Flix, a streaming service that promises the best in "faith and family entertainment." Along with producing the *God's Not Dead* franchise, Pure Flix has distributed

---

[*] *Good Christian Fun*, April 21, 2021.

[**] The most recent entry in the series, 2021's *God's Not Dead: We the People* features a God-fearing hero defending a group of Christian homeschooling families from the terror of a progressive government official trying to regulate them.

[***] Along with its high box office take, the film has been politically influential: According to reporter Talia Levin, Donald Trump even hosted a screening at his New Jersey golf club.

some of the bigger Christian hits in recent years, including the Jennifer Garner–fronted *Miracles from Heaven*, the Kendrick brothers' prayer-warrior movie *War Room*, and *The Star*, an animated retelling of the Christmas story through the perspective of the animals in the manger. The company was acquired by Sony in 2020 under its own faith-based subsidiary, Affirm Films. Then, in 2023, Pure Flix merged with Great American Media, a venture of a former Hallmark CEO, rebranding the streaming service with the unwieldy moniker Great American Pure Flix.

Logging into the service is a bit like entering a strange hall of mirrors. The grid of thumbnails that populate the screen are hilariously similar—hundreds of movies and TV shows all marketed the exact same way to reach the same niche audience. Rows on scrolling rows of uplifted faces glowing with shafts of sunlight—aptly called *God rays*, a Google search informs me. Judging from these thumbnails, Christians love horses, sports, and blond women. There are a lot of titles like *Going Home* and *Learning to Love*. Some of the thumbnails use a big graphic to show off a high Rotten Tomatoes score, I guess because that is a rarity. Browsable categories include "Faith Favourites" and "Romance," the latter of which seems well-populated. In fact, I watched two 2000s-era movies on the site—the made-for-TV anti-abortion drama *Sarah's Choice*, starring Contemporary Christian Music star Rebecca St. James, and *The Wager*, a strange, meandering story about a famous actor whose imminent Oscar nomination is threatened when he decides to try to live his life according to Jesus's Sermon on the Mount—that, despite being vastly different and both kind of bummers, were appended with the tag *hopeless romantics*.

Pure Flix also has a "Lifestyle" section under the Great American Media branding that features blog-style videos from well-manicured, Southern hosts who teach you how to make Buffalo chicken dip from their spotless, echoey kitchens.

In fact, the saga of Great American Media is an interesting illustration of the siloing of Christian entertainment. The company was formed in 2021 by Bill Abbott, former Hallmark CEO, and mimicked most of the programming and stylistic decisions of the Hallmark channel, including a focus on Christmas movies, even signing deals with former Hallmark Channel actors. In April of 2022, Great American Media hired Candace Cameron Bure—the former *Full House* star who was a longtime staple of Pure Flix and Hallmark movies and known, like her brother Kirk, for her fervent evangelicalism—in an executive role that would see her both acting in and developing original content for its platforms.

This timing suspiciously coincided with the Hallmark Channel releasing *The Holiday Sitter*, its first ever Christmas movie featuring a gay male couple in the romantic leads. A month before it was about to premiere, a profile entitled "Candace Cameron Wants to Put Christianity Back in Christmas Movies" appeared in the *Wall Street Journal*. In the profile, when asked if the movies she worked on with Great American Family would include any 2SLGBTQIA+ love stories, Bure responded, "I think that Great American Family will keep traditional marriage at the core."* Elsewhere in the article, Bure stated that her move was motivated by the Christian values behind the channel. "My heart wants to tell stories that have more meaning and purpose and depth behind them. I knew that the people behind Great American Family were Christians that love the Lord and wanted to promote faith programming and good family entertainment."

There's an odd dissonance within Christian moviemaking, in which those creating the media refuse to incorporate any outside, secular ingredient—whether that be the existence of gay people

---

* Despite stating that Bure doesn't speak for the company, and that her personal views don't necessarily reflect those of Great American Media, CEO Bill Abbott evaded refuting Bure's claim about "traditional marriage" to *Variety*.

or non-Christian actors—yet actively acknowledge how bad faith-based movies can be. In all the interviews I read with the Kendrick and Erwin brothers, all the think pieces in *Christianity Today*, there was a self-conscious addressing of the poor quality of Christian cinema. I understand this as someone who grew up Christian. We may have been religious, but we still had *eyes*. We could see the poor acting in *Left Behind*, the ridiculous graphics in *Bibleman*, hear the corny music cues in *The Jesus Film*. There was a desire for the kind of slick, glossy Hollywood appeal that major films like *The Passion of the Christ* offered. And there was also a realization of how easy it was for a religious film to turn preachy, schlocky, unsatisfying. Jon Erwin told *Christianity Today*:

> It can be a mistake when you're trying to wedge Christianity into a film that you're making. The beautiful thing about Christianity is that the themes of Christianity are so appealing at a fundamental level.... When you make a movie about hope and forgiveness and grace and love, these things are incredibly appealing to any audience. It's the nature of the story you pick, making sure you're passionate about that, and making sure at some core level it's meaningful and it's inherently what you believe. That's what we do, as opposed to making a film that's like everything else and then putting a little Christianity in there. Then it feels forced and then it comes out totally cliché.

All well and good, except for the fact that the interview is about *October Baby*, one of the most forced and clichéd movies I think I've seen in a long time. "We believe that we can help advance the Gospel to reach religious and non-religious audiences by creating bigger, blockbuster films," the Erwins' website says. "With each film, we are earning the right to be heard by audiences as we push for excellence and quality in everything we do. And we believe this is our time."

♥ † ♥

There was *one* Christian movie that I loved as a kid. I was ten years old when it came out, the prime age to be swept up in a tale of chaste romance and weepy inspiration. My best friend and I were obsessed. We would sit on the huge, plush couches in her parents' basement, pile ourselves with knitted blankets, and put the disc in the DVD player. There was that gentle, plucky music, there was the DVD menu with its sun-dappled photo of the romantic leads with their arms wrapped around each other: *A Walk to Remember*. Press Play.

Released by Warner Bros. Pictures and directed by Adam Shankman (who would go on to direct *Hairspray* and judge *So You Think You Can Dance*, among other things), the movie is not Christian in the Kendrick brothers sense of the word. But the storyline—and, importantly, the main character, Jamie (Mandy Moore)—is. The film was adapted from a book of the same name by romance writer Nicholas Sparks (of *The Notebook* fame), and follows the doomed love story of a Christian girl who is dying of cancer and the Bad Boy who turns his life around for her.

And I, too, fell in love with Jamie Sullivan. Not just in the sense of nascent bisexual stirrings, either. The character was a perfect fantasy for a couple of shy Christian girls unsure about how to square a dedication to their faith with all sorts of other budding desires, for romance, identity, to be really seen by someone. In the movie, Jamie is the ultimate goody two-shoes, mocked for her frumpy clothes, earnest participation in every after school extracurricular, and geeky telescope hobby. And yet she wins over Landon (Shane West) with sheer magnetism, with undying kindness and sweetness. The ultimate evangelical version of a Manic Pixie Dream Girl.

At the end of the movie, Jamie dies offscreen—after a quickie marriage to Landon to provide some romantic satisfaction while keeping things chaste—and huddled in my friend's basement, I would feel the gratifying welling-up of tears behind my eyes, that special kind of cry evoked by a quote, unquote, *inspirational* story. That blend of bittersweet enjoyment, cathartic and devastating, the kind of thing that feels good because it feels so bad, like the story of the dog who waited at that train station for his dead owner for ten years.

Is that what evangelicals find so inspiring about Christian films?

Rewatching the movie now, the emotional beats seem corny and contrived, the tear-jerking cancer storyline kind of rushed and problematic. My emotional reactions were limited to squeals of nostalgia (a young Paz de la Huerta?!).

The highlight of the movie was Jamie's big performance in the school play, where she sings basically the entirety of a Switchfoot song (interpretable as about love *or* Jesus!) onstage, hilariously as part of a musical that she apparently wrote herself that seems to be about Prohibition-era gangland Chicago. She enters onstage in a big hooded cloak, and then drops it to reveal a modest but pretty dress in pale blue silk, her formerly lank hair meticulously curling-ironed into a cloud of chocolate-brown waves. This is the moment Landon falls in love with her: She's beautiful, onstage, stunning them all with her pure, tinkling voice. No wonder my friend and I wanted to be her.

This, I suppose, was the kind of Christian representation I was hoping for as a kid in evangelical spaces. But even back then, I remember having the sense that the character was a little too perfect to really be interesting. Like the kind of escapism and hollow inspiration offered by Pure Flix, the Kendrick brothers, and the like, I wonder what the function of a feel-good movie really is. Do Christians really need that much reassurance that God, that the things they believe, that they themselves are good?

♥ † ♥

On the opposite end of the spectrum—what you might call a *feel-bad* movie—is *The Passion of the Christ*. I had never seen it in its entirety, only that clip played over and over in Good Friday assemblies of my youth. From what I can remember, the film was cued up to the point when Jesus is being nailed to the cross and played until he says his final words and slumps forward into death. As someone who has to cover their eyes even in boxing movies, the bloody horror of it was too much for me.

But for the sake of journalistic integrity, I felt I had to watch it. A very kind friend who possibly did not know what she was getting herself into volunteered to watch it with me, and we squirmed and shrieked on her couch for two hours. (I still couldn't look during the nailing-of-the-hands scene, but the sounds of piercing flesh brought back some very visceral memories.)

What was the point of such hyperviolence, rendered so extreme as to almost become comical? When Jesus took up the cross, my friend and I, baffled, checked the timestamp—there was still an hour of movie left. In lingering, almost loving shots, the camera shows Jesus falling, again and again, often in slow motion, as he tries to carry the cross on his back—skin torn to shreds, body bathed in his own blood, sweat and blood crusting on his face. We counted seven falls.

One imagines that the point is to convey the horrors, the cruelty, of what Jesus suffered. When I mentioned the *Passion* to my partner and another friend who'd been raised in the evangelical church, they were both able to tap into some long-dormant store of knowledge about the science of crucifixion. *Did you know they actually typically nailed crucifixion victims to the cross through their wrists, because there's a point where a nail can pierce through without hitting any bones or veins, and it takes longer for them to die? Did you know they pierced his side with a spear to see if he was really dead because water will run from a wound in a dead body?*

I think I was subjected to similar lessons on the horrors of crucifixion, though I didn't retain the knowledge since even typing the above sentence made me feel woozy. I suppose the stated intention is to show the depth of Jesus's love and sacrifice: Look what he was willing to do to save you from sin! Look what he went through—willingly! Perhaps this is meant to be another type of *inspirational* film.

Jim Caviezel, the actor who played Jesus, certainly seems to think so. The actor has been vocal about how playing Jesus both strengthened his faith and caused him to be ostracized by Hollywood for his Christianity. In a rambling 2013 interview at the evangelical Rock Church in San Diego—available on YouTube—Caviezel variously skips between stories of the immense physical toll the role took on his body and digressive sermonizing about the importance of repentance.* Among the horrific injuries that Caviezel recounts during filming were being accidentally whipped during the scourging scene (causing a 14-inch gash on his back), dislocating his shoulder while carrying the cross, losing about 50 pounds of body mass due to illness, catching pneumonia and having his lungs fill up with fluid, being struck by lightning, and requiring open-heart surgery after filming ended. Despite the danger of this role—which I would say amounts to, at the very least, some labour violations—his main complaint about the set is that "Mel Gibson would take God's name in vain." (He claims to have scolded him for this while dressed as Jesus.)

Caviezel recounts:

> At the end of filming, when I was on the cross, my body was blue. There was no make-up, my body was actually blue. . . . Between takes, they would take

---

* The introduction of the slightly goofy, sycophantic pastor who's interviewing him gives a good gloss on how evangelicals felt about the film in retrospect. After asking those who haven't seen it to raise their hands, he says, "Okay, we'll slap you later, no problem. Just a little film that did over a billion dollars worldwide and kind of revolutionized the theatrical industry, but no big deal."

me down . . . and it would snap my shoulder out of joint. I was just beyond. At that point I was so sick that it would be ripped out and I would barely feel it anyway. I was so gone. But something's wrong with my heart. And the man [I assume a set doctor, though this is unclear] put a stethoscope on my heart, and he said, "Mel, he can [sic] die." And at that point—one of the greatest things about Mel Gibson was, he's a gambling man. He said, "Jim, what do you think?" And I said, "This is between me and God." . . . I knew that if I died making this movie, so many people would be saved. . . . I know if I die, I'm going to heaven.

♥ † ♥

Meanwhile, there was a fair amount of pushback against the violent imagery upon the film's release. Reviewers were divided on the efficacy of it—Roger Ebert famously called it "the most violent film I have ever seen"—but the film became one of the highest-grossing rated-R movies in history. Two different people reportedly died of heart attacks while watching the movie in theatres.

But it's impossible to see such suffering in a vacuum, to not demonize those doing the nailing and the side-piercing and the jeering.

The antisemitism in the movie is shockingly overt. Not only are the Pharisees and the crowds of Jewish onlookers portrayed as bloodthirsty and lacking basic human empathy, the Roman leaders—including Pontius Pilate and "Claudia," a whole cloth–invented, pure-of-heart Roman woman there to look beautiful, plead Jesus's case to Pilate, and stare sadly out of windows while Jesus gets beat within an inch of his life—are portrayed with such sensitivity that it sneakily denigrates Jewish representation by elevating the portrayal of gentiles. As *New York Daily News* film reviewer Jami Bernard—who called the film "the most virulently anti-Semitic [sic] movie made since the German propaganda films of World War II"—laid out in 2004:

> Jews are vilified, in ways both little and big, pretty much nonstop for two hours, seven minutes. Gibson cuts from the hook nose of one bad Jewish character to the hook nose of another in the ensuing scene. He misappropriates an important line from the Jewish celebration of Pesach ("Why is this night different from all other nights?") and slaps it onto a Christian context. Most unforgivable is that Pontius Pilate (Hristo Naumov Shopov), the Roman governor of Palestine who decreed that Jesus be crucified, is portrayed as a sensitive, kind-hearted soul who is sickened by the tortures the Jewish mobs heap upon his prisoner.

In a later column, Bernard writes of receiving virulent hate mail and death threats in response to her review. Certainly, there were groups committed to the narrative that the film was not antisemitic; the Catholic League launched a "counter-offensive" against the claim, but their compilation of "incendiary remarks" about the film does more to prove than refute the claims. Charges of antisemitism, of course, did not arise out of thin air, and were even plaguing Gibson during filming and post-production. According to an *Entertainment Weekly* article from the time, after screenings of the film, Gibson responded to complaints about a particular scene in which Caiaphas, the Jewish high priest, says of Jesus, "His blood be on us and on our children," a phrase pulled from the Gospel of Matthew that has historically been used within Christianity to stoke anti-Jewish hatred. Gibson responded, promising to remove the scene, though according to Bernard's review, the line remained in the film with subtitles removed.

In 2006, Mel Gibson was pulled over by the police for driving while intoxicated and was caught on film in the midst of an antisemitic rant. I was 14 at the time and shocked. I heard the hosts on HOT 103, the pop radio station, discussing it while my mom drove me to school, heard it transformed into monologue jokes on David Letterman, which my dad watched every night. I had no context—I didn't know then about Gibson's father, Hutton Gibson, who, like Mel, was part of the ultra-orthodox Traditionalist Catholic movement and had made many public antisemitic remarks, including denying the Holocaust. I didn't know about any of the criticisms *The Passion of the Christ* had garnered, before, during, and after its release, about antisemitic overtones, including charges that the script had borrowed liberally from extra-biblical sources, some of which have been criticized for antisemitism. In fact, I knew very little about antisemitism in general. My Christian school had taught me extensively about the Holocaust, but it was presented as something mainly left in the past, the singular vision of Adolf Hitler uncoupled from any larger ideology.

Antisemitism has unfortunately been a legacy of Christian teachings for centuries, particularly as it stems from the conception of Jesus "fulfilling" Jewish prophecy as well as the representation of the Pharisees, the Jewish sect sometimes—as in the *Passion*—represented as responsible for Christ's execution. In the early 1980s, the Catholic church sought to correct these teachings, putting forth a conference of experts to study relations between the church and Judaism and eventually creating documents with guidelines on preaching about and presenting Judaism and the Jewish people within sermons and liturgy. Other denominations have created similar documents.

The 1985 document "Guidelines for Catholic-Jewish Relations" states:

The presentation of the Crucifixion story should be made in such a way as not to implicate all Jews of Jesus'[s] time or of today in a collective guilt for the crime. This is important for catechisms and homilies, especially during Lent and Holy Week, as well as for any dramatizations of the events, such as Passion Plays.

It also mandates the "explicit rejection" of "the historically inaccurate notion that Judaism of that time, especially that of Pharisaism, was a decadent formalism and hypocrisy," noting an increasing consensus among scholars on "the closeness on many central doctrines between Jesus'[s] teaching and that of the Pharisees." Despite making his movie almost two decades later, Gibson could not seem to follow even this guideline for church Easter plays in putting his Passion on the big screen.

♥ † ♥

Many of my teachers, on the other hand, fell into a segment of Zionist evangelicalism, and I was also taught that the Jewish people had a "special bond" with God; I remember a teacher telling our class with dead-set confidence that Jewish people held some kind of Godly exception and would be joining us Christians in heaven for eternity.

This belief, part of the theology of dispensationalism, is a common tenet of Christian Zionism, which has become a near de facto belief in American evangelical circles, bolstered by preachers, politicos, and evangelists like Billy Graham, Pat Robertson, and Jerry Falwell. *The Passion of the Christ*, attempting to mitigate charges of antisemitism, ends up treading a line where it creates a distinction between the Pharisees and Jewish high priests, who are portrayed as Jesus's killers and true followers of Jesus, respectively.

These are the "good" Jewish people who evangelicals could also read as their Christian forebearers.

One Night with the King (2006), a retelling of the biblical story of Esther, does something similar. In dramatizing an Old Testament book of the Bible in which the Jewish people are the persecuted and oppressed underdogs, it presents Judaism as some kind of proto-evangelicalism that is headed on a trajectory toward American nationalism. Haman, the villain of the film, aims to stamp out a growing trend of democracy imported from Greece. At one point, he asks rhetorically whether the Jewish prophesy of a Messiah, a "King of Kings"—he's one step away from winking at the camera and mouthing *Jesus* while saying this—is not "the very essence of democracy." Besides not being historically accurate or having anything to do with the movie's plot, these lines suggest a direct connection between democracy and Christianity and hinge on the underlying belief that Christianity should be integrated into politics and that secular government is sinful and somehow undemocratic.

Christian nationalism categorizes America as both a "Christian nation" and depends on a reading of Christianity that centres around right-wing American politics. There is another Christian movie (in a way) of the 2000s that shows the reach of Christian nationalism into the mainstream evangelicalism of the decade: *Jesus Camp* (2006), a documentary focused on an evangelical Christian camp that featured scenes of kids pledging allegiance to the Christian flag, marching in army uniforms, preaching, and participating in conservative political advocacy. The film's strategy of presenting an impartial view of its subjects makes it all the more alienating to watch—these kids are drinking in Christian media and regurgitating it as zealous ideologues.

In 2023, Caviezel did a YouTube interview with infamous Christian nationalist and alt-right sympathizer Jordan Peterson to promote his film *Sound of Freedom*, in which he also seemed to be there to promote human trafficking conspiracy theories. Like his work on *The Passion of the Christ*, he frames his acting process as a horrifically trying ordeal, a necessary sacrifice in order to spread the message of the film, and that making this fictional film is somehow part of a supernatural fight for the souls of the nation.

This was the tactic taken by *The Passion*'s PR team, who supplied American churches with marketing kits and suggestions on how to incorporate the film and its teachings into sermons. Some churches led group outings for congregants to see the film, and one Christian businessman in Texas even bought six thousand tickets to screenings to hand out in his community.* That kind of action reminded me of how I was bundled into a youth group van to go see *The Nativity Story*, how my partner's youth group bought opening day tickets to *One Night with the King*. Unflinching, unquestioning support: That was what was required of Christians toward these films.

Despite the moniker of Jesus's life as the "greatest story ever told," I came out of my Christian movie marathon with a sense that there is some essential difficulty between the Christian story and narrative structure. Jesus's life might have formed a good basis for a heroic myth, but stories about Christian triumphs or human forgiveness easily come off as preachy, low-stakes, or overly pat. Human nature is hard to explore while censoring for "sin," and it's hard to turn a scene of someone delivering a sermon into a cathartic, visually compelling climax. You end up with the bland pablum of *Facing the Giants* or the torture porn of *The Passion of the Christ*.

All Christian films are, by nature, morality tales; they have a message, which makes them didactic. Typically, that's not an ingredient in quality narrative fiction. This works a little better

---

* Chilton, "The Blood, the Outrage and *The Passion of the Christ*," *The Independent*, 25 February 2019.

in children's programming—all children's media is expected to be a bit didactic, meant to teach even if subtly, which strangely makes *Veggie Tales* easier to watch than *October Baby*. Perhaps this is also why Christian film seems to have abandoned the wide-net approach and siloed itself more cleanly into a conservative Christian market.

The Christian film trends that arose in the 2000s—independently financed "message" films with all-Christian casts, inspirational alternatives to genre films—have, if anything, concentrated in their potency and shifted from the realm of single church–funded visionaries to larger-scale independent production houses. In 2025, if you trust what's posted to IMDb, Mel Gibson is set to release *The Passion of the Christ: Resurrection*, a sequel which will apparently elucidate "the three days between the crucifixion and resurrection when Jesus Christ descended to Abraham's Bosom to preach and resurrect Old Testament saints," a plot which seems even more alienating than the violent visions of the first installment, albeit in a different way. Samuel Goldwyn Pictures, the distributor of countless independent Christian movies, is set to distribute, and the news of its production seems largely untouched by secular media—likely because "seculars," as Caviezel calls them, are not the target audience. I noticed that more recent Christian films actually have much higher Rotten Tomatoes scores than the 2000s-era entries I'd watched—not because they were better films but because the average was compiled from very few critic reviews, and most of those reviews were from evangelical publications and blogs. Since the inflection point of the *Passion*, it seems Christian and secular films have drifted apart again. (I'm guessing evangelicals won't be happy with the upcoming *Narnia* reboot with Greta Gerwig at the helm, though it remains to be seen.)

Recently, a controversy around the film *Bros* reminded me of my childhood feelings toward Christian movies. Billy Eichner, the writer and star of the romantic comedy, urged members of the 2SLGBTQIA+ community to see the movie opening weekend in order to prove that queer mainstream films were worthy of investment for movie studios. Despite the fact that it was my queer identity and not my religious affiliation that was being called upon, the urging felt familiar. Once again, I was being asked to validate a representation of some part of my identity through box-office receipts. While *Bros* is conservatively 100 percent more enjoyable to watch than *The Passion of the Christ*, in my mind, both show the danger of a representational framework that relies on the buying power of different subcultures to validate their inclusion in the mainstream.

The only thing I remember about that *Nativity Story* screening with my youth group is that I was so bored I kept almost falling asleep. (I've never been a big fan of historical *or* biblical epics.) Still, at the end, I stood and clapped alongside my friends and youth group leader. It wasn't really the story that mattered. It was that it was being told at all.

CHAPTER FOUR

PLEDGES AND PURITY RINGS

THE RISE OF ABSTINENCE TEACHINGS FOR A GENERATION WHO WERE TOLD THAT TRUE LOVE WAITS

Onstage at the 2008 MTV Video Music Awards, a dark-haired Katy Perry[*] coyly unpeels a banana built into the top of her stage costume while singing a cover of Madonna's "Like a Virgin." When the chorus repeats, she sings: "Like a Jonas, touched for the very first time / Like a Jonas, put your promise ring next to mine." On the words *promise ring* she taps her hand against her crotch.

The Jonas Brothers, the three-piece Disney-star pop outfit, took a beating that night. British comedian Russell Brand[**] was the show's host and peppered his stand-up set with jokes denigrating the brothers' public statements about their decisions to wear purity rings, rings which symbolizes a pledge to remain sexually abstinent until marriage that had become popular in evangelical Christianity in the previous decade. But *American Idol* star and fellow purity-ring-wearer Jordin Sparks had a different message, taking a moment to make a brief aside to camera: "It's not bad to wear a promise ring because not everybody—guy or girl—wants to be a slut," she said, before clapping her hands and saying, "Okay!" as she moved on to the teleprompted lines.

---

[*] The artist formerly known as Katy Hudson, Christian music star.
[**] Who is now, in a strange twist of fate, an extremely right-wing evangelical Christian.

This VMA performance offers—along with a heaping of nostalgia for side bangs—a perfect encapsulation of the messy pop culture moment that was coming to an end along with the first decade of the millennium. Abstinence—saving sex for marriage—had grown since the 1990s from a fringe evangelical Christian talking point to a downright movement, one so large it had spilled into mainstream popular culture. Jordin Sparks and the Jonas Brothers were only the latest in a decade-long line of pop stars pledging to keep their "purity" with the signifier of that little ring on their finger: Selena Gomez, Demi Lovato, Miley Cyrus, Hilary Duff, Britney Spears, and Jessica Simpson.

I was eight years old at the turn of the millennium, so the 2000s neatly encompassed the entirety of my transition from child to teen—my whole junior high and high school years. From the vantage point of my Christian high school in the middle of Canada, these Disney Channel pop stars who praised God and vowed to stay pure for their future wives and husbands seemed like a natural extension of the culture around me—even the signs of a cultural shift. Was being a Christian becoming *popular*?

In reality, larger political forces, many driven by capital, were spurring these social shifts in the U.S. Historian Sara Moslener links the rise of the modern evangelical purity movement to a reaction against the countercultural movements of the 1960s (including the sexual revolution), and in response to the sexual fears of the AIDS crisis years. From its start, the movement was expressly political. True Love Waits, a ministry that grew out of the Southern Baptist denomination in the early '90s and would later become one of the biggest abstinence-advocacy organizations in the world, initiated itself in 1993 by bringing several dozen youths to Washington, D.C., to pound more than 100,000 cards bearing abstinence pledges into the lawn of the National Mall.

"The purity movement received strong support from evangelical institutions and organizations," researcher Kristin Kobes

Du Mez writes in her book *Jesus and John Wayne*. Along with support from the Southern Baptist Convention and the Christian homeschool community,

> countless local churches promoted purity teachings, and purity culture found expression in an array of consumer products. Families purchased silver "purity rings" to provide girls with a constant reminder of the value of their virginity, and of their obligation to guard it vigilantly. "Purity balls" started popping up across the country, offering families opportunities to enact their commitment to sexual purity through public ceremony. At these events, fathers provided a model of masculine headship by "dating" their daughters, and girls pledged their sexual purity before their families and communities.

Silver Ring Thing—generally credited with popularizing the purity ring—was founded in 1995. The organization put on concert-style events with a live show that used music, videos, scripted skits, and preaching to convince teenagers of the value of abstinence, the whole night ending with a purity pledge and each participant taking home a ring.

In all my research for this book, I have not been able to trace a definitive basis for the Christian teaching that the Bible outlaws premarital sex. Most evangelical Christian books will tell you that sex is only appropriate between *one man and one woman within the confines of marriage, forever*. This neatly eliminates divorce, queer relationships, polyamory, and relationships that are not a legal marital union from moral righteousness. But the Bible verses used to justify it refer only to "sexual immorality." There are verses mandating heterosexuality (seemingly—plenty of scholars disagree with the translations and contexts that surround them). But there is no verse that says, "No sex before marriage."

Despite this lack of clear biblical mandate, politically influential and conservative Christian players in the United States increasingly pushed for abstinence as the only moral option for young people, and this belief became ever more synonymous with Christianity. And it didn't remain cloistered on one side of the church-state line. The U.S. federal government began funding abstinence-only education under Ronald Reagan, funding which only increased under Bill Clinton and George W. Bush. Since 1981, more than $2 billion of federal funding has been allocated for abstinence-only programs in the United States. The Community-Based Abstinence Education funding stream, which ran under President George W. Bush from 2001 to 2009, allocated $733 million in federal funds to abstinence programming. True Love Waits actively campaigned for increases to this funding—that's what the mass purity pledge on the National Mall was about—and held a special session between purity activists and Bill Clinton.*

Given this influx of federal money, it's no wonder that the purity-focused speakers and organizations who had previously made their mark in small community settings would expand their teachings to go mainstream: The rise in government funding coincided neatly with the rise of purity rings, bracelets, necklaces, shirts, hats, books, journals, devotionals, DVDs, planners, and many other purity-centric products, not to mention events and curricula. Researcher Linda Kay Klein notes that Silver Ring Thing itself received $1.4 million from the U.S. federal government and was sued in 2005 by the American Civil Liberties Union (ACLU) for evangelizing at government-funded events.

This kind of funding slowed during the Obama administration but picked back up under Trump. All of this, even though studies have shown that teens who pledge to be abstinent are no more likely to abstain from sex than a control group, have

---

* Klein, *Pure*, pp. 22–25

roughly the same number of partners, and become sexually active at the same average age. Studies have also shown that evangelical adolescents are, compared to their peers, less likely to expect sex to be pleasurable and more likely to expect sex will make them feel guilty (even more so for girls, who are 92 percent more likely to experience sexual guilt than boys). Overall, studies find that purity teachings are not even effective by their own standards—they do not meaningfully delay sex for young people—but that they do increase shame and sexual anxiety and decrease sexual pleasure. A U.S.-based 2007 study authorized by the country's congress showed that over a decade, abstinence-only education did not meaningfully reduce rates of teen sex.[*]

2008 might have been the last mainstream burst of enthusiasm for teen abstinence. In the following years, those Disney stars quietly slipped off their purity rings, and the wave of teen celebs replacing them didn't take up the pledge. Now, 15 years after that decade, my demographic—those teens who received abstinence-only sexual education, who attended Silver Ring Thing shows or wore True Love Waits necklaces, who listened to pro-abstinence music and read books about how to maintain our purity—have grown up. Now, we have a name for that time: *Purity culture*, a pervasive culture stressing sexual propriety through the use of concepts like "pure" and "impure," extending to sexual abstinence as well as compulsive heterosexuality, modest dress, and "traditional" family structures.

That decade, in which I felt immersed in purity culture, had a major impact on my life. And as I reflected on the ways it had shaped me and hurt me, I knew I wanted to hear how it had affected others.

Throughout this chapter are the voices of friends and acquaintances who generously shared their experiences with abstinence teachings and purity culture in response to interview questions. These experiences encompass several different Christian denominations,

---

[*] Klein, pp. 25–28; "Study Casts Doubt on Abstinence-Only Programs," *The Washington Post*.

countries of origin, and generations, and yet common threads run through most of them, the most common being shame about sexuality and discomfort with their own bodies and minds.

♥ † ♥

† Looking back, what troubles me the most about the abstinence teaching that I received is how I accepted it as the one and only way to properly be a Christian. I accepted it as totally biblical and thought that any belief or behaviour outside of it made someone a marginally committed Christian. It bothers me that I couldn't imagine legit Christians having a different theological or moral understanding. I also feel like it kind of messed up my view of sexuality. I think that the teaching I received scared me away from forms of physical care in relationships and from relationships in general. I viewed marriage as the goal of any relationship, which meant I put so much weight on any relationship I entered.

† I think the teaching that clicked the most with me was the idea that your virginity/abstinence was somehow tied to your love for God and your love for your future spouse. Even though it wasn't considered cool to save yourself for marriage, the church had given me a sort of superiority complex that made me think that my marriage and sex life would be so much better than everyone else's because of my faithfulness to God's teachings about sex.

† I remember being skeptical of abstinence teachings, even then. I didn't say anything about it—mind you, I was already feeling judged by the church and didn't like it. I didn't want any further attention.

† Sexual purity extended not just to what we did with others but what we did by ourselves, too. So, the young men of the church were told to find themselves "accountability partners" they could unburden themselves to every time they masturbated, referred to colloquially as

falling *in my church setting (as in, "It had been a couple of weeks, but yesterday I fell again, guys."). The guys were even encouraged to download what was essentially spyware onto their home computers that would send an alert to any emails connected to the account (again, usually a youth pastor) if we looked at a pornographic website. There was no real absolution to be gained from these confessions. The point was just to publicly, or semi-publicly, reckon with your rebellious, sinful, inherently broken nature.*

† I do remember being confused that there weren't verses in the Bible that were more explicit about one partner only/no premarital sex rules. A lot of the verses I was pointed to seemed to be about divorce and male pride around childbearing. I did, however, find a whole book of poetry in the Bible about a woman and a man who are lovers and not yet married, delighting in one another's bodies, but I don't think anyone in my denomination ever acknowledged the Song of Songs outside of a wedding homily.

† I got involved in an evangelical youth group where it was, like, a no-brainer that you're not going to have sex before marriage, and what you really needed was to be careful because it could just happen all of a sudden.

† In all honesty, staying pure also seemed like a way to honour your parents, showing them that you were listening to a teaching of theirs that you could prove by not living with your partner before you married them and by sleeping in separate bedrooms on family vacation.

† I believed that "normal" women didn't want or enjoy sex—it was something you did for men because they were driven by their biological needs. Children were a natural and almost guaranteed result of having sex, so you could only have sex within the confines of marriage. This made me feel ashamed to ask for what I wanted from a partner or to masturbate. I stayed in a marriage where the sex was terrible for

far too long without fixing it. Sex scenes in books and movies made me squirm; I felt like they were "lowbrow" content.

† *I actually learned about sex from the encyclopedia.* World Book, I think. *There was a set in my classroom at school. One day, I pulled out the S volume and looked up* sex. *After reading that entry, I read* pregnancy *and* penis *and any other words that felt vague in my mind. But the encyclopedia was also confusing—I remember that a penis was described as "finger-shaped," which baffled my imagination. I also had no idea what my own anatomy was like, and I was terrified to look/probe.*

† *I remember one of the women speaking to my youth group. She was literally 30 and she was like, "I'm still waiting." I remember kind of admiring her and also thinking it was insane. By the middle of Grade 10, I was starting to deconstruct things and be like, I just don't believe this. And one of the things that really clicked to me was all these girls in the Bible are getting married when they're like 14. Yeah, good job, you waited to have sex until you were married—you were fucking 14.*

† *Sexual sin was THE BIG sin, and it represented all that Jesus died for.*

† *I feel like, for a certain kind of person, purity culture really fuels a kind of melancholy. I'm supposed to be sad about it; it's supposed to be fraught, a dark night of the soul, "Why can't I beat this temptation, God?" There was an honour-based, chivalric, even deep concern for women in a lot of Christian pop culture if you chose to read it there. You could find care for women if you looked for it, if you needed it to be there. And as someone who grew up in an abusive household where I didn't feel like my dad had any care for my mom, I needed it to be in there. The part that went awry was, I felt like I was supposed to show that care and respect for women by not touching them. Half the*

relationships I had that had some romantic aspect when I was younger got fucked up because I was like, "The way I'm supposed to show I care about is by never touching you!"

† Sex was bad, scary, dangerous, impure, wrong, disgusting, damnable, and I badly wanted to be what I was taught was an exemplary human being.

† Purity culture did not just teach me not to have sex before marriage. That was the least of it. It taught me to be hyper-vigilant about my own thoughts, to assume that what felt good to me or what I wanted was actually evil, to fight myself and think of myself as constantly failing God.

† It felt all-pervasive and inescapable. I internalized what I was taught, but at the same time, it was an uneasy internalization. I never felt completely comfortable following the teachings of purity culture. I just assumed whenever I failed to live up to the ideals of purity culture that it was a personal failing. That I alone was at fault. It never occurred to me that it might be the system I grew up in that was problematic. That it was purity culture that failed me, not the other way around.

† Purity culture and the heteronormative project it supported were absolutely what kept me from knowing that I was queer until I was 24. Heterosexual, monogamous marriage was the only kind of intimate relationship I could hope for or correctly desire, so I desired it desperately. As someone who longed for connection and ached to be loved, I focused on the only God-approved way to find that connection and love.

† I remember my older sister telling me when I was 15 years old that the Bible never actually says sex before marriage is wrong, and I was just so mad at her for even suggesting that because it made me feel so wrong-footed. Like my whole foundation was uncertain. If the sexual

experience wasn't black and white like I had always been taught, what if that meant other things weren't black and white, too?

♥ † ♥

In the Christianity I grew up with, it was like sex could exist only in the metaphorical register. Perhaps it was because we were restricted from straightforward sexual education that would have taught us the appropriate and correct terminology for things; maybe it was because there was no clear instruction against premarital sex in the Bible, and therefore every sexual activity became couched under nebulous terms like *sexual immorality* and *purity*.

Our teachers, pastors, or parents wouldn't dream of using anatomically correct words, and we wouldn't dream of asking questions that might betray desires too sinful to be talked about. Our sexual selves, and in particular, our virginities, could not simply *be*; they had to be spotlighted in elaborate object lessons intended to "prove" the necessity of waiting for marriage. Virginity had to be bigger than itself, had to become purity, that word loaded with value and goodness. Just like we needed metaphorical object lessons (your body is a flower, your promise is a ring), virginity itself needed a metaphorical vehicle, had to be represented by the sweet perfection of a good Christian life. Even the word *waiting* became loaded with metaphor and implication. It presupposed an inactivity, a static-ness, and an assumption that marriage was coming for all of us.

Maybe it would have been easier if there was a verse in the Gospel of John or something: "Verily, I tell you, you shall not let a man insert his penis into your vaginal canal until the night of your wedding, after exchanging vows, at the airport Holiday Inn Express on the eve of your Hawaiian honeymoon." Or a loophole handed down from on high: "Thou shall not masturbate, unless you're alone at home and the porn you look at is appropriately wholesome."

Instead, youth pastors the world over reached into the most creative parts of themselves to find the perfect metaphorical stand-in for what would be lost if young Christians didn't Wait for True Love.

Examples are easy to find in the pop culture of the time, particularly in the cottage industry of abstinence books that promised to help teenagers battle their purity demons and enable parents to tell their kids about sex without actually, well, talking to their kids about sex. Such books were, of course, popular with evangelical teens of the time, too.

I Kissed Dating Goodbye by Joshua Harris, an infamous entry in this category, was published in 1997 when Harris was just 23. In the book, Harris warned young Christians about the dangers of premarital sex and the glorious promises of abstinence, and did so while laying out his vision for a new kind of dating—what he called *courting*—based around building friendships, going on group dates, and restricting physical intimacy to the point where a couple might have their first kiss on their wedding day.[*]

The book—which I will reiterate was written by an unmarried 23-year-old Christian who seemingly had never done more than kiss a girl prior to its publication—opens with an imagined anecdote. A bride and groom are stepping up to the altar on their wedding day. They are both so happy. But what's this? When the bride looks past her groom, she sees a line of . . . women? Who are these women that she's marrying by association? Well, when you marry someone, you marry everyone they've ever "given [their] heart to."

---

[*] Harris has since denounced his own book and ordered the publisher to discontinue its publication. After decades of backlash from former evangelical teens (there's a great roundtable on the book archived on The Toast), Harris officially recanted his advice and apologized in 2016 and again in 2018 through a documentary entitled *I Survived I Kissed Dating Goodbye*. He also promptly made his detractors angry by trying to monetize the opportunity with a new anti-courting self-help series. In 2019, Harris announced that he and his wife were separating and that he was no longer a Christian.

I didn't read *I Kissed Dating Goodbye* as a teen, except for some excerpts given to us in lieu of sex ed in my Christian school's health class, but I was familiar with the iconic cover of a young man tipping a fedora over his face. The book that haunted me was *Every Young Woman's Battle: Guarding Your Mind, Heart, and Body in a Sex-Saturated World*. A sequel or companion book to a popular Christian self-help title, *Every Young Man's Battle*, the book is focused on teaching teen girls to be "sexually pure," not only by remaining abstinent but by refraining from masturbation, immodest dress, sexual thoughts, and non-heterosexual attraction. I recently reread the book, wondering what I would find outside of my foggy memories of what it contained; it was shocking to read. All the things I thought I'd been implicitly taught were there in stark black and white—the shaming, the homophobia, the rape apologism, the instruction toward constant self-surveillance, everything.

There were also metaphors—so many metaphors! The book instructs readers to think of how far they can go sexually as a traffic light, their sexuality as a table, an unhealthy relationship as "two ticks without a dog, just sucking the lifeblood out of each other," masturbating as "feeding a baby monster" whose appetite will grow, the way you dress as equivalent to how a chef plates and presents a dish, and a woman who's been sexually abused as a wedding present—fine china and silverware—that has been used for yardwork and as dog dishes.

The book also contains a classic metaphor, a version of which has been used and even acted out in sermons to teens all around the globe:

> Imagine two paper hearts, one red and one black. Apply glue to each and press them together, allowing plenty of time for the glue to dry. Once the two hearts are bonded, pull them apart. What happens? Black fibers remain stuck to the red heart

and red fibers still cling to the black. The object lesson is this: When you get attached to someone, you will always keep a part of that person with you, tucking those memories into your trunk of emotional baggage and eventually dragging them into your marriage where you may be tempted to compare your husband to one or all of your previous boyfriends. Also keep in mind that some parts of your heart, once given away, can never be given to someone else, such as first love, first kiss, and first sexual experience.

Other versions of this paper heart lesson involve tearing pieces off a paper heart and giving them away, but the message is the same.

So many of these metaphors are about spoiling something, about not being able to go back or return an object to its pure, pristine state. They throb with panicky fear—fear of heartbreak, fear of comparison between once and future lovers, fear that someone (usually a woman) will be "ruined." For a religion based on a God who self-identifies as infinite love, Christianity seems convinced that there is not enough love to go around, that tying yourself to someone or keeping a part of them with you could only ever be a bad thing.

♥ † ♥

† *I remember them giving two analogies consistently. One: Take a piece of duct tape, put it on their arm, rip it off, put it back on, rip it off, and it would become less and less sticky as they kept putting it on and pulling it off. And they were like, your virginity is like this piece of duct tape: It becomes useless once you give it away to a bunch of people; it doesn't even stick anymore. It has no value. So, you want to be able to give your husband a fresh piece of duct tape, I guess, is the analogy? The other one was the one where we were a flower, and*

we were a whole gift to our future husband, and every time we had sex with someone, we lost a petal—and imagine finally finding your husband and all you have to offer him is a flower stem with no petals left. At least in the second analogy, I was a flower, not a piece of duct tape. But in all of the analogies, I was certainly not a human being.

† There was a strong message of saving yourself for marriage in youth group and the sinfulness of sex before marriage. You didn't want to spoil yourself for your future partner. The imagery of a Christmas present was used as a metaphor for our virginity, and if you open it early, you will be very disappointed on Christmas morning. Not to mention the guilt involved!

† Early in university, I remember a pastor using the duct tape analogy. They got a male and female student to stand with their arms next to each other. Then they put a piece of duct tape across their arms, symbolizing the way that sex binds you to that person. Then they ripped off the tape. While the tape comes away, it pulls out hairs so that neither person is the same; a little piece has been removed.

† One teaching that sticks out to me was about how having sex with someone ties you to them, bonds you, so that even when you break up, a little part of yourself stays with them. Basically, bit by bit, you lose yourself. This ended with us all praying for God to cut those ties, to bring back those parts of you. I actually don't hate this. I think it's not necessarily about the sex, but being in a relationship with someone is a bonding experience. I still do pray for parts of myself to return.

† The most disturbing object lesson I remember was during a camp staff training session with just females, where the camp director's wife wheeled in a cart heaped with chocolate and said, "When all those boys at camp look at you, this is all they see. And it's your job to cover yourself so they don't see that and just want to consume you."

† At the church we had switched over to right around the time I started dating, they were right in the middle of doing purity teachings: separating the girls and boys and teaching them different things . . . having the girls make promises and taking the boys outside to play soccer. My sister found out through a guy friend that they never had any of the same talks with the boys.

† We had two science lessons about abstinence in my chemistry class at Christian school. In one, my science teacher lit a candle and told us it represented sex within marriage: long-burning, warm, light. Then he lit some chemical compound that sent coloured sparks into the air. That was sex outside of marriage—fleeting and purposeless. In the other lesson, he handed out beakers of a clear solution to everyone in the class. All the liquid was clear, but one of the jars had a different solution, which represented an STI. We were allowed to mix our solutions together (ew) or choose to remain "abstinent." Of course, everyone went ahead and mixed, because there was really no upside to not participating; you had to just kind of stand in the corner with your hand over your beaker. Afterward, he went around and dropped another solution into each beaker, and if the "STI" element were present, the solution would turn pink. Every beaker in my class turned pink. I remember someone yelled, "We're a bunch of sluts!"

† Nobody told me I had to wear a purity ring; I just saw them talked about online or in Christian media from the U.S. I remember pestering my mom to drive me to the Christian bookstore for a purity ring, and they didn't actually sell any jewelry specifically branded for that, so I had to settle for one that just had a bunch of crosses on it. It was made of a really cheap metal that was soft and pliable, so the ring got squashed and became unwearable quite quickly. I got a replacement, and then that one got misshapen right away, too. There's some kind of metaphor in there! I put a lot of pressure on myself; I felt like I could only wear a purity ring if I were absolutely

pure of thought and deed, so it ended up being a symbol of my failure to live up to these impossible standards more than anything else.

† At my youth group, there was one night when a woman with her own purity/female empowerment organization came to talk to us about sex and relationships. She gave us a handout with a list of 101 things to do with your boyfriend/girlfriend instead of having sex. I remember that one of the items was "build a snowman."

† I studied at a Christian liberal arts university. In my third year, a few friends and I started the SIFF crew—Spanking It is For Fools. Yup. A bunch of guys who would hang out semi-regularly and encourage each other not to masturbate through code language (i.e., "I haven't surfed in two weeks."). I think this experience was actually part of me changing my views when I realized that probably 95 percent of the guys at that university were in the same boat, feeling shame around their sexuality as they tried their best to repress it.

† When I turned 16, my dad took me out for supper (one-on-one—I don't think that had ever happened before in my life). We both dressed up, and he gave me a necklace: gold, with a gold key pendant encrusted with crystals. This was "the key to my heart." He explained that, until that day, he had carried the key to my heart and was responsible for protecting me, but now I was going to wear it and commit to purity until I could give the key to my husband. I wore the key every day for seven years.

† I absolutely pledged to be abstinent. We didn't have a formal pledge, but in my heart, I was 1,000 percent waiting until I was married to have sex. We didn't do purity rings at my church, but we did have a day at youth group where they brought everyone a piece of paper, and on the paper, there was a triangle, kind of a Maslow's Hierarchy of Needs vibe. There were horizontal lines across it going all the way up, smaller and

smaller chunks of the triangle. And at the very top, the small triangle was labelled sex, and at the very bottom, the big long line was labelled platonic friendship or something like that. We were all encouraged to draw a line on our sheet, in front of everyone, where we would commit to not moving above before marriage.

† I remember being told if you have sex with one person, you are also "going to bed with" everyone that they have ever had sex with.

† As a "renter" of a female body from God, I was terrified; of my body and its changes, of my responsibility to God and family to remain pure, and that I would end up pregnant from touching a doorknob—if, somehow, semen found its way from someone's penis, to their hand, to the door knob, and from door knob, to my hand, to my vulva—because that's a sane, logical, and scientific belief, and in no way a sign of my mental illnesses or spiritual traumas or the conflagration of the two. I truly believed that if I touched the sexuality of my body or brain, or that if my body or brain touched some form of sexuality outside of marriage, that I would burn in hell for eternity. These fears were continually stoked by religious retreats at which anti-choice propaganda videos were frequently screened. (Pam Stenzel, I hope you feel my constant ire.)

† They had us walk around and shake hands with each other (the handshake represented sex), and at the end we found out that one of the hand shakers had an STI, and we had to figure out how many people were now infected. So, of course, everyone was dying of AIDS by the end of the object lesson.

† My youth leader did a talk on sex where she had a paper heart in her hand. She said that every time we had sex with someone who was not our spouse, it was like we were tearing this paper heart in two. Every time we would have sex with someone, another rip in the paper—until all we had left were these little paper shards she dropped on the floor.

† There was a popular skit where a paper heart was ripped into pieces. The heart was ripped apart, then Jesus came along, and there was this new heart all of a sudden. But it was always being played by a girl who gave her heart away, never the other way around—never a boy. Then again, when I was a teenager, that was the most magical skit to me for some reason.

† There was an object lesson that I used at camp with my teen cabins that I called purity boxes. I do not remember exactly how it worked, but it involved a clear plastic box that had different-sized gumballs in it. And the gumballs represented sexual partners, and the box represented your life, or the space available in a woman's life, I think? I think the message was that if you have a bunch of little relationships, those are going to fill up all your life space, and the giant gumball that would have been your husband wouldn't have room to enter your life because your space was wasted on cheap sex. Lovely.

† The speaker began by saying how wonderful young life is, how wonderful young love is, how it's God's way of showing how much he loves us. It's up to us, however, to show how much we love God by not having sex. When we have sex, we give a piece of ourselves to our partner. At this point, the speaker put a stick of gum in his mouth and started to chew. He then passed around a flower and asked us to remove a petal when it came by and pass it to the next person. The person who received only the stem was asked how they felt to receive just the stem and no petals. How did it feel knowing that the flower gave all its beauty away before it could reach you? Don't give your petals away, they're what gives you value. When his talk ended, he spat the piece of gum into his hand and offered it to a student in the front. What do you mean you don't want my gum? Oh, it's because I've already chewed it? Yeah, disgusting, isn't it? It's already been in my body; of course you don't want it in yours. Our bodies were the flower. Our bodies were the gum. Our bodies were disgusting and wasted if we had sex before marriage.

† *In retrospect, I wish my parents had been a bit more critical about the messages they allowed me to absorb from Christian culture. They (particularly my mom) were pretty concerned about the messages I was getting from secular culture, but that same care didn't seem to extend within evangelical media. I think she trusted Christianity too much.*

♥ † ♥

I read *Every Young Woman's Battle* several times as a preteen—not, I think, because I was so entranced by its message but because it was teaching me things. Before rereading the book, I still remembered that it was where I learned what oral sex was and how I learned that boys were not the only ones who could masturbate. Outside of that book, my only sexual education was of "how babies are made" and "your body is changing" and the like: practical, biological info about periods and procreation. In health class, my teachers preached abstinence but were fuzzy on the details of what happened after you were married. In Grade 7, our teacher put out a shoebox with a slit in the top where we could drop anonymous questions. She answered two—very memorable answers, one about having shower sex (with your eventual husband, of course) on your period, and the other about curing yeast infections with yogurt—before returning to the next class sans box to tell us she'd revoked the privilege because our questions weren't mature enough. (I wonder now if she just didn't want to answer them.)

Every Young Woman's Battle was attempting to speak frankly, to talk to teens on their level, which made it educational. It also made it scintillating. I remember lying in bed, paging through the chapters that contained testimonials supposedly from teens who'd written to the author to tell their stories of becoming "addicted" to pornography or "stumbling into sin" with their boyfriends. They were cautionary tales, but I read them like they were Penthouse

Forum, wiggling under the covers, letting my imagination roam and a warmth grow between my legs.

I doubt Shannon Ethridge, the book's author, would be happy to hear about my reading experience. But that was my main memory of the book before a copy arrived in my mailbox, wrapped in the paper packaging of a second-hand, online book retailer. I was shocked when I began turning the pages and found every terrible teaching I'd thought I'd atmospherically absorbed about purity culture handily collected in one volume. Even the testimonials didn't live up to my memory: They were short and vague, something only a sexually frustrated mid-pubescent girl with an active imagination could use for sexual fantasy fodder. My used copy quickly filled up with curse-laden marginalia.

It's hard to convey how bad this book is. If I can demonstrate with a brief list of examples, here are some actual things this book contains:

- Bible verses with all the pronouns changed to the feminine form (sometimes to the detriment of the actual meaning of the quotation)
- A chapter on weight that culminates in the assertion that "looking good" is important because "you represent God"
- A list of "practical ways to avoid being sexually abused or raped," one of which is to not sexually arouse your date
- The characterization of lesbian relationships and affairs between married people as "sex and love addictions"
- Some untrue "facts" about the prevalence of infertility as a result of having an abortion or STI
- A section titled "Why Is My Abstinence So Important to God?" that claims abstinence leads to

"perfect" physical, mental, emotional, spiritual, and relational health
- The assertion that "even if you do not choose wisely and marry Mr. Wrong, when you recite your wedding vows, he automatically becomes your Mr. Right. It's God's will that you be a committed wife to this man, through good times and bad, regardless of the character flaws that may surface down the road"
- Characterizations of husbands as head of the household and financial provider, while wives are the "helpmeet" and "cheerleader," must take care of the children (husbands "help out with the parenting"), and must give up her own ambitions for his
- An afterword called "If You Desire Other Women" that points queer readers to conversion therapy organization Exodus International[*]
- Multiple mentions of Mel Gibson's attractiveness

I never took an official purity pledge that I can remember or wore a purity ring, but like many of the friends that I interviewed, it was the default setting in the context in which I was raised—being a Christian meant being abstinent until marriage and viewing marriage as the goal of any relationship. The ways I was taught this seemed frivolous and strange, like the object lessons I was constantly being shown in youth group. I still have a Rolodex of these moments in my mind: the health class where my teacher played the music video for Lady Gaga's "Poker Face," pausing every few seconds to explain the dirty, sinful lyrics; the teacher who handed us a list of ways to make ourselves more "dateable," one of which was to do crafts like gluing leaves and pressed flowers to your school

---

[*] Conversion therapy, a form of therapy that attempts to "help" gay individuals become straight, has been formally banned in Canada since January 2022. It was officially condemned by the American Psychological Association in 2009 but had a large presence, particularly in the U.S., throughout the 2000s. Exodus International, the organization suggested by *Every Young Woman's Battle*, ran for 37 years before shuttering in 2013 and issued an apology.

notebooks; the guest speaker who told our high school an anecdote about seeing a girl littering outside of a Tim Hortons and "thinking to myself, *that girl's not ready for dating.*"

Despite my recently-activated teenage libido (thanks, *Every Young Woman's Battle*), I wasn't especially interested in dating, or sex, in real life; sex still seemed scary unless it was safely ensconced in fantasy, and I hadn't yet learned to understand the bounds of my own nascent desires. Why, for instance, I seemed to have so many fewer crushes than my friends, why most of my male peers grossed me out, why I got little butterfly thrills in my stomach when my hand brushed against a female friend's, or why I spent so long staring at the girl who sat in front of me (just jealous of her hairstyle—right?). Deep in denial, the silly-seeming abstinence lessons from my teachers and youth pastors rolled off my back, became something I could laugh about with my friends after class. What was more insidious was the "battle" *Every Young Woman's Battle* and its ilk was encouraging me to fight, this calling to be "pure," not in action but in every thought, every private moment.

"You can bounce inappropriate thoughts right out of your brain by rehearsing appropriate responses to them," the book says. This is the way I was taught to view my interior monologue, like a goalie playing defense, always on.[*] I would lie in bed at night, unable to sleep, "tempted" to "fantazize" about sex, my barely-formed preteen brain swarming with hormones and the vague but unshakeable conviction that the way my body was reacting to whatever latest thing—the Christina Aguilera "Dirrty" video, perhaps—meant something was definitely wrong with me. I can physically remember the feeling of this kind of stress and the shame when I "gave in" to simply *thinking* about sexual things. How sad this is, now, to remember, as an adult who

---

[*] The book also has several helpful suggestions for how to "redirect" your sinful thoughts toward more holy aims. For instance, you can chase sexual thoughts out of your mind by listening to abstinence anthems, "Wait for Me" by Rebecca St. James or "Dismissed" by ZOEgirl. Instead of fantasizing about a guy, you can pray for his future wife. And, my favourite, "When you see a good-looking guy . . . simply say to yourself, Lord, you sure know how to make awesome works!"

has been in a stable, long-term relationship for ten years. I want to go back and shake my younger self, yell at her, *Relax! You're doing nothing wrong!* (Maybe explain to her where the clitoris is while I'm there.)

♥ † ♥

† *I was pretty confident that everyone outside of the church had AIDS and/or herpes and/or babies, and I was one of the righteous few who was going to have a good marriage one day.*

† *In the version of Christianity I grew up in, abstinence was not just about having sex with others. Sexual explorations on your own, masturbation basically, that was also a sin. So, in my teens, my mom gave me a copy of* Every Young Man's Battle, *and she had pre-highlighted all the bits she thought I should pay extra attention to. There were notes in the margin and stuff, things starred and underlined. The book took the place of an actual conversation, which she was obviously uncomfortable having with me.*

† *I do remember a teacher once saying that masturbation was only a sin because it usually involves lust, but if you could masturbate without thinking about a woman lustfully then, in theory, it wouldn't be a sin. Obviously, my teenage brain constructed some elaborate mental gymnastic equipment to try to thread that needle.*

† *In youth group, we used to occasionally split into guys and girls. One time, when it was just the guys, we talked about masturbation. What I remember in particular was that our youth pastor and one of the adult youth leaders had a bit of a debate over whether you can masturbate without it being a sin. The youth pastor said absolutely no, all masturbation is sinful. The youth leader thought that you could masturbate without sinning if you didn't think about sexual thoughts. So, yes, I have masturbated while thinking about the Toronto Raptors.*

† My parents talked to me about sex when they walked in on me attempting to lose my virginity to my boyfriend, as I wanted to break up with him and didn't think I had a reason, so I thought guilt over having sex would be a good enough one . . . If that doesn't directly show you the effect gendered teachings and purity culture had on my brain, I don't know what will.

† My high school art teacher had what he called a "sweater of shame" behind his desk for any female students who came into his class dressed "inappropriately" (by his definition). He encouraged other students to mock anyone who had to put the sweater on and delighted in telling us it was never washed. He framed this as a protection he was taking for himself because he had a wife at home he loved and didn't need to be distracted by other female bodies at work. But who needed protection in this situation? Him, or the young teens who came into this 30-something man's classroom and were sexualized by him?

† I had been masturbating since I was five years old, and I knew that it was shameful and that something was wrong with me.

† Purity culture taught me all about the power of female bodies, and it taught me to fear female bodies; female bodies are the location of original sin. My female body had power over men, and that was to be feared and shamed. I remember this fear of the male gaze beginning young, like when I was nine or ten. Dance costumes could be particularly contentious with my mom, who told me that we looked like sex workers. I was ten and being told that I looked like a hooker. By my mother. For wearing a competitive dance costume.

† I think evangelical Christianity doesn't allow sexiness to be part of your life. You can't be sexual, and you can't derive sexual joy from something unless you're going to "capitulate" to it, basically. It's this weird way of working with sexual content that doesn't work in the

real world, where it's like, you're only allowed to be turned on if you're going to have sex to have a kid.

† I used to love swimming, but after my body decided to grow size 30F breasts by the time I was 19, I stopped swimming both at home and in public. I didn't want to make my dad or my brother uncomfortable with my "curvy" body. I didn't want to cause men to stumble. I didn't want people to look at my body and immediately see "sex."

† I think there's a flattening of sexual experience that purity culture creates where it's like, if you're watching pornography, it's all bad, so there's no difference between watching a scripted pornography scene, or watching a video of rape, or watching a sex tape that was filmed or released without the person's consent. They're all levelled onto the same plane.

† There was a lot of pressure on girls to protect the purity of the boys by dressing modestly (tank tops with straps three-fingers wide, shorts/skirts with hems an inch below the tips of our fingers). At camp, if we wanted to swim, we had to wear shorts and T-shirts over any two-piece bathing suit, but boys were allowed to bare their chests in their swim trunks.

† My boyfriend and I would describe each sexual act we engaged in, including sexting and individual masturbation on our own time, as "messing up." I asked about and monitored my boyfriend's use of porn, and guilt and shame were a big part of how we experienced our sexualities independently and together.

† From a young age, I've always masturbated quite a bit and never had an issue with it. For a long time, I didn't even know what it was called, just that it felt good and helped me sleep, and provided a foundation for thinking about exciting fantasies. But in my first year at a small Christian college, I picked up Every Young Woman's Battle from the library and remember thinking, Whoa! Whoops, okay, this

is obviously something I'm struggling with. I'm going to do what this book says and enter into this battle against immoral, bad lustfulness, and it will help me feel closer to God. *So, the first night, I valiantly tried to pray rather than masturbate when I couldn't sleep, and almost immediately, I thought,* This is so dumb. I don't feel bad about this and it's helpful and it feels good and I don't actually WANT to stop . . . I don't think that this is my battle. *And that was my short-lived experience with that.*

† *I assumed that I would meet my husband while I was younger and that it would fall into place. Things haven't, and my ideas around this have shifted as a result. If I had gotten married young, like my sister did, I might not have needed to change.*

♥ † ♥

Even within Christianity, there has been a backlash against purity culture in recent years.

When I solicited the personal experiences and memories scattered throughout this chapter from friends and acquaintances, I expected responses from people I knew who had deconstructed their evangelical upbringings and left their faith behind. But I was surprised by how many responses I received from friends who are currently Christian, who have a theological education, and who are regular churchgoers.

After its boom in the 2000s—maybe as we Y2K-era puritypledgers age—purity has become less of a Christian buzzword, and abstinence as a rallying cry has nearly fallen by the wayside. Today, Silver Ring Thing has become Unaltered Ministries, which, rather than an explicit mandate of promoting abstinence, now says on its website that its mission is to "lead students to fullness of life in Jesus Christ." The famous ring is no longer silver and no longer a purity ring—now, it's a UN Lifestyle Ring (as in unaltered, not

United Nations), made of cheap-looking white or black silicone, advertised as "an external symbol and reminder of the internal commitment to live within God's unaltered, unchanging design."

Are these vague-sounding platitudes mere dog whistles for the same hurtful theology that shaped my young life? Probably. Contemporary evangelical media has not reversed course on the belief that sex belongs only in the context of heterosexual marriage, though it seems evangelical and fundamentalist authors and influencers now pay lip service to the idea of purity culture breeding shame and try to frame their messages in less overtly shame-based ways.

Elsewhere in evangelicalism, there are—and have always been—divergent streams of thought that undermine purity culture. The No Shame Movement, launched by a Black evangelical Christian woman in 2013, is an online platform for unlearning the teachings of purity culture. Some longstanding denominations and churches also fall under the evangelical umbrella—such as the Metropolitan Community Churches, founded in the 1960s, or Indianapolis-based LifeJourney Church, founded in 1990—that were specifically created as spaces welcoming to 2SLGBTQIA+ Christians.

The problem is that the mainstream view is dictated by powerful, politically conservative groups and denominations that spread their ideology through cultural products. As Linda Kay Klein relays in her book, despite the diversity of belief and opinion within evangelicalism when it comes to other political and theological topics:

> The sexual purity message is one of the most consistent elements of the evangelical subculture. Among my interviewees, a remarkably similar language and set of stories about gender and sexuality surfaced. The same adages, metaphors, and stories from books, speakers, and events were described

to me over and over again, though those I spoke with grew up around the country and in some cases the world.

I had a similar experience, even with my small sample set of responders—similar analogies, experiences, and pop culture touchstones popped up in multiple people's answers. Researcher Donna Freitas found that evangelical college students proved to be "diverse in their politics, nuanced in their expressions and beliefs about Christianity, and perfectly willing to swim in a sea of doubt and life's gray areas," but "their pursuit of purity is one area where almost all of them could see only black and white."

As historian Sara Moslener writes, "Sexual purity isn't, after all, about what ultimately is good for the physical and psychological well-being of the individual. Sexual purity, with its promises of marital bliss and sexual ecstasy, is a most compelling metaphor for the Christian faith and the promise of eternal salvation." The promise of purity is the promise of Christianity itself: Hard work and self-denial lead to future reward, whether that reward is eternal life in heaven or a perfect, holy sex life post-marriage. Like all attempts to deny sinful pleasures, abstinence had the air of noble sacrifice that seemed to mean it would earn some reward in the end—and a complete inability to connect with or live in the present.

♥ † ♥

† *I was a youth pastor in the early 2000s in an evangelical Mennonite church, and I am sure if asked, I would have said you should wait for marriage, et cetera. But generally speaking, it wasn't a subject I focused on. I was more into teaching the youth about contemplative prayer and social justice. I feel abstinence teaching was wrong and super damaging, and I'm embarrassed that I may have ever encouraged anyone else to buy into it.*

† In our sex ed classes, which were rare, no one offered us free condoms or dental dams. There was no talk of consent or what good, healthy sexual connections might look like. Instead, we received an abstinence-based curriculum: The only safe sex was no sex. STIs were only mentioned as a scare tactic. Of course, everyone in the classroom was presumed straight and cisgender. There were no discussions or even acknowledgments of queer and trans folks. That silence spoke volumes to me as a bisexual and non-binary person and ensured I stayed firmly in the closet throughout my childhood.

† I remember feeling very hemmed in by the heteronormative nature of the teaching, though I didn't understand that at the time. I just knew I didn't want to live the kind of life that was being held up as ideal, which was marrying young with a boring Christian man who would provide financially for you while you cranked out a few babies and let go of any career goals you might have had. I used to think about being celibate instead of getting married. I also didn't want to have kids, which I didn't understand was even an option.

† When my university boyfriend and I broke up, I remember literally saying out loud to him, "I'm so sad; now I'm going to have had sex with three people." Even after I stopped identifying as a Christian, there was still this very strong, lingering understanding that to have had sex with multiple people was so abhorrent and bad. I remember telling myself, okay, the max you can have sex with is five people. I had all these rules for myself that I had never really reflected on; they were just these lingerings of the indoctrination I had been given growing up. And I really connected it to morality, to value. Like, good people wait and only have sex in relationships. Bad people have one-night stands.

† My parents have no problem with homosexuality or with my sibling being trans, but to me, I still have that internalized—even though it's not really what I believe, there's still this current of, no, this is not okay, this is what I should believe. *Same with sexuality.*

I feel like deep down, I still think you shouldn't have sex before marriage—even though I did.

† When I look through my journals from the early 2000s, I am obsessed with purity and my struggles with maintaining it. I hadn't even kissed anyone at this point. But I considered "purity" to include my thoughts and emotions, and not just the content of those thoughts and emotions but also the intensity/frequency COMPARED TO my thoughts and feelings for and about God. I felt like I was "cheating on God" if I thought about a boy more than I thought about God. This was all part of the rhetoric of purity culture in my Christian circles, too. Jesus was the Lover of my soul. My first Love. The One who desired a sacred romance with me. Until I was married, I belonged only to God.

† I was "excessively pure." That was a big thing. And that was part of the reason why the sort of assumed male relationship with pornography, and the way they would talk to the boys in youth group, was so uncomfortable for me because it caused you to segment your brain and put the sexual part of you in a different part of your brain. And it was tied up in gender confusion, too, because it was like, well, that's great—if that part's over here, then I can just get to be asexual, agender. It doesn't matter what my gender is because if I'm not participating in any sort of sexual activity, then I don't have to worry about what my sexuality is or what my gender identity is. So, I think I hid inside it to a certain extent.

† When my best friend started having sex, she didn't tell me. By the time I found out, she had been having sex for a while and with my younger friend from youth group she had been seeing. I felt betrayed and angry. Turns out, she was right not to tell me. I continued to shame her for a long time until I realized how stupid this was. I've apologized several times, and we're still really close, but I feel awful.

† My friend and I used a software to keep ourselves accountable that would send the other person an email with links when you went on a

porn site. It's a funny reality where, because you're being accountable to each other about a very specific type of thing, it gave us permission to talk about it—not in a sex-positive way but in a more apparent way than the typical oblique Christian "I'm struggling." But my friend had this idea that if he was demoralized, he wouldn't do proper self-care habits—if he masturbated, he would eat sadness peanut butter in his bedroom and then wouldn't brush his teeth out of self-loathing. His teeth would rot, and then he would get an abscess and die. And that was Satan's plan to kill him. He thought he had such a great, powerful purpose for his life; Satan was fighting hard to get him with peanut butter.

♥ † ♥

I thought I had escaped it.

Sure, I would be *technically* a virgin when I got married. I wasn't brave enough to actually have premarital sex. But I no longer believed premarital sex was a sin, and my partner and I had talked openly about our views on sex. I was well-forewarned by my mom's birds-and-the-bees talks and later talks with my few married friends (and, really, more my non-married, non-Christian friends) about exactly where everything goes, the importance of—as a coworker charmingly put it—"warming up the oven before you try to bake the bread," the fact that it might hurt the first time, the fact that I might or might not bleed.

We had sat through a belated round of personalized sex ed focused on contraceptive options at the Women's Health Centre, and I had chosen an IUD and had it inserted in advance of the wedding so as to have some time to get used to it, but not far enough in advance to make anyone worry we were "honeymooning before the wedding." I had finally learned how to properly unroll a condom. It was all coming together.

I knew about those people who were supposedly so confused, so wracked with guilt, when suddenly forced on their wedding night to make the mental switch between "sex is sinful" to "sex is pure and good." I felt pity for them. That wouldn't be me. I was too smart for that. I hadn't sat through all those sermons with too-cool faux-hawk sporting youth pastors yelling about how *sex within marriage is great, as long as you wait, sex is wonderful and beautiful, and I love having sex with my smoking hot wife!* for nothing!

And if all else failed, I had the guarantee: I had waited, so it would be good. That was the deal, after all. Save yourself for one person and you have spectacular, mind-blowing sex forever.

It's right there in *Every Young Woman's Battle*: "[A married man and woman] can have guilt-free sex however many times in whatever way they want until they die."

(I think she meant "for the rest of their lives," but the point still stands.)

And yet, and yet. "Mind over matter" failed me.

For the first couple of years of my marriage, I struggled with vaginismus, an involuntary tightening of the pelvic muscles that can make penetration painful or impossible. I cried, frustrated, because my body was reacting in a way I couldn't control or prevent. It was this experience that made me realize how my Christian upbringing had alienated my body and my mind from each other. I didn't really know how to listen to my body. I didn't understand my body. I didn't even think of my body as a part of me, just a shell that housed the important stuff—my soul, my mind—that would occasionally ruin my day with pesky things like period cramps or sexual temptations.

After those challenging years, I didn't feel that contraction, that wall go up again, for a very long time. And then one evening, while I was researching this chapter, it happened. I'd been spending the previous week reading *Every Young Woman's Battle*, writing angry exclamation points in the margins and laughing at its weird metaphors and silly-sounding advice, barging into my partner's office to read them the most wild and damaging excerpts. I didn't think it was affecting me. And then, suddenly, that familiar pain was there, and I was rolling back onto the bed and crying so hard I couldn't say anything. Purity took my body captive again and my language with it.

♥ † ♥

† *It's no surprise that I did not learn about sexual consent through purity culture. It's no surprise that after I experienced my first sexual assault at the age of 19, I had no idea what happened to me was assault. You do what you're told, right? You do what you're told to make people happy, even when you don't want to.*

† *I feel like sexual repression had a really bad effect on all my relationships—from not taking opportunities given or jumping into sex way too soon, even with the right person. I haven't had a sense of balance. By the time I actually did lose my virginity, it felt like I'd done it on my terms, and it was a positive experience. I've had sex in romantic and platonic relationships, but I still feel rigid and closed off sometimes.*

† *I am an openly queer, gender-fluid woman in a non-monogamous relationship. I feel liberated in my thinking about my sexuality, but my body/emotions still carry a lot of baggage from the before times. I don't have the sexual life I would like to have. I wish my sexuality felt easy/natural/effortless, but it still triggers fear, shame, frustration, or numbness.*

† *I think, in general, I've always been a pretty bad Christian—not for lack of trying! I tried so hard to fit into the church for so many years, but it never worked. I remained an outsider in many ways. And I think at the crux of my outsider-ness was that I couldn't stop questioning what the church kept telling me because so many parts*

didn't make sense. I WANTED them to make sense so badly because I wanted to fit in. But I need to fully understand something before I can accept it fully, and a lot of the church's teachings kept falling short.

† Basically, for every important decision that you have to make, you hand it over to, like, God, or some spiritual authority, and you learn not to trust your instincts or your own desires. Which is why it was such a healing decision to have sex before marriage. I guess I did feel like I could finally trust myself with that decision. But I struggle because it's my default—when I have to make a decision, I ask people, and I need to get, like, six opinions about it. When I should just know myself, know what I want.

† I now identify as queer, I'm very sexually fluid, I've been in polyamorous situations, I have tried a lot of things. Once I really separated from the church, I remember thinking, I need to explore, I need to figure out what I actually like. I had never orgasmed at that point with a partner. And that wasn't entirely Christianity's fault, but it was certainly related because even talking about it with your partner or the fact that sex isn't a gift to a man, it's an experience for two people to come together, was something that I had to work on and figure out. I had to realize it's a pleasure-based activity by design.

† Maybe, in a way, it protected me during my teenage years and early 20s from men with bad intentions. So, in a way, abstinence was a protection.

† It was difficult to change my perspective overnight from anything sexual being a sin to it suddenly being a good and God-ordained activity. The first few years of marriage were difficult, and honestly, it's been a long, slow process of accepting my body as sexual. I've come a long way, but there's still an inherent idea that my body as a sexual entity is bad, or that sexual desire is a bit shameful.

† *My current relationship with my sexuality now is complex. Ever changing. Fearful. Shameful. Occasionally optimistic.*

† *In some ways, the biggest shift in my view of sexuality is that I don't actually need to worry about it so much. Purity culture seemed to make sex the most important thing—a super serious sin and the pinnacle of intimacy with a partner.*

† *It took me until my late 20s or early 30s to fully embrace my queerness and come out to people I know. I felt really sexually repressed for a long time, and in some ways still do. There are still parts of my sexuality that I'm only comfortable with alone, and I would like to be able to share them with my partner someday.*

† *I sometimes wonder how I would approach my sexuality if I were not married today. How sexually active would I be if I were in a relationship or going on dates? If my partner and I have kids someday, what would we teach/tell them? I still think that intimacy is something to take care of, including sexual intimacy. But is sex all about intimacy?*

† *I grew up having sexual feelings and came to feel like they were wrong, and I was wrong and broken for having them. A lot of self-suppression happened in more ways than just sexuality. It took a long time for me to come around to accepting my human nature and feeling comfortable in my own skin. I still sometimes struggle.*

† *Purity culture broke me sexually. It made me sexually broken. The thing that told me I was sexually broken is the actual thing that made me sexually broken. My sexuality is still broken because of purity culture and its insidious teachings.*

† *It wasn't until I was married that I realized that I am pansexual. I could recognize people in my life who I had sexual and romantic*

feelings for but never thought I could pursue because of their gender. I really mourn the relationships, connection to others, and connection to myself that I could have had if heterosexuality had not been compulsory in the church I grew up in.

† *I didn't have a healthy understanding of what good sex could look and feel like because good sex was never discussed in my church upbringing. We were all just supposed to magically have amazing, mind-blowing sex once we got married—but how do you do that when you spend the first 20-odd years of your life trying to separate your mind and body, viewing your sexuality as a dirty, sinful thing? Even today, when I am having really pleasurable, consensual sex with someone, I can sometimes be overcome with waves of fear and self-loathing that manifest physically as trembling, overwhelming nausea, and a racing heart, like a panic attack.*

† *I thought of every bit of my sexuality as lust and knew that the feelings I had would only be ones that were normal or allowed once I was married. Sometimes, in my worst moments, I still think of men as unable to control their lusts and being at the mercy of their body's reaction to mine.*

† *Purity culture didn't teach me to view my own body, or other people's bodies, in a healthy way. It didn't teach me to think ethically about sex or relationships; it just taught me to avoid specific things. I got married in my early 20s, believing in the basic messages of purity culture and following them. I was married for over half my life and have separated in the past year—so it's complicated.*

† *I wish I could feel sexually confident. I wish I could own my body and my sexuality, but I still feel like I'm renting it from a God that I don't believe in and that it belongs to men who've hurt me in the past. It may never feel as safe and as natural as I want it to. But I'm not giving up on it. I'm not giving up on myself.*

♥ † ♥

How could something so silly affect us all so much? is what I wondered when I reread those books, listened to those cheesy Christian pop songs, read about the cringey metaphors and object lessons. All the jokes about purity rings, the horrible fedora cover of *I Kissed Dating Goodbye*, the comedy of Christian romance novels, the heightened language of battling and guarding your heart, the deeply dorky Silver Ring Thing skits, the tacky romanticism of Waiting and Dating Jesus—all of it was so goofy, and yet here were all these friends and acquaintances; here I was. We'd been deeply, permanently affected—some broken, even—by this culture.

Being raised with these views on sex had taught me to compartmentalize my sexual self and the rest of me; it had taught me to even hate my sexuality. Now, as an adult, trying to integrate those pieces of myself, remembering the old feelings of guilt and shame and confusion, felt alienating. I was so far from it; I remembered the hot, burning shame but couldn't feel it anymore, and the things that sparked that shame now seemed trifling and stupid. And yet there was my body, seizing up again, there was the feeling that I didn't know who I was, what I liked, there were my friends telling me, *I still feel broken*, telling me, *I still don't feel comfortable talking about it*, telling me, *I still don't feel comfortable with myself*.

One friend, in an interview, told me about the strange realization that she could make her own decisions, that she no longer felt pressure to ask God or seek guidance from a spiritual counsellor when she made a choice. *Your body is not your own, your life is not your own; you belong to God*, we were told.

To think your body might belong to you, or better yet, *be* you, that you might be one holistic thing, that you can be sexual and spiritual, that you need not be either, that you know yourself and know what's best, that bad sex and heartbreak are not the end of the world, that sexual abuse is not your fault, that there is no such thing as pure and impure, that your gender and sexuality are differentiated, that it's good to think deeply about how you feel and what you want in life, that pleasure is important, that intimacy is not the same as purity, that the stakes are not life and death. That's what I want for me, for everyone.

CHAPTER FIVE

DECLARATIONS OF WAR

THE WAR ON TERROR, THE CULTURE WARS, AND THE CHRISTIAN PERSECUTION COMPLEX

The book was thick and printed to look worn, with a textured cover imitative of old leather binding. Its pages were cut raggedly, the paper stock hefty. These things made the book seem important, and its appearance is probably what drew me to it as a burgeoning literary snob.

It was hard to find books I wanted to read in the small school library, where the catalogue had to be free of any whiff of controversial content; I was too old for the shelf of *Boxcar Children* books and too snobby for the Amish romance section. I was probably ten or eleven at the time, in Grade 6, trying to make the leap out of the children's stacks and into young adults'.

So, I picked up the thick brown book with the embossed crest on the front, over which hovered the title: *Jesus Freaks*. Along the bottom left corner, *Stories of those who stood for JESUS: the ultimate Jesus Freaks*.

The book was a co-production between the international nonprofit organization Voice of the Martyrs and Christian rap-rock band DC Talk, whose contribution mostly seemed to lend the book the title of their album (and song), *Jesus Freak*. Inside was a collection of stories of martyrs: Christians who had been persecuted, even killed, for their faith.

There were no chronological or geographical bounds to these stories—any tale from any time, anywhere in the world, was included. Most of them were terrifying, but I couldn't stop reading. From the moment I opened the book, I was hooked. For the following week, I spent most of my spare time reading it. I stayed up late poring over it like it was a *Goosebumps* book—thrilling myself with every horrifying page.

The stories were shocking in their cruelty, stories of Christians being abused, tortured, and tested by oppressive regimes and invading forces. The martyrs' willingness to stand firm in their beliefs—to submit to torture or death rather than renounce their Christian faith—was meant to be inspirational, but I was hung up on the irrationality of the oppressors. Who could do such terrible things to other human beings? And beyond that—why was God so pleased, from 1 AD to 1999, to let Christians be nailed to crosses and dropped in frozen lakes and whipped and beaten and bloodied and scarred?

Twenty years later, I'm sure I still remember some of the stories. What feels murkier is how they were packaged and presented—what rationalizations did the book have for God allowing human cruelty? What was I meant to take away from those stories, other than nightmares about being forced to spit on a Bible under penalty of death? Luckily, it's easy to find out because used copies of *Jesus Freaks* can be obtained online for less than five dollars plus shipping.

♥ † ♥

While I waited for my package to arrive, I decided to find out more about Voice of the Martyrs, the organization responsible for the book. I remembered them as the source of the printed pamphlets about martyred Christians around the world that used to be stocked at the back of my childhood church foyer. I had perceived them as some kind of Christian version of Amnesty International.

According to the organization's website, which has the slightly too on-the-nose URL www.persecution.com, Voice of the Martyrs was founded in 1967 by a Lutheran priest named Richard Wurmbrand. Born in Romania in 1909, he spent 14 years in prison under the Communist regime between the 1940s and 1960s, including three years in solitary confinement. Despite these imprisonments, Wurmbrand was determined to continue preaching Christianity. The website calls him "The Iron Curtain Paul," though without the biblical Paul's bloody past and supernatural roadside conversion.*

"In May 1966, [Wurmbrand] testified before the U.S. Senate Internal Security Subcommittee, where he stripped to the waist to show 18 scars from torture wounds covering his torso," the website says.

Today, the organization is worth $50 million USD and focuses on providing "practical relief and spiritual support" to persecuted Christians around the world. In practice, this seems to mostly mean putting out media to share the stories of those persecuted Christians, as well as some evangelism-focused ministry projects, like Bible translation and distribution and funding missionaries. (In 2020, the organization got in trouble for launching Bibles tied to balloons into North Korea.**)

I suppose I always understood this organization as trying to reach countries where Christianity was outlawed or religious freedoms were curtailed. But somehow, as a preteen, I'd failed to notice how this gave Voice of the Martyrs its overt Cold War–era agenda—in fact, the organization was named *Jesus to the Communist World* until switching to its less overtly political moniker after the fall of the Soviet Union.

---

* As the Bible tells it, Paul was a persecutor of Christians himself until he was struck by a blinding light and the voice of God on the road to Damascus and decided to change his ways.

** CHVN Radio, "Balloons Launched into North Korea Banned by South Korea."

When I received my copy of *Jesus Freaks*, just as faux-leather and faux-distressed as I remembered, I was surprised to find its pages loaded with evil communists—and not only that, evil Muslims, too. The more contemporary entries in the book take place in countries where Islam is a state religion.

> "When you catch the infidels, beat them! Allah will be very pleased," Zahid encouraged them. The crowd of young men, the youth group of his mosque, waved their sticks and iron bars and cheered in agreement. Zahid's arrogance and hatred swelled. He felt he was doing well as a young Muslim priest. . . . To Zahid, as many Muslims, Christians are heretics and should be punished.

> "The Communist army then brought three hundred government students to scream at us in an organized 'demonstration of the people.' These government students surrounded our school shouting, 'Everything belongs to the government! Your pigs and fish are ours!' The soldiers then took all the animals that the Bible school had been using for food. Finally, the soldiers gave up trying to convert us to follow Marx and Lenin, the founders of Communism."

> Mary Khoury and her family were forced to their knees before their home. The leader of the Muslim fanatics who had raided their village waved his pistol carelessly before their faces. His hatred for Christians burned in his eyes. "If you do not become a Muslim," he threatened, "you will be shot."

> The Communist soldiers had discovered their illegal Bible study. As the pastor was reading from

the Bible, men with guns suddenly broke into the home, terrorizing the believers who had gathered there to worship. The Communists shouted insults and threatened to kill the Christians. The leading officer pointed his gun at the pastor's head. "Hand me your Bible," he demanded. Reluctantly, the pastor handed over his Bible, his prized possession. With a sneer on his face, the guard threw the Word of God on the floor at his feet. He glared at the small congregation. "We will let you go," he growled, "But first, you must spit on this book of lies. Anyone who refuses will be shot."

The Muslim prisoners were sympathetic. "It is better that you are Christians," they told Mira. "It is a good life. Muslims are not at peace; they are always fighting each other."

Throughout the book, communists and Muslims are bloodthirsty, heartless, and rabid—except for those whose "hard hearts" are moved by the plight of the suffering Christians, who are so overcome by the light of Christ that they turn to Jesus. These stories sit side by side with those of Reformation-era torture by Catholics and Bible-times atrocities from sneering emperors and haughty Roman guards. It has the strange effect of a forced equivalency, positioning all these various "enemies," divorced of their context, within a single compendium, as if Christianity stands in direct opposition to all of them. But Christianity is a religion, not a political ideology or a system of governance.

The bogeyman versions of communism and Islam that are portrayed through the characters in these stories form a strange and surreal spectrum. One end represents the horrors of a purely secular society where religion is outlawed, the other the oppression of an enforced state religion. But from all my experience with evangelical Christianity, it never seemed as though the utopian vision was a moderate, peaceful land of happy religious pluralism where people were free to worship as they wished. While the martyrs in *Jesus Freaks* were victims of religious persecution, they didn't seem to be fighting for everyone to have religious freedom, just for Christianity to persevere. In fact, evangelicalism has always been defined by a desire to convert others to Christianity.

Even Voice of the Martyrs' attempts at political advocacy seem unfocused. Under an appendix section titled "What Can I Do?"—after the more important suggestions like "write a skit" and hold a fake underground church service ("have people who are dressed as police invade your meeting")—the book suggests writing your elected officials, United Nations ambassadors, "officials of foreign governments," and local newspaper editors to voice your concerns about Christian persecution. "Write a letter to or e-mail your elected officials in Washington and in your state capital," it suggests. "Inform them of specific human rights violations committed against Christians in various countries around the world. . . . Request that they investigate these violations and propose sanctions against the governments of these countries until these violations end." Perhaps in an attempt to keep the content evergreen, these instructions seem vague. "Propose sanctions"?

By burying its politics under religion, Voice of the Martyrs' advocacy becomes less about principles and cohesive ideology and more about preserving the rights of their own interest group. It reminds me of Christians I knew who claimed to be guided not by politics but purely by their own Christian morality. But surely it's no coincidence that, like old-school action movies, the persecutors of Christians in each *Jesus Freaks* story also happened to be America's political enemy at the time.

In reality, there are no claims in *Jesus Freaks* toward the importance of religious freedom—only the freedom to be Christian. Which makes me think the real goal is Christian hegemony.

♥ † ♥

I was an "end of history" kid. I was born in 1992 and raised partially in post-Soviet Eastern Europe. Trailing my mom through clean-scrubbed, lax-security airports, attending my international school, I was being prepared for a certain kind of world. A globalized world, where technology was zipping forward, where yesteryear's crude wars would no longer be fought and diplomacy would rid the world of genocide, famine, and disease and smooth global culture until it gained the slick, seamless texture of a Microsoft ad.

That didn't happen.

I was nine on September 11, 2001. Watching the Twin Towers fall over and over in the news coverage on my aunt's TV, I felt that feeling tragedies can spawn, the overwhelming bafflement at the pain of being human—or, at least, at the possibilities of what we as humans could do to one another. It was the first time I really remember staring at a television screen and being aware that I was seeing other people die.

While I was old enough to be shocked by the spectacle of destruction, I was still too young to comprehend the geopolitics of the situation. In the weeks following, other kids at school told panicky rumours about terrorist plots meant for our humble Canadian prairie city. I vacillated between fear and disbelief. The U.S. president, with his little round serious face, declared war—not on a country but on the concept of Terror itself. Adults, unable to work what was happening into child-size bites, explained to me that terrorists didn't want anything in particular, they just wanted to scare people. A horrifying thought—random acts of violence writ huge. *Safety* and *security* became words constantly in the air, over the TV and radio waves. So did *freedom* and the *Patriot Act*. The news seemed choked with fear.

That war, for me, played on, far away, only glancingly touching the edges of my life. Years passed. Bombs went off in subways and were found in shoes and water bottles at airport security.

We all started unlacing our sneakers in airport lines. Bombs fell, too, far away from where I lived. The news showed me people—civilians—screaming in languages I didn't understand, being pulled from rubble, seeping blood, cradling lost limbs. The president stood in front of his *Mission Accomplished* banner. His little round face lost its blankness, and now I could perceive in it an anger that was meant to be righteous. I learned more new words—*invasion, pre-emptive strike, casualties, nation-building*—words that hid the reality of violence because that violence was meant to be justified, because America had been targeted, persecuted. The president spoke about "enhanced interrogation techniques"; the words clanged against the photos of naked bodies, cowering or forced into positions like dolls belonging to a cruel child, faces cloaked under bags and hoods. There were pictures, too, on the front page of my local newspapers of caskets draped with red maple leaf flags, daily counts of bodies "coming home," as the news liked to put it.

No, history didn't end, and I grew up the same way my parents and my grandparents' generations did, with the backdrop of a world at war. Like them, with the privilege of viewing it from afar. We were away from bodily danger, affected only by the ambient psychic stress. Cold War kids hid under desks as War on Terror kids checked compulsively for suspicious packages, ready to say something when they saw something.

I should say: white kids.

In the white enclave of my private Christian school, I didn't even have the tools to understand the Islamophobia that was pulsing through all of this, radiating through the very air, let alone the matrices of marginalization that meant others in my city, my school, my country, had a very different experience of this time.

For my part, I felt powerless and cruel. I was living my little life, and people were dying everywhere. When it came to the wars in Iraq and Afghanistan, I didn't understand why, and my teachers had trouble explaining to us the exact political forces at play.

Martyrdom, though—there was some death and destruction that could be explained. That, I was supposed to understand.

♥ † ♥

While the persecutors in *Jesus Freaks* are nearly inhuman in their lust for Christian blood, their victims are angelic. There are a few stories in the book of young women standing up to persecution under communist regimes—one has no name and is simply identified as "Girl." The adjectives used to describe these young women are almost parodic: They are always fresh and beautiful, attracting soldiers' eyes with their cleanly scrubbed, cherubic faces. Why their physical attractiveness is pertinent to the story isn't explained. They are described as glowingly angelic. They are demure in demeanour but steadfastly brave in accepting pain and death for their beliefs. Often death. These are stoic martyrs for the cause. Some accept sexual assault as well—just another trial and tribulation for the glory of God.

The facile language hides what seems to me an ideologically complicated proposition. The very idea of God's power, as laid out in this conception of Christianity, is confusing. So, God has the power to spare some persecuted Christians—meaning that when Christians are killed, God is choosing not to save them? Their deaths are for God's "glory," but even in these stories, they rarely lead to the miraculous conversion of the torturers. The biggest audience for these stories is evangelical Christians, who are presumably already "in" and won't be converted, either. And if hearing about these tragedies spurs them to action, are they meant to help people who are being persecuted for their faith? Wouldn't that undermine the use of persecution as a testament to God? In terms of practical action, other than the halfhearted suggestions about writing letters to representatives and staging mock police raids, the book mostly tells readers to pray for the

Christians being persecuted around the world—or pray that persecutors' "hard hearts" will be opened to God.

The strange thing is that it's always a win-win situation. The book contains stories of those who were brutally killed but also those who were miraculously spared. Some people were burned at the stake, while others were magically impervious to the flame. Some people took their beating with the radiant stoicism of a true believer and were killed; others did the same, and their captors were converted to Christianity, fell on the ground, and spared them. In some stories, the Christian sacrifices themself to save another's life; in others, they willingly give up their own children, family, or friends. Despite all these different outcomes, the book treats each story as equally holy and miraculous. But what is the moral or theological cohesion of these tales? How can God be asking all these people to die for him and yet saving some of them, letting them off the hook? More dark is the question: If he has the power to save some, why not all?

In a section entitled "Why Did They Have to Die?", *Jesus Freaks* nods toward these questions. However, it says, "The purpose of this book is not to try to explain away the deaths of the martyrs, but to honor their conviction, commitment, and faith—and to build yours."

"Some deaths seem senseless—but God sees things differently than we do," the book assures us. Martyrs have made a sacrifice, one that has acted as a witness to their faith and thus "grown" that faith—"Many have died so you could experience the faith and freedoms you enjoy today." Ultimately, their deaths should not make us grieve, the book says, because these martyrs knew that by dying, they were simply entering into their eternal life in heaven.

Don't be horrified, or sad, then, about the stories in this book, this introduction seems to be saying. Don't think too much about the why or the how of it. Don't question their veracity. Simultaneously treat them as parables and as Gospel truth.

♥ † ♥

In 2003, the United States launched its second invasion of Iraq, alleging that Iraq was developing weapons of mass destruction. One year later, in 2004, the CIA admitted there had been no "imminent threat" of such weapons before the invasion.

That same year, Bill O'Reilly ran his "war on Christmas" segments on his Fox News show, *The O'Reilly Factor*. Titled "Christmas Under Siege," each spotlighted different affronts in this new battle, from Denver disallowing religious floats in its holiday parade to Macy's department stores supposedly no longer greeting shoppers with a "Merry Christmas!" In an accompanying "Talking Points Memo" still available on the Fox News website, O'Reilly wrote that these "anti-Christian" bellwethers were all part of a systematic attack on organized religion. "Secular progressives realize that America as it is now will never approve of gay marriage, partial birth abortion, euthanasia, legalized drugs, income redistribution through taxation, and many other progressive visions because of religious opposition," he writes, laying out a very strange progressive platform. Apparently, Christians' weak flank is their holidays: "But if the secularists can destroy religion in the public arena, the brave new progressive world is a possibility."

He adds ominously, "That's what happened in Canada."

Canadians pride themselves on an excess of politeness, define their politics on "peace, order, and good government" rather than the bold swipes at freedom and liberty preached by our American neighbours. At least, that was the propaganda I absorbed, growing up in quiet Manitoba. I remember feeling visceral shock as a young teenager when, visiting a friend's house, I heard her dad loudly rehashing his favourite points from the radio broadcast he'd been listening to—Rush Limbaugh, a favourite of the hyper-conservative faction known for his loud, angry, and offensive rants, Republican sway, and unsparing use of derogatory language (calling women *feminazis* was probably his least offensive catchphrase). I hadn't heard that kind of angry, brazen politicking before.

Not like that, at least. Of course, I had heard something like it—the quiet, Canadian version. The dog whistles that flew right over my head. The hardline anti-gay beliefs held by Canadian conservative politicians like Preston Manning or Stockwell Day, for instance, hidden under layers of misdirection and a veneer of tolerance, seemed different than American radio hosts pouting about "Adam and Eve, not Adam and Steve." Prime Minister Stephen Harper's controversial choice to end a speech with "God bless Canada" wouldn't have merited discussion south of the border. But there was racism and religious intolerance lurking underneath this seemingly calm respectability.

The Christian school I grew up attending seemed to present itself as an apolitical space. But don't I have memories of teachers and guest speakers coming to my classrooms, telling us kids how lucky we were to go to private school, where we could pray in class and didn't have to pass through a metal detector on our way in each day? Didn't a representative for Gideon's Bibles pass around little red books to my fifth-grade class and tell us all about how sad it was that the government wouldn't let him go to every school, that he was being shackled from sharing the word of the Lord with children like us? Didn't members of my Grade 8 class cheer when our teacher announced that George W. Bush had won a second term?

That phrase "war on Christmas" has always had a dark motivation lurking within it. Histories of the concept generally start back in the 1920s, with Henry Ford's collection of antisemitic pamphlets, which he published in his newspaper, *The Dearborn Independent*. Then there was the anti-Civil Rights, anti-communist John Birch Society in the late 1950s, who claimed that "UN fanatics" were somehow perpetrating an "assault on Christmas." The actual phrase "war on Christmas" was likely first penned by Peter Brimelow, a white nationalist blogger whose web page was charmingly identified by the ACLU as "racist, anti-semitic, and anti-immigrant." He coined the term in response to a "Happy Holidays" greeting on the Amazon.com home page. O'Reilly's 2004 segment likely brought the idea further into mainstream culture. The next year, in 2005, the book *The War on Christmas: How the Liberal Plot to Ban the Sacred Holiday Is Worse Than You Thought* (!) by John Gibson, another Fox News contributor, codified the titular phrase.

As a nine-year-old, I hadn't heard there was a war going on. That is until a friend looked over my shoulder and saw me carefully colouring in the bubble letters I'd drawn on a school pre-holiday craft project: MERRY XMAS. I can still remember the exact tenor of her voice, a high-pitched, slightly wild tone, as if she was yelling about some life-or-death situation. "You're taking the Christ out of Christmas!"

I'd thought *Xmas* looked pretty cool. It was how my mom always abbreviated it on the calendar in our kitchen. I remember feeling a hot rush of shame, realizing that yet again I'd discovered some rule in my school that I didn't know about but seemingly everyone else did.

It wasn't enough to be allowed to celebrate Christmas—everyone had to celebrate along with you. And there was a right and wrong way to do it. Secular Christmas was commercial; it had lost its way, forgotten its true meaning. We should all look to the brave animators of *A Charlie Brown Christmas*, who dared to put the biblical Christmas story from Luke in their TV special, I remember a guest speaker at our school assembly telling us. I was just happy that we got to watch a TV show instead of being in class.

In 2014, Kirk Cameron released *Saving Christmas*, a film which has achieved the rare feat of a zero-percent score on Rotten Tomatoes. Basically an angry Facebook rant come to life, the movie acts as a culmination of ten years of persistent assertion from these Fox News types that secular society is mounting strikes against Christian holidays. Cameron apparently takes a slightly different ideological position than O'Reilly and my childhood classmate, which is not simply that Christmas celebrations should include Christ but that all of them *already do*, whether you know about it or not. His movie includes biblical justifications for Santa Claus, nutcracker dolls, and Christmas trees, among other things. As Wikipedia puts it, in a lovely example of rhetorical brevity, "Cameron [says] that Christmas trees were God's idea since God created trees."

It's easy to make fun of the War on Christmas, with its juxtaposition of hysterical pitch and objectively goofy practicalities—Fox News anchors yelling about red Starbucks cups spring to mind. But this hysteria comes from a deeply necessary, needy place, the paradox of the evangelical mindset: Christians must somehow both rule the world and be persecuted by it.

Evangelical Christianity is inextricable from American culture, the culture which, largely, produced its modern iteration. And to me, it seems these cultures share a strange kind of imperialism: The will to dominate coupled with an intense sensitivity to attack. Any perceived slight will cause a lashing out. After all, a war necessitates an enemy. If someone has declared a War on Christmas, that is sufficient justification for striking back or even making a preemptive strike.

This doesn't square all that well with the actual teachings of Jesus, the man of "turn the other cheek" fame. "If someone takes your coat, do not withhold your shirt from them," Jesus instructed his followers in Luke. The red-faced, sweaty Christianity epitomized by 2000s news pundits with foghorn voices seemed likely not only to withhold the shirt but to claw and bite to get the coat back.

♥ † ♥

Jesus Freaks's opening page carries a dubious fact about the prevalence of Christian martyrdom: "It is said that there are more Christian martyrs today than there were in 100 AD—in the days of the Roman Empire. According to the World Christian Encyclopedia, there were close to 164,000 Christians martyred around the world in 1999. An estimated 165,000 will be martyred in 2000."

When I reread the book, I did so over several days, in short bursts. It was hard to take so many horrifying stories one after another, even the ones that I felt (or knew) were fake, or the ones so ancient (martyrs of the early church or Reformation, in centuries past) as to feel disconnected from present reality—though these have the downside of being even more visceral, often involving crucifixion or live burning. Others were so strangely presented or used such weird or anachronistic language that they were actually just funny. Sometimes I felt bad laughing. If there was ever a book that needed content warnings, this was it—beheadings, tortures described in a little too much detail, brutal sexual assaults, and the violent murder of children were lurking around random pages. And, of course, there were the centuries-old stories of saints being flayed, dragged behind horses, crucified, and burnt at the stake. I couldn't believe I'd read this as a kid.

> "We have your nephew," said the handwritten note. "If you surrender to us, we will return the boy to his parents." Brother MT stared at the message. It was from the leaders of the New People's Army (NPA), the military arm of the Communist Party of the Philippines. People in many parts of the Philippines have been threatened and persecuted for years by this group of terrorists. . . .
>
> MT had counted the cost and was prepared to give his life for the Gospel, but he was not prepared for this! He knew there was no hope that his surrender would save his nephew. He knew they would both be killed; still, he hesitated.

The boy's parents insisted that MT ignore this order and continue his evangelistic outreach. As a result, the parents gave their son for the Gospel. Peter was killed on Good Friday, April 17, 1992. He was tortured for three hours and suffered very much. . . . Finally, he was beheaded.

Reading this now, the semi-jubilant tone—"the parents gave their son for the Gospel," on Good Friday—strikes me as horrific. I certainly don't find this account of parents giving permission for their eight-year-old son to die inspiring at this point in my life.

In the face of the sorrows and terrors of life, I think it can be an easy comfort for religious people to say, *It was willed by God. He's in a better place. It was all for the greater good.* But where does that grief go? There is no room in stories like these for the kind of deeply human, visceral pain that anyone who loses a loved one would feel. There's no room for the parents in that story to hate Brother MT for getting their family mixed up in something so awful.

But whatever were gains to me I now consider loss for the sake of Christ. What is more, I consider everything a loss because of the surpassing worth of knowing Christ Jesus my Lord, for whose sake I lose all things. I consider them garbage, that I may gain Christ and be found in him, not having a righteousness of my own that comes from the law, but that which is through faith in Christ . . . I press on to take hold of that for which Christ Jesus took hold of me. Brothers and Sisters, I do not consider myself yet to have taken hold of it. But one thing I do: Forgetting what is behind and straining toward what is ahead, I press on toward the goal to win the prize for which God has called me heavenward in Christ Jesus.

Philippians 3:7–14
(New International Version)

When I was eight years old, in Grade 4, the above passage haunted me. In class, my teacher handed out printed sheets of purple paper designed to look like certificates. The Bible verses above were printed on it like a kind of pledge. Underneath was an image of a ribbon, like you might get for placing first at a country fair. There was a line where we were meant to sign and date the certificate, pledging our dedication to press on toward the goal to win the prize for which God has called us heavenward.

For some reason, I took this assignment incredibly seriously. I think I had a latent guilt about not being *Christian enough* that was hanging around me. All I know is, the moment I put my pen to the page to sign my name, I began to feel panicked. How could I pledge such a thing? I wasn't ready to dedicate all that I was to Jesus, to throw everything I loved in the garbage and live only for the Glory of the Lord. *But I should be*, I thought. I took the paper home and taped it to the wall of my bedroom, right above my desk, so that I could look at it as a reminder every day. I would win the prize of heaven.

One of the most famous contemporary martyrdom stories, the one that ricocheted its way through turn-of-the-millennium Christian pop culture, was "The Girl Who Said Yes." I can't remember where I first heard the story. It might have been told to me on the playground, almost as salacious gossip; a teacher or a pastor might have used it in a lecture or a sermon. I might have read it for the first time in *Jesus Freaks*, which includes a short version of the story in the preface to the book. In any case, when I was growing up, it felt ubiquitous.

There was an entire book about it, in fact: *She Said Yes* by Misty Bernall, the aforementioned girl's mother. It tells the story of Cassie Bernall, a 17-year-old who attended Columbine High School in Colorado and was killed in the 1999 shooting. As the book tells it, shooter Eric Harris asked Cassie Bernall if she was a Christian. When she replied yes, he shot and killed her.

Along with the book about her life and the story's inclusion in *Jesus Freaks* were several other Christian pop culture monuments to the girl who was quickly labelled a martyr. She became a lesson used in countless sermons to churches and youth groups across a country rocked by the then-unimaginable spectre of a mass school shooting. A Christian metal band, Flyleaf, wrote a song called "Cassie." And famous Christian Contemporary Music artist Michael W. Smith won a Dove Award for his song "This Is Your Time," the music video which starts with a real home video clip of Bernall speaking to the camera about how she is "inventing the kingdom" by being "a good example to non-believers" and Christians alike.*

In the years since the Columbine murders, this story has been told and retold. But as early as a few months after the shooting, the account was contested by surviving eyewitnesses. From the vantage point of years, and several reportorial and FBI investigations later, the actual events in the library where Bernall was killed are fairly clear. Harris did not, in fact, ask if Bernall was a Christian before shooting her; he looked under the desk where she was hiding and said, "Peek-a-boo." A terrifying end, in a different way—one that requires grappling with the senselessness of the violence that some humans are willing to inflict on others.

Despite the many "causes" blamed for the shooting after the fact (including music, goth style, and violent video games), it seems Columbine shooters Dylan Klebold and Eric Harris had no clear ideological motivation for the spree and no targeted victims but rather sought to kill as many as possible at

---

* Incidentally, this clip is followed by a shot of Smith lowering an old-timey movie camera from his face and looking sadly to the side, which is a very strange visual—is the video suggesting that *he* filmed her?

random. There is certainly no evidence that they desired to kill Christians, specifically.*

Interestingly, in terms of narrative crafting, fellow student Val Schnurr, who survived the massacre, is believed to be the one who told Harris that Bernall was a Christian in that library. According to a *Vox* retrospective on the impact of Columbine on Christian martyrdom stories, though Schnurr told her story at youth rallies following the event, there doesn't seem to be any substantial legacy of her tale in Christian pop culture, perhaps because she was Catholic and not part of the Protestant evangelical Christian mainstream.

In the case of Bernall, a tragic loss of life was transformed into something else: a parable of sorts, an example of how Christians should be. Growing up in my evangelical world, I heard this story weaponized as a way to tell me that was what was required of me as a Christian: willingness to die for my religion.

There was also an implication that this was always an imminent threat. At any point in the normal course of a day, you might have a gun thrust in your face and a shooter demanding you explain your faith on penalty of death. And to deny Jesus would be the ultimate failing. This was, as Michael W. Smith puts it in "This Is Your Time," a "test" that all young Christians should hope to pass.

I remember laying up late at night, unable to sleep, imagining such a scene. Would I be able to claim Jesus in such a circumstance, or would I deny him like Peter in the Bible? Guiltily, I always had to admit internally that I would never let myself be killed. There was nothing that scared me more than death, particularly violent death.

Clearly, this meant I was not a good Christian. I was not living up to the certificate I'd signed; to the call of Philippians.

---

* A second martyr story from the Columbine shooting, the death of a Christian teenager named Rachel Scott, was also turned into a book in the form of Scott's journals, which were published under the editorial guidance of her parents. Years later, in 2016, Scott's story was transformed into a movie called *I'm Not Ashamed* by Christian movie studio Pure Flix. The film was not well-reviewed, and according to *Vox*, made the implicit assertion that Klebold's and Harris's violence was somehow motivated by the fact that their school taught them about evolution in science class.

As an adult, other questions about the way Cassie Bernall was used, the way her death was narrativized, preoccupy me. What were the implications of this martyrdom framing? Did the story mean to suggest that everyone killed at Columbine was killed for being a Christian?

In a way, it obscures the reality of the Columbine killings as well as the painful loss of Cassie Bernall's life. After all, isn't the senselessness of the violence of a mass shooting more terrifying than ascribing some kind of motive? It might be a comfort to those who knew Bernall to see her as a martyr, but does it erase some element of her humanity? Does it erase the stories of other victims? Does it stand in the way of other lessons we might learn from such a tragedy, such as the need for gun control or mental health support in schools?

Columbine was one of the events that primed Christian teen culture for its obsession with martyrdom. Living passionately for Jesus meant being ready to die for him at any time, as well as going against the grain of culture in regular daily life. This was the theme DC Talk's song "Jesus Freak," the namesake of the martyr book—proudly taking back the insult, being willing to be a "freak" for Jesus.

For those not steeped in evangelical Christianity, it might be hard to understand why this politically powerful bloc considers itself a persecuted minority.

New Testament scholar and historian of Christianity Candida Moss contends in her 2013 book *The Myth of Persecution* that this sense of persecution is foundational to the way modern Christianity figures itself. Drawing on the history of martyrdom stories in Christianity, she shows how, throughout history, Christian myth-making has presented the religion as one that is persecuted and marginalized. The Christian Gospels (the books of Matthew, Mark,

Luke, and John in the Bible) that tell the story of the life of Jesus were written in a time when Judea, where Jesus and his early followers lived, was controlled by the Roman Empire, portrayed in the Bible as a violent occupying force. "Blessed are ye, when men shall revile you, and persecute you, and shall say all manner of evil against you falsely, for my sake," Jesus tells his followers.

Of course, this verse comes from the King James Version, a translation undertaken by a Christian leader of an imperial power—a mythmaking project, not one of historical interest and accuracy. (The Geneva Bible contains about four hundred instances of the word *tyrant*, most referencing a king, while the King James Version, suspiciously, contains none.) While England was busy colonizing the globe, English Christians were building a mythos of their religion as a persecuted underdog.

Actes and Monuments, published in 1563 by John Foxe (a Protestant English historian), collects polemic stories of Christians murdered for their faith—the 16th-century version of *Jesus Freaks*. Today, it's known as Foxe's Book of Martyrs. At the time it was published, Foxe's book was the largest publishing project undertaken to that point in history (pulling from several scholars in Early Modern print history, Wikipedia derives the description: "A single volume book, a bit over a foot long, two palms-span wide, too deep or thick to lift with only one hand given it exceeded 1,500 pages, and weighing about the same as a small infant"). An explicit propaganda device of the Reformation, it was widely read by Protestants at the time of publication, and its popularity continued for hundreds of years. Catholics, too, carried on the tradition of martyr stories with their emphasis on the lives (and deaths) of martyred saints—St. Lawrence, who was grilled alive (and apparently told his tormentors to flip him over for even charring), or St. Sebastian, who had to be clubbed to death after his first assassination by arrows didn't take.

Foxe's book creates a lineage of martyrdom leading up to the lives of Protestant Reformation leaders, like William Tyndale and

John Calvin, by compiling this compendium. It starts with the deaths of the disciples and continues through Roman persecution under Nero; Papal persecutions and Catholic inquisitions; accounts of the lives and deaths of reformers, beginning with Martin Luther; and persecutions in Scotland and England under King Henry VIII and Queen Mary, respectively. Christianity had divided along Protestant and Catholic lines, but by including the apostles and members of the early church, Foxe was essentially claiming them, impressing a sense of continuity between the biblical saints and contemporary Protestants.

But according to Moss, scholars of early Christianity "agree that there is very little evidence for the persecution of Christians" in the time of the early church. "For the first two hundred and fifty years of the Christian era, there are only six martyrdom accounts that can be treated as reliable. . . . When we look closely at even these stories, however, it becomes clear that they have been significantly edited and changed."

The problem with the distinction between "martyrdom" and "murder victim" is that it's a matter of perception. Moss notes that many early martyrdom stories contain theological ideas that didn't exist in the period in which the death took place. "The fact of the matter is that there are no stories about the deaths of martyrs that have not been purposely recast by later generations of Christians in order to further their own theological agenda," she writes.

The "Actes and Monuments" included in Foxe's book are a prime example, written in the aftermath of sometimes quite bloody conflict between Catholic and Protestant factions of Christianity, following a narrative that cast Protestant Reformers as noble martyrs and the Catholic Church and its figureheads as sadistic killers.

Moss contends that stories of martyrdom are always a political and rhetorical tool (whether they be provably true or fictionalized), always casting an oppressor and enemy in the role of persecutor. Whether that be other Christians on the other side of a theological schism, as in Foxe's case, or those on the other side of a political or religious divide, as in *Jesus Freaks*'s tales of bloodthirsty communists and Muslims. The stories in *Jesus Freaks* explicitly align Christianity with a certain set of American political ideologies.

One of the significant problems with this is, of course, these accounts are being offered as some kind of proof of Christianity's oppressed status—while simultaneously removing any context or reference to how the religion has been co-opted to oppress others. For instance, countries like the Philippines, where Brother MT was targeted by communists in *Jesus Freaks*, have endured decades of violent political instability in the wake of colonization led by Christian missionaries. Converting people in other countries is assumed to be a noble goal and so integral to the evangelical worldview that it's worth breaking the law to smuggle Bibles into China, Vietnam, or North Korea. But the effects of spreading evangelical Christianity in other countries, like Uganda—which, as shown in the 2013 documentary *God Loves Uganda*, has become a hotbed for human rights violations against 2SLGBTQIA+ people under evangelical leadership—go unexamined.

Moss writes:

> Martyrdom continues to matter . . . Persecution remains an integral part of how Christians think and talk about their history and themselves. It endures in the claims of Christian politicians and commentators that they are persecuted and under attack, and it is powerful precisely because it refuses to acknowledge its own power. Everyone agrees that a country that is invaded by enemy forces is morally justified in defending itself. In the same way, when the powerful and politically secure claim that they are persecuted, oppressed, and attacked, then they can claim that all of their actions are born out of self-defense. They can act aggressively and

even violently and maintain the moral high ground in the knowledge that they are the victims.

♥ † ♥

In the face of the War on Terror, in retrospect, the Christian response was a rapid increase in Islamophobia. Just over a decade after the fall of the Berlin Wall, the threat of communism in the evangelical American ethos was ebbing, and Islam arrived to take its place. "In the 1990s, as evangelicals looked for alternatives to a foreign policy agenda long framed by Cold War categories, many had turned their attention to the persecution of Christians in other nations, attention that often ended up focusing on the oppression of Christian minorities in Islamic nations," historian Kristin Kobes Du Mez writes in *Jesus and John Wayne*, describing the exact phenomenon that takes place over the pages of *Jesus Freaks*, though it was published two years before the September 11 attacks. Prominent Christian leaders, like Franklin Graham and Pat Robertson, began denouncing Islam with increasing fervour, even comparing Muslims (as a whole) to Nazis. James Dobson of Focus on the Family took up the talking point of terrorism as a threat not just to the nation-state but to its supposed microcosm, the American family, saying, "The security of our homeland and the welfare of our children" are both "family values."*

When the Twin Towers fell on September 11, in the minds of the Christian Right, it was as if this narrative was coming true, writ large. The Muslim persecutors of Christians in *Jesus Freaks* were now a threat not just to people in their own countries—they were after the "Christian Nation" of the United States of America. "They hate our freedoms" was the popular political reasoning for these acts of terrorism; in Christian circles, this was quickly

---

* Du Mez, p. 220.

latched to the already much bandied-about idea of Christianity as being about "freedom in Christ."

This mentality was not merely an American phenomenon; it certainly extended to conservative Christian groups in Canada as well and continued well beyond the early 2000s. As late as 2015, Conservative Prime Minister Stephen Harper—a member of the evangelical Christian and Missionary Alliance Church—set up a hotline for Canadians to report "barbaric cultural practices," his party's code word for Muslim religious rites such as the wearing of head coverings.*

Du Mez notes that in the frenzied response of the years following September 11, the Christian pop culture machine started churning out a new breed of celebrity, spawning book deals and speaking tours: the "ex-Muslim terrorist." Some of the book titles published in the decade in question:

> *From Iraq to Armageddon: The Endtimes Clock Is Ticking, The Final Showdown Approaches*
> *Iran: The Coming Crisis: Radical Islam, Oil, and the Nuclear Threat*
> *Secrets of the Koran*
> *Married to Muhammed*
> *The Islamic Invasion*
> *The Final Move Beyond Iraq: The Final Solution While the World Sleeps*
> *Why We Want to Kill You: The Jihadist Mindset and How to Defeat it*
> *Unveiling Islam: An Insider's Look at Muslim Life and Beliefs*

The final entry on this list was written by brothers Ergun and Emir Caner and sold 200,000 copies. Supposedly written by

---

* *The Globe and Mail*, "Conservatives Vow to Establish 'Barbaric Cultural Practices' Tip Line."

former terrorists, the book was meant to reveal the secret intent of Islam to destroy Christian civilization. Ergun Caner became a prominent evangelical figure; however, it became clear as the book's popularity grew that many of his stories were shifting and overembellished. Eventually, Muslim and Christian bloggers fact-checked his claims and discovered that he had not been raised in Turkey, as he said, but in Sweden and Ohio; he'd never been involved in "jihad," and his "thick Middle Eastern accent" was fake. Caner has not admitted to these falsehoods, but among the evidence are the many erroneous claims about Islam that fill the book and at least one instance, documented by the *Huffington Post*, of Caner speaking "an entirely made-up language" on stage.

Other "former terrorists" included Walid Shoebat, Zachariah Anani, and Kamal Saleem, who spoke at churches and published books filled with graphic stories of Christian persecution at the hands of Muslims. Stoking fear in the evangelical public was a good way for the Christian church to maintain moral superiority while making it seem rational, even justified, that their response be a militant, violent one.

"Conservative evangelicals had regained their footing in 2001," Du Mez writes. "The election of George W. Bush placed a kindred spirit back in the White House, and the terror attacks ensured that foreign policy was once again framed by a clear battle between evildoers and Christian America." But was the increasingly militant tone of evangelical faith in response to the terrorist threat, she asks, or "were they creating the perception of threat to justify their own militancy and enhance their own power, individually and collectively?"

As the war in Iraq dragged on, U.S. forces' death tolls mounted, and support for Bush and the war generally waned—dropping less among conservative evangelicals than the general population but still diminishing. Islamophobia was useful in whipping Christian culture into a frenzy—a frenzy that was both financially lucrative for Christian leaders, organizations, speakers, and publishers and helpful in strengthening and motivating their base. Fear, it was clear, was a useful tactic in mobilizing Christians politically. Perhaps this explains the rapid acceleration, in the aftermath of 9/11, of another so-called war, the Culture War.

With the rise of neoconservatism in the 2000s, political difference was no longer centred mainly around differences in policy; political issues became moral issues. Building on the legacy of the Moral Majority and the Christian Coalition, the Christian Right in the U.S. consolidated its political base around issues it deemed pressing for preserving the moral health of the nation. "You appeal to where the demographic is. You say, 'We're concerned about children, we're trying to strengthen the family, we're trying to reverse the coarsening of the culture,'" then–executive director of the Christian Coalition Ralph Reed revealed to reporter Dan Gilgoff. "That's a totally different kind of marketing than saying, 'We're evangelicals and we're here to take over.'" It was more than the War on Christmas; among the war's many battles were prayer in schools, marriage equality, abortion rights, and the separation of church and state. When then–chief justice of Alabama Roy Moore (who would later become known for a senate race in which his sexual relationships with underage girls came to light) fought for his "right" to display a large block of granite engraved with the Ten Commandments outside the state courthouse, he presented his case like, well, a martyr. Focus on the Family founder James Dobson flew down to offer his support of Moore, and in a speech in Montgomery, Alabama, he compared Moore's refusal to move the Ten Commandments statue to the actions of civil rights hero Rosa Parks.

Dobson took up many Culture War causes and was the most hardlined and politically active in his opposition of national arts funding, abortion rights, and "same-sex marriage," issues he framed under the mission of "defending the American family." He demanded that the national Republican party listen to his evangelical bloc; after all, they had delivered George W. Bush the election. He wasn't far off—2004 marked a shift in voter patterns, with religious commitment tying with race as the single best predictor of voting behaviour (more than union membership, income, or urban/rural residency). A third of the electorate was comprised of voters who attended church either weekly (backing Bush over Kerry 58 to 41 percent) or more than weekly (64 to 35 percent), according to Gilgoff's research. Republicans couldn't ignore "those that put them in office," Dobson told Fox News in 2006. "There's going to be some trouble down the road if they don't get on the ball," he said.

Gilgoff wrote:

> In its capacity as a political machine, Focus on the Family is the culmination of a dream nearly half a century in the making. The dream was to somehow persuade millions of evangelical and fundamentalist Christians, who'd withdrawn from American public life for decades, to rise above their separatist impulses and join the political fray, and in such large numbers that they could tip local, state, and even national elections or flood Congress with enough phone calls to stop a bill in its tracks.

Yet in the same kind of doublethink required for valorizing martyrdom, Dobson, too, harped on the power of evangelicals as a voting bloc while presenting his position as a defensive one, fighting to hold up some kind of conservative vanguard against the powers of liberal persecution. By the end of the 2000s, according to a series of focus-group studies from 2009, Republican voters viewed themselves as a "maligned minority."

For my own part, on the other side of the border, I was being taught I was lucky—lucky to live in a "free country," lucky to be able to practice my faith without fear of communists knocking down my door, lucky to be attending a Christian school where we could pray openly and weren't mandated to follow the provincial curriculum's guidance about teaching, say, evolution or sex ed. And yet, despite all this luck, we were meant to feel persecution lurking around every corner. We were meant to stand strong in the sweeping tide of liberalism and *post-modernism*—a term that, in the evangelical lexicon, represented an existential threat that usually encompassed any contemporary social politics that they disagreed with. Even though most of my social groups—between school and church—were made up of other Christians, I somehow absorbed the expectation that as I moved about the world I was going to be confronted with tests to my faith. I needed to prepare answers and arguments. I needed to be ready to stand up for my beliefs, whether that be to angry communists with guns or misled college professors eager to force their secular humanism upon me.

In reality, when I told non-Christian friends and acquaintances that I was Christian, I mostly received bored nods in reply. At my first job, when I mentioned needing to take Sunday off to attend church, a coworker asked, "Are you, like . . . devout?"

"I guess," I replied and then changed the subject. I felt bad about that reply for years. That had been my chance, my moment to Save someone, to convert my searching coworker to personal faith in Jesus Christ! And instead, I changed the subject. Yet another of my failures as a Jesus Freak.

Chillingly, the Christian persecution complex has not abated in the past two decades. In conversations in recent years, I've heard acquaintances express surprise about the rise of Christian nationalism in Canada—the belief that one's country is a "Christian nation" and should be governed by a set of Christian values and principles—let alone the smug superiority I've heard from Canadians discussing the situation in the U.S. through the

Trump years. But as I write this, evangelical groups in Canada and the U.S. are waging a new culture war, this time on trans youth—the same old talking points applied to a different "enemy." This has serious consequences and will cause far more collateral damage (to use a War on Terror euphemism) than the War on Christmas—trans people are in immediate physical danger, subject to rising violence, and are precarious at the policy level, in danger of losing vital, lifesaving healthcare.

At the same time, evangelicals' sense that they are the ones being persecuted remains strong: Donald Trump announced in September 2024 that, if re-elected, he would create a presidential task force to combat "anti-Christian bias." In pandering to Christian nationalists, he's sold his own $60 Trump-branded Bibles and promised his Christian supporters that they "won't have to vote anymore" if he's elected, suggesting some kind of move toward a Christian autocracy. At the same time, he has built on the racist and xenophobic pillars of his first presidency, targeting migrants and stoking fear of immigrants—even going so far as to claim in the second 2024 presidential debate that Haitian immigrants in Ohio were eating their neighbours' pets.

The Christian teachings I grew up with didn't always seem so vehement, ugly, or warmongering, but they often carried a dark undercurrent that I now understand to be hate. Often, too, such hate was disguised by weaponizing these persecution narratives, always framed as a defense of something—family, morality, faith, freedom—rather than what it really was: an outright attack on a marginalized group.

Ultimately, the concept of martyrdom allows Christianity at large to have its cake and eat it, too, to demand special treatment at the same time as it cries foul for its perceived victimization. The power that refuses to acknowledge its own power, as Candida Moss says.

There is no helpful, healing, or peaceful resolution to persecution, Moss also notes. "You cannot collaborate with someone who is persecuting you. You have to defend yourself. . . . There can be no compromise and no common ground."

♥ † ♥

Voice of the Martyrs' founder Richard Wurmbrand has his own story in *Jesus Freaks*, though it's not clear who authored it. I was surprised to read that his first infraction—the act that supposedly put a target on his back and led to his arrest and torture by the Communist government—was kind of in opposition to other Christians.

> It was a year after the Communists had seized power in Romania. The government had invited all religious leaders to attend a congress at the Parliament building—over 4,000 attended. First, they chose Joseph Stalin as honorary president of the congress. Then the speeches began. It was absurd and horrible. Communism was dedicated to the destruction of religion, as had already been shown in Russia. Yet bishops and pastors arose and declared that Communism and Christianity were fundamentally the same and could coexist. Out of fear, these men of God were filling the air with flattery and lies.
>
> It was as if they spat in Jesus Christ's face.
>
> Sabina Wurmbrand could stand it no longer. She whispered to her husband, "Richard, stand up and wash away this shame from the face of Christ."
>
> Richard knew what would happen. "If I speak, you will lose your husband."
>
> Sabina replied, "I do not wish to have a coward for a husband."

Pastor Wurmbrand took the stage. To everyone's surprise, he began to preach. Immediately, a great silence fell on the hall.

"Delegates, it is our duty not to praise earthly powers that come and go, but to glorify God the Creator and Christ the Savior, who died for us on the cross.". . . The atmosphere began to change. The audience began to applaud. He was saying what they had all wanted to say, but were afraid to.

The book's introduction claims that "Our culture understands heroism. But we don't understand martyrs." It's true, there is something compelling about sacrifice, particularly if it is selfless. But this seems like an odd dichotomy—heroism versus martyrdom—for a book so hagiographically valorizing martyrs to set up. "I do not wish to have a coward for a husband," Wurmbrand's wife prompts. These ideas of cowardice and bravery flatten the martyr just as the role of evil persecutor flattens the enemy, preventing any cooperation or coexistence.

Later in the story, after describing the tortures he faced while under arrest, Wurmbrand says that it was important for him to learn to pity and love his torturers—in fact, that he was divinely inspired to do so. "Only love can change the communist and the terrorist," he says.

But when I look at these stories, I don't see any love. I see loopholes, ways out—ways to politicize faith without saying it, and ways for aggressors to feel like victims.

CHAPTER SIX

FIRST THERE WAS NOTHING, AND THEN IT EXPLODED

CREATIONISM MEDIA AND CHRISTIAN EDUCATION

In the year 2000, while George W. Bush was clawing his way into office on the wave of Christian family values (and with the help of the Supreme Court and various ballet snafus*), Canada was also having an election.

One of the candidates, Stockwell Day, was the subject of a CBC documentary which dug into his evangelical background and Christian beliefs, in which it was alleged (by a professor who reported to have seen Day speak at Red Deer College) that Day believed Earth to be six thousand years old, and that humans and dinosaurs both walked the earth at the same time.

Having grown up in a conservative Christian enclave in Canada, I tend to push back against the assertion that Canadian society is all that different from our U.S. neighbours when it comes to religious fundamentalism—it exists here, too. But to me, the Stockwell Day dinosaur scandal represents most clearly the difference in the sort of liberal-centrist resting point for Canadian society. In America, I believe, this spurious assertion

---

* For those too young to remember, the Supreme Court's controversial *Bush v. Gore* decision stopped the recount of Florida ballots in the 2000 U.S. election, despite tens of thousands of ballots uncounted and miscounted by the state's voting machines, pushing Bush one electoral college vote over the threshold to win the presidency.

would have provoked little more than an eye roll, if not downright support from a portion of the general population. But in Canada, blowback was swift. Warren Kinsella brought out a Barney the Dinosaur toy on TV and journalists whistled "Meet the Flintstones" at Day. Four years later, covering Day's appalling comments on AIDS, *The Tyee* was still referring to the politician as "The Man Who Walks with Dinosaurs."

It was easy to mock Day for believing such a thing—or rather, for disbelieving a mountain of evidence, from fossil records to plain old math. *Young Earth creationism* of the kind Day was espousing—the belief that the creation of Earth happened literally as it is described in the book of Genesis, in six days, a mere six thousand years ago—has a veneer of silliness to it that is hard to shake. It does, indeed, call to mind the Flintstones—chomping on a brontosaurus burger, throwing a bone for your baby dino to catch. It is not, to be fair, a scientifically credible theory, but also the *way* in which it is uncredible is pretty, well, incredible. Perhaps you've seen creationism textbooks with illustrations of Adam and Eve in the garden, a vegetarian T. Rex biting at a hanging banana from the tree above their heads, Noah's family riding dinosaurs.

While Stockwell Day was fielding questions in Ottawa, I was probably sitting in a darkened church sanctuary, hearing a very similar talk to his infamous speech at Red Deer College. A white man in glasses and a button-up shirt—there were many of them, I remember none of their names—was probably pacing slowly across the stage with a microphone in his hand. He was probably telling us about the flaws in carbon dating. Or maybe about the geological records that prove that the flood described in Genesis—the one that wiped out the whole earth except those animals loaded two by two onto Noah's ark—had really happened. Or maybe about a miracle of nature—some occurrence in the animal kingdom so perfectly attuned that it couldn't possibly be the product of randomness, of fate. It had to have been *made by someone*. Intelligently designed.

Yelling "Wilma!" at Stockwell Day is funny, but the real critics were worried more about these beginning-of-the-world beliefs as a bellwether for other positions and the policies that might result from them. And they were right to worry. This battle over creationism, one often framed as a fight pitted between science and religion, was also about something else entirely: education and Christian nationalism.

♥ † ♥

Creationism refers to a belief in the creation story laid out in the first chapter of Genesis, the beginning of the Bible. "In the beginning, God created the heavens and the earth." A strong start.

The basic story of this first chapter of the Bible is an itemized run-through of God's creation process. He creates by speaking things into existence. Verses follow a pattern: "And God said," followed by dialogue from God, *let there be light*, or sky, or animals. He creates and then names one element of creation per day over six days: first day and night; then the sky; the land and vegetation; the sun, moon, and stars; birds and ocean-dwelling animals; land animals and humans.[*]

On the seventh day, God decides to rest from all his work, and to bless that seventh day of rest, creating the Sabbath and the seven-day week.

For creationists, this is not an ancient myth with anything to say about the organization of human society, the power of language, the mysteries of the eternal, or metaphors about the rise of agricultural civilization. Instead, this is a literal and scientific reporting of the origins of the planet Earth.

---

[*] There's not much info about what existed in the universe prior to the creation story; all we get is Genesis 1:2, a very poetic and mysterious verse: "Now the earth was formless and empty, darkness was over the surface of the deep, and the Spirit of God was hovering over the waters." (New International Version)

Any challenge to this way of thinking is typically traced back first to Charles Darwin's publication of *On the Origin of Species* in 1859. While Darwin's research was accepted in some corners of Christianity, others—particularly evangelical Protestants—found the idea of evolution to be an affront to their belief system. Dissent boiled to a head in America in the 1920s, when the Scopes Monkey Trial—the trial of a Tennessee schoolteacher who violated the state's law against teaching evolution in state-funded schools—pitted fundamentalists against modernists and non-religious folks. The issue seemingly faded from North American public consciousness for a few decades, typically seen as an embarrassing loss for fundamentalism. By the end of the century, it had ramped back up to a fever pitch. In the 2000s, waves of U.S. court challenges would be launched, aimed at introducing creationism into schools, and high-profile Christian media would take on the issue publicly, pitching it as yet another front in the Culture War.

Today, those who believe the Bible is an accurate rendering of how life came to be fall generally into two camps. There are Young Earth creationists, who are dedicated to the idea that each day in the Genesis story represents a literal 24 hours, and based on the timelines laid out in the Bible, through genealogies and dates, Earth cannot be more than a few thousand years old—six thousand being the usual consensus among Young Earth creation scientists.

The other camp are creationists who believe in *Intelligent Design*, a term that rose in the late '90s and early 2000s as a way to distinguish more scientifically probable theories of life's origin that still incorporated the biblical story (and, arguably, to rebrand creationism in order to more easily push it into schools, but more on that later). While there is, of course, a wide spectrum of belief encompassed by this term, most often it prioritizes a fundamental belief that life was created, whole cloth, by God, whatever His methods. Proponents of Intelligent Design may allow for some metaphorical language—viewing the days in the creation story as long stretches of time, perhaps, rather than 24 hours—but stop short of viewing the Christian creation story as a myth.

As a kid attending Christian school, I was aware that creationism was the minority opinion in general society. Yet from all the ways it was presented to me, I had no proper conception of how commonplace "belief in" evolution (as it was always put) was, or the soundness of the theory. Creationism was, of course, presented as a perfectly viable alternative theory, and I had no concept of whether or not that was true of the world outside my Christian bubble.

So how many people really *did* believe Earth was created in six days, a few thousand years ago?

In the United States, this appears to be a large portion of the population, especially when looking back on the first decade of the millennium. Gallup Polls run every year since the early 1980s seem to suggest that in the early 2000s, just under half the U.S. population supported creationism. This stat is often quoted in material from both creationist and secular sources, either to prove the acceptability of the belief or to show some kind of astonishing anti-science bent in the general U.S. population.

In actuality, as mathematician Jason Rosenhouse points out in his book *Among the Creationists*, the Gallup Poll suffers from some fraught issues around language that might complicate the picture. "People's religious views are generally too complex to capture with simple questions," he points out, noting that a small difference in phrasing leads to extremely different data on this point. In the case of the Gallup Polls, conflation of Young Earth creationism with general Christian belief seems to have inflated the numbers.

A different poll, run by a group of political science researchers in 2010, found that only 18 percent of people agreed with the statement that "the earth is less than ten thousand years old," while 50 percent agreed that "the Bible describes the creation of life exactly as it occurred in six days," and 60 percent agreed that "all people are descendants of one man and one woman—Adam and Eve." This shows a lot more variance in the types of belief systems Christians have around the origins of the universe.

Still, a 2008 Pew Research Center poll showed only 23 percent of evangelical Protestants agreed that evolution was "the best explanation for the origin of human life," meaning that most evangelicals have some kind of problem with evolution. That poll placed the segment of the U.S. population defined as evangelicals at 26.3 percent, so overall believers in creationism (70 percent of evangelicals by this poll's metric) still might have represented a pretty slim sliver of the overall population.

For my part, I knew vaguely what evolution was—had probably seen it laid out in simplified form on some wall-mounted sign at a natural history museum—but would not have learned or thought much about it if not for Bible class.

Because I attended a Christian school, our science curriculum was exempt from teaching us about evolution, and I remember very little instruction on, or even mention of, the matter (though I did drop biology as soon as possible, after I was told one of the assignments involved dissecting a fetal pig). And that probably would have been fine for me—I wouldn't have thought much about it. As a teen, I was interested in the arts, not the sciences, and I really had no care about how the world began, be it six thousand or 83 million years in the past. To be honest, I didn't care about much that happened more than a hundred years prior (and wasn't written by someone named Austen, Wilde, or Brontë).

But in my high school, students were also required to take a class every year that we simply called *Bible*. In Bible, our teacher, a passionate student of the art of debate and the burgeoning field of Christian "apologetics"—which attempted to "prove"

Christianity through rational argument—was determined we learn not so much about evolution but why it was *wrong*. In doing, he accidentally ignited probably my biggest crisis of faith up to that point in my life.

♥ † ♥

We watched many horrifically boring documentaries in that class, all of them about the science behind Intelligent Design and disproving evolution. Talking head after talking head of creationists explaining how the origin of the universe could only be the way the Bible described: a flash of light, a word spoken by an eternal being. First day and night, and then the sky, the earth and seas, the sun and the moon, the animals of the air and water, land animals and humans—Adam, that is, and Eve from his rib. And then a day of rest, because, God said, it was Good.

This, they explained, was credible—not like that dubious theory of the Big Bang.* Which, as a creation scientist proved in one of these films by trying to recreate the exact conditions in a test tube, was impossible.

There was one line from one of the documentaries that I always remembered. "What the Big Bang essentially says," a creationist tells the camera, chuckling derisively, "is, first, there was nothing—and then it exploded."

He says this as if it's a ridiculous, undefendable impossibility. Ignoring, of course, that this is almost exactly what he believes. That a shadowy force of a being, omnipotent and eternal, sitting outside of time with no beginning and no end, one day spoke *let there be light*. And then it exploded.

♥ † ♥

---

* The Big Bang Theory, of course, is a scientific proposition about the specific point of origin of the universe and is not the same as Darwin's theories of evolution or natural selection, but creationists like to conflate these two things.

What these documentaries made clear was that Christianity hinged on the belief in creation and thus the disbelief in evolution.

The trouble was, they were having the opposite effect on me. The documentaries were convincing me that Intelligent Design was impossible and evolution kind of the only alternative.

The turn of the millennium was also the rise of a popular form of Christian apologetics. Convinced that the religion was losing the battle with secular society on the frontlines of scientific discovery and philosophical relevance, a large segment of the Christian publishing industry suddenly flooded with books meant to rationally argue, and indeed *prove*, the veracity of the Bible's claims.

This vision of Christianity did not appeal to me as a teen any more than it does now. At the time, I was upset with the implication by my teachers, the documentaries, and the creationist speakers for making things harder for me. The line they typically took was that biblical literalism was necessary because if one element of the Bible was untrue, how could you trust the rest of it? If Eve wasn't really pulled from Adam's rib, how can we believe that Jesus came to die for our sins? This births a backward scientific method, a backward philosophical precept, in which an outcome is determined, and one must find the evidence and arguments to prove it.

But this idea cuts both ways, which means that they seemed to be forcing me to throw the baby out with the bathwater: If one element of Christianity was unconvincing, I was meant to disbelieve all of it.

However, I'd also been taught that to lose one's faith was the worst thing that could happen to you. My family, my friends—my entire social world was Christian. I wouldn't dare step outside of that.

This shouldn't have to be so difficult was the feeling hanging over my head throughout high school. If this belief system was so *rational*, so provable, and so beneficial, shouldn't it be strong enough to stand up to pressure? Why was it so difficult to believe?

♥ ☦ ♥

There is a famous—or perhaps infamous—scene in the 2006 documentary *Jesus Camp*, which followed families attending a fundamentalist Christian summer camp. Its lingering shots of weeping children praying in tongues, or marching in camouflage get-ups to war metaphor–laden worship music, were chilling enough to secular audiences to snag the doc an Academy Award nomination for offering this peek into the evangelical subculture. But the scene that feels the most weighted with lingering relevance is of a homeschooling family starting their day. Gathering around the kitchen table, the kids put their hands on their hearts and pledge allegiance to the Christian flag, a white field with a navy square in the corner, kind of like the American flag with all the stripes erased and the stars replaced by a giant red cross.

In the HBO documentary *Questioning Darwin*, the mother of a similar homeschooling family explains the importance of shielding her kids "from what's going on in the world," and making sure that they can "defend their faith."

"I'm sure that they will be attacked when they are older and they go out into the workforce," she says. "One of our children is very interested in science. . . . We warn our son that there are going to be many people who are not going to agree that God created this world in six literal days. They're going to tell him it's a fairy tale. He needs to have strong faith and believe God's word to be able to defend that later."

In *Among the Creationists*, Jason Rosenhouse relays a similar line of thinking from participants in a creationist conference session on homeschooling. "An issue that arose repeatedly, both from the presenters and from the audience during the question period, was that of protecting their children from the perverse influence of 'the culture,'" he reports. "It was clear that, from their perspective, evangelical Christianity was a tiny island of righteousness adrift in a sea of secular evil." During the question period, Rosenhouse asks the conference speaker "if he ever worried they are being *too* protective of their children": "Eventually, the kids will leave home and go out into the world. They are inevitably going to encounter all those ideas the parents find so threatening. Perhaps it is better they encounter them under circumstances where their parents still have influence." The speaker's reply, he says, is a "wonderfully" terse, "No, we don't worry about that."

Of course not, I thought. I imagined asking that same question to the parents and teachers at my high school. The suggestion, I can imagine, would seem tantamount to asking why they didn't just let their kids smoke drugs at home where it was safe. In the panicky, fearful world I'd grown up in, these were questions of extreme moral import. Life and death, really.

♥ † ♥

I once participated in a student group that was assembled to give some feedback to our Bible teacher about the course and how it was run. This was the year after high school, and I think we were all very passionate and optimistic about giving other students a better experience than we'd had in school—laced with the hubris of 18-year-olds who believe they've figured out all the best ways to fix the world. We convened in my friend's living room and aired our grievances—politely—in slightly coded language. I remember talking a lot about the adversarial energy in the room, and the tendency to turn every class into an issue debate rather than a space for learning.

There were a few things I felt I couldn't say—about how depressed and anxious the class had made me feel, about how difficult I felt it was to maintain any kind of faith or spirituality outside of the rigorous boundaries drawn by that teacher (among others) about the right and wrong way to believe. There were many things I didn't even know how to give voice to, things I am now able to recognize. The blind rage that filled me during debates about "same-sex marriage" that I thought was purely some kind of reaction to injustice, that I now understand as being shot through with a deep fear and shame. I can see now the harm I did to my own psyche by constantly pushing the little thought *they're talking about me* to the back, back, back of my mind.

But I think people like my teacher came by their tactics honestly. They thought we wanted to engage intellectually; they thought a religion that had no answers and didn't want you to ask questions would turn people off, which was likely true. I don't think they recognized that judgmental faux intellectualism can be just as off-putting.

Famously, for an entire year, this teacher would make classes study a book by Christian apologist Josh McDowell called *Don't Check Your Brains at the Door*. The premise of the book was that teenagers lose their faith when they go off to university because they've been steeped in an unintellectual, non-rationalized version of Christianity that asks them to "turn off their brain" (or "check it at the door," a reference that I didn't really understand as a 13-year-old).

Like the evolution documentaries, though, this book had the effect of pushing me further from the kind of religious certainty my Bible teacher espoused, where every question had an answer, and furthermore, every probing, skeptical question was actually some secret atheist ju-jitsu. These questions were really just trying to trip you up and were not an honest exploration of a very complex and ancient religion. It was all about finding the perfect answer, a kind of mic drop so that when someone came at you with *Why do bad things happen to good people?* you could yell something about free will, and then drop kick them or something.

The formal structure of the book was to introduce "difficult questions" or misconceptions about Christianity, and then offer answers and corrections. The only problem was the answers and explanations were not satisfactory. It hadn't really occurred to my budding consciousness that the Bible had been stitched together from a bunch of religious texts and translated and retranslated and copied out over and over through the ages, until I read the chapter of this book that supposedly answered the question of why such a book could be infallible. As the author waxed on about monks who hand-copied each line of the Bible with such accuracy that a misplaced ink blot would have them restarting the entire chapter, I felt a cold sinking feeling in my stomach. *Wait, this isn't convincing. I don't like this. This doesn't make sense.* So many human decisions and interpretations were at play in this history, more than I had ever really considered before, and I was supposed to learn how to rationalize all of them? That couldn't be right, could it?

♥ † ♥

Not every Christian I knew shared this approach, of course. In more academic terms, it's a matter of hermeneutics: Whether one chooses a mode of reading with an eye to literary symbolism and figurative language or follows *sola scriptura*, the belief that every word of the Bible is literal, divinely inspired, and infallible.

A belief in inerrancy is relatively new in the theological history of Christianity, having arisen in the late 19th century. A group of conservative American Protestants spearheaded this push toward fundamentalism, an effort to return to what they saw as the core principles at the heart of Christianity. They were driven by a number of factors, including what journalist Marci McDonald calls the "twin assaults" of Charles Darwin and Karl Marx upon their faith.

One of the world's most prominent creationists is Ken Ham, the founder of the organization Answers in Genesis and, famously, both the Kentucky-based Creation Museum and the Ark Encounter, a theme park housing a full-sized replica of Noah's ark. In his book *The Lie: Evolution,* he writes that the biblical creation story "is foundational to all other doctrines of Scripture." In his view, "*Every single biblical doctrine of theology, directly or indirectly, ultimately has its basis in the Book of Genesis.* Therefore, if you do not have a believing understanding of that book, you cannot hope to attain full comprehension of what Christianity is all about."

I wanted to hold onto my religious belief, and I was annoyed that my school environment was making it difficult. My family, and even the churches we attended, had never seemed to consider an anti-evolution stance fundamental to Christian belief. But at school, it was *all* a zero-sum proposition. All my internal dispositions, all the intellectual orientations that felt natural to me, seemed to be outlawed, and my religion was suddenly tightly tied to political affiliation, personal opinions, and whether or not I thought certain scientific facts were true. Why did it have to matter? No one's material circumstances were being affected by the age of Earth, I thought. Couldn't some of us just think Noah rode a dinosaur and some of us think God did the Big Bang, and we could all shake hands and be done with it? Couldn't I just be left alone?

But no, as my teacher told it, if every word in the Bible was divinely inspired, then any one error would cause the entire thing to crumble. If scientists were able to prove that it wasn't true that the entire Earth was destroyed in a flood or that Jesus didn't really rise from the dead, then the whole of Christianity had lost its foundation. (Luckily, both these things were provable—we watched documentaries about them.)

This is what really shook me to my core. What kind of faith was so tenuous that had to be gripped so tightly?

♥ † ♥

Questioning Darwin offers a fairly non-judgmental view of believers in creationism and so-called *creation scientists*, merely granting them space to air their beliefs. One interviewee, a pastor named

Peter LaRuffa, offers this explanation of his strict adherence to biblical truth:

"If somewhere within the Bible, I were to find a passage that said, '2 + 2 = 5,' I wouldn't question what I'm reading in the Bible. I would believe it, accept it as true, and then do my best to work it out and to understand it."

Creationists understand, like everyone else, that the Bible includes "many literary genres," Rosenhouse points out. "They argue, however, that if you are going to interpret a passage non-literally there should be strong contextual grounds for doing so." Being that the writing style of Genesis is in line with other books of the Bible that present straightforward historical narratives, they argue that it's irresponsible to interpret it metaphorically. "There is nothing in the Genesis creation account to label it as a parable, or an allegory, or an accommodation to limited human understanding," Rosenhouse writes.

These subtleties of interpretation are helpful to remember, to understand why people would believe in something like Young Earth creationism. They don't believe out of ignorance but because all these rational explanations are, up to a certain point—when errors of science or logic are introduced—sound. There is no reason to write people off on the basis of assumed stupidity. Of course, for creationists, it's all about the hermeneutic being applied—starting at 2 + 2 = 5 and going from there. Or, a slogan that Rosenhouse reports hearing often at the creationism conferences he frequented in researching his book: "Same facts, different starting points."

This is what creates the house-of-cards feeling I experienced as a young Christian. Often, in the Bible, God or faith are metaphorized as a rock, the substance of belief figured as building on a solid foundation. But the faith I was given didn't have good structural integrity. When confronted with some hard-to-deny evidence, like fossil records that showed evolution happening, Christian leaders had to fall back on unconvincing arguments:

Maybe the fossils were falsified by evil scientists or put there by God to trick people (for a mysterious purpose unknown to us).

I remember one of those creationist speakers at my school telling us confidently that Darwin had actually recounted his theory of natural selection. As if confessing a long-held secret, Darwin supposedly "admitted" on his deathbed that his theory had been entirely made up and that he had decided to become a born-again Christian. Then he went forth in peaceful surrender to the kingdom of heaven, hallelujah.

Of course, I can find no evidence for this claim in my research.

In fact, Darwin was quite a devoted member of the church in his day, and as various historians interviewed in *Questioning Darwin* point out, his religious faith in essence led him to the research that eventually resulted in *On the Origin of Species*. It was through his travels, scholars in the film claim, that Darwin was exposed to what he considered the depths of human depravity, particularly as he saw the evils of slavery firsthand. He also encountered the random, senseless cruelty of nature: natural disasters that claimed lives and destroyed habitats, animals that mauled and devoured one another with abandon. The horrors of the natural world didn't seem in line with his belief in an essentially loving God.

Just as proponents of Intelligent Design view any beautiful aspect of nature as proof that it was created, the horrors and redundancies of the natural world can easily be seen as a sign that something else must be at play.

I found it interesting to see these diametric starting points of evolution and Intelligent Design, which both share the same foundation: a belief in a certain type of God—a just and loving God who would surely want to create useful, beautiful things and would certainly not want to create things just to hurt and degrade us human inhabitants of his Earth.

Of course, the other interesting part is what comes after—devoting one's entire life to stress-testing these presuppositions, or merely searching for "evidence" that will fit your claim.

"If [Darwin's] professors had taught him that this world is not the way it used to be, that it changed because of sin, maybe, if he had been taught the truth about the history in Genesis, he would have responded differently to the death and suffering issue," Ken Ham supplies in his interview in the documentary.

♥ † ♥

Ah yes, the "death and suffering issue." That pesky thing.

Creationists have a ready-made answer for this "issue," which is called *Original Sin*. Supposedly, in the story of Genesis, God created a perfect world. Any imperfection was therefore introduced after the meddling of Satan—who, taking the form of a snake, convinces Eve to eat a forbidden fruit and to then convince Adam to do the same (women, am I right?). This apple-eating was the Original Sin from which every other injustice flows. After this sin, Adam and Eve were cast out of the Garden of Eden. Dinosaurs, who had previously been herbivores, decided to start using their sharp teeth to kill smaller animals. Disease and pestilence burst forth. This is commonly referred to as *The Fall*.

So, this is what is referred to when, in response to any question about the unfairness, cruelty, or meaninglessness of life, an evangelical Christian will respond, "We live in a fallen world."

♥ † ♥

Speaking of senseless cruelty, Ken Ham's brother was afflicted with a rare brain disease that caused him immense pain. Writing in one of his books, Ham says of his brother:

> Did Rob deserve to suffer the way he did? The answer is "yes." When you think about it from a Christian perspective, we *all* deserve much, much more than the suffering afflicting Rob. Because of our rebellious

condition, we don't even deserve to live. But God didn't annihilate us. He has allowed us to live—while at the same time giving us a taste of what life is like without God.

♥ † ♥

Amongst a sea of green, fern-like plants, a shirtless man is extending his hand. Actually, he's completely naked, but the greenery covers anything below his waist, giving him the appearance of floating in a strange, leafy pond. He has bulging pectoral muscles and glossy dark hair swooped gracefully back from his face. He is reaching out a hand, and a big cat—a cougar, perhaps?—is sniffing his fingers. Not with the ready-to-pounce body language you might expect but with the tentative curiosity of a housecat. Other animals look on: a mountain goat, zebras, and—jarringly out of place—two penguins.

This is one of the dioramas on display at the Creation Museum, the attraction in Petersburg, Kentucky, run by Ken Ham and his organization, Answers in Genesis. Opened in 2007, the museum originally cost $27 million.

"Just under three years later, it celebrated its three-millionth visitor," Rosenhouse reports in *Among the Creationists*. He visited the museum at the turn of the decade to offer his impressions: "This is not a fly-by-night operation or an amateurish set-up run out of someone's basement. You would never mistake it for the Smithsonian, but the exhibits look good and the environment is generally pleasant," he writes, adding that along with the indoor displays the museum grounds include "an attractive botanical garden," walking trails, and a petting zoo.

Based on my own online perusal of the museum's exhibits, displays, and video content, I would consider Rosenhouse's description of the centre's quality, let's say, generous. Of course, as a scientist wandering through a museum devoted to demonizing scientists, he does have qualms. He writes:

> [There is a] philosophical question of whether 'museum' is the proper term . . . The appeal of a real museum is the opportunity to see actual physical exhibits and artifacts. By viewing such things, you experience something you cannot get just from reading a book. Walk among actual fossils, say, or bits of memorabilia from Charles Darwin, and you feel connected, if just in a small way, to history. There is very little that is comparable at the Creation Museum. . . . You can stay home and read creationist literature, or you can go to the museum and see it in placard form.

Beyond the scientific displays, however, the Creation Museum houses a lot of displays that just sort of generally depict the horrors of modern culture or the despicable things that human beings have gotten up to in the past, chalking all these up to a belief in evolution.

"According to human reason, everyone does what is right in his own eyes," a placard in the museum explains. "Once people abandon the authority of God's Word, there is no sure foundation for morality and justice in the world."

One area of the museum called Graffiti Alley is a hallway cast in scary red lighting, where faux brick has been scrawled with graffiti tags and the walls are papered over in a collage of images and headlines about violence, abortion, and gay marriage. Many of the papers are made to look torn out of newspapers and magazines. A prominent photocopy of a *Newsweek* cover is splashily emblazoned with the headline, "*The Case for Killing Granny.*" Some of the graffiti reads *Today man decides truth* and *Whatever.*

In another room, the Cave of Sorrows, the museum projects black and white images of horror onto the walls, including clips of the Nazis and intravenous drug use.

"It's not God's fault that there's death and suffering in the world," Ken Ham says in *Questioning Darwin.* "It's our fault because we sinned, in Adam."

♥ † ♥

As Rosenhouse puts it, after looking at a display of Noah's Ark: "One diorama shows the panicked unsaved desperately trying to escape the rising waters. The ark, meanwhile, floats safely by. The image is disturbing. The ease with which creationists summon forth threat and menace against those who demur from their perspective is one of their least endearing qualities."

Listening to the creationists featured in *Questioning Darwin*, I thought it seemed telling how offended they are by being equated with animals. A common response to the idea of evolution usually falls along the lines of a scoffing, "You think I'm descended from a *monkey*?" It feels knee-jerk, disgust-loaded.

Evolution, in this conception, offends at the suggestion that humans are not "set apart" from nature in the way that evangelical Christians wish them to be.

A lot of this thinking is derived from a section of the first chapter of Genesis, directly after God creates everything, where He commissions humanity to "rule over" the earth:

> So God created man in his own image, in the image of God created he him; male and female created he them.
>
> And God blessed them, and God said unto them, Be fruitful, and multiply, and replenish the earth, and subdue it: and have dominion over the fish of the sea, and over the fowl of the air, and over every other living thing that moveth upon the earth.

The militaristic language of subduing and dominion, or "ruling over," has survived in newer translations like the New International Version. Evangelicals typically interpret this passage to mean that humanity is special, alone among all living things created in the image of God, and divinely tasked with bending the natural world to our human will. Aside from leading to some questionable anthropocentric viewpoints about human nature and the environment, this concept of dominion has been equally used to justify intensely racist beliefs, casting certain groups of people as of a lower order of nature, somehow animalistic, and therefore less than human. A later story in Genesis, in which Noah's sons are separated into different parts of the globe, and one cursed to "servanthood," was used by colonial powers for generations to justify slavery.

Ironically, in the Creation Museum this story appears as an explanation of "our differences," meaning racial differences, while another display attests that the acceptance of evolutionary theory drastically increased "biological arguments for racism." (There is no proof cited for this claim, but it seemingly rests on the assumption that evolution could be weaponized to categorize different races as more or less evolved.) "Human reason can be used to justify evil of every sort," the display warns. Highlighting one racist justification while sweeping the other under the rug to make your point seem, well, icky at best. As does ignoring Christianity's history of antisemitism and the professed Christianity of the Nazi party by linking Nazism to a belief in evolution.

The Creation Museum almost doesn't seem real to me, like a parody come to life. But sure, the creationists in America are kooky—of course they were building giant replicas of Noah's ark and museums full of dioramic Adams and Eves. But actually, there is a creation museum in Canada, too.

A Canwest News Service poll in 2009 showed that nearly one-third of Canadians believed that humans were "created by a 'spiritual force,'" compared to 41 percent that "accept the premise that we have evolved 'from a lower species such as apes.'" Sure, a much lower segment of the population than in the U.S., where the 2008 presidential election included questions on evolution in the primary debates. But still a demographic that can wield some serious political power, especially when one of their own is in the Prime Minister's seat. In fact, by the end of the 2000s, as Marci McDonald points out in her book *The Armageddon Factor*: "At a time when Barack Obama had just named a Nobel Prize-winning physicist as his secretary of energy, many in academic circles winced when [Prime Minister Stephen] Harper handed the science portfolio to an obscure Conservative backbencher who had dropped out of university to become a chiropractor."

A couple years before that, in rural Alberta, a man named Harry Nibourg was opening his own Creation Museum.

Alberta is famous as the discovery site of the Albertosaurus, and Drumheller—where the dinosaur's fossil was found—is now home to the Royal Tyrrell Museum and calls itself the "Dinosaur Capital of the World." But even Drumheller has its own share of conservative Christians "who regard the museum's account of history as secular propaganda, and help stage the town's other main tourist attraction, the annual Canadian Badlands Passion Play," McDonald writes, referring to the annual dramatization of Jesus's crucifixion performed on a massive six-acre stage in the badlands.

It was 2007 when Nibourg opened his museum—a non-coincidental timing meant to make a splash. "Only days after [Ken] Ham unveiled his 65,000-square-foot showplace designed by a former special-effects wizard from Universal Studios, Harry Nibourg opened his one-room creation-science museum in Big Valley, Alberta, earning a front-page spread in the *Globe and Mail*," writes McDonald.

Nibourg, a self-described redneck, worked on Alberta's oil rigs and was converted after listening to a coworker's cassette tape about Armageddon. After a deep dive on End Times theorizing, Nibourg became a creationism buff, a hobby which eventually spiralled into his passion project, the Big Valley Creation Science Museum, that takes up a proud storefront on the town of Big Valley's main drag. According to its website, the museum is still open, though due to limited staff, it opens by appointment—visitors have to make reservations in advance. Its mission is "to display the evidence of His [God's] handiwork and refute the lie of evolution."

The museum certainly looks less than impressive from the photo gallery available online. It seems to be housed in a small bungalow, which, above one window on the vinyl siding, has a large statue of a raptor protruding from the front. Inside are several displays—mostly of rocks and fossils—underneath titles like *Evidence from Geology* and *Age of the Earth*. Still, the testimonial of a "visitor from Montana" claims, "I spent more time in this museum than I did in the Smithsonian."

By the end of summer 2007, more than eight thousand people had visited the museum, including Christian school field trips and international visitors. Inside, they'd find a donated exhibit, a genealogical scroll containing a genealogy that leads from Henry the Eighth all the way back to Adam and Eve.

"For conservative Christians like Harry Nibourg, an attack on the factual accuracy of Genesis calls into question biblical quotations on issues such as homosexuality that have provided the rationale for the culture wars," writes McDonald. She notes, "No one stresses that connection more firmly than Ken Ham, who routinely warns that 'compromise on Genesis has opened a dangerous door'—one that has led to nothing less than a breakdown of society."

While the Royal Tyrrell museum, less than an hour's drive away, has awe-inspiring prehistoric skeletons, it "can't deliver the one commodity that Nibourg's postage-stamp gallery serves up: absolute certainty," McDonald writes.

♥ † ♥

Meanwhile, in Christian school, I was being taught with that same certainty. It was perfectly possible for Noah to have taken two of every kind of animal on the ark, just as it was possible that a 40-day-and-40-night rain had caused a flood of the entire globe which would last for a full year. There was scientific evidence for this, I was taught; in particular, I remember a teacher fervently telling us a theory about a sort of water-filled sac that once ringed Earth's atmosphere. If this were true, the atmosphere at that time would have been quite different, meaning that our preconceptions about certain biological facts—the size of animals, the age it's possible for humans to live to, et cetera—would have been irrelevant. When God decided to flood the world, he ruptured the barrier holding back this water, both creating the giant flood and the atmospheric conditions we have on Earth today. As for the whole loading-every-animal-on-a-boat thing, Rosenhouse reports one Young Earth scientist has proposed a figure as low as 16,000 when it comes to how many kinds of animals were on Earth at that time. Noah, his family, and 16,000 animals (or 32,000, I suppose, if they were in pairs) floating on a boat for a year. Seems reasonable.

What went unaddressed was why God would decide to murder nearly everyone on the planet, and even so, why he would choose such a convoluted method to do so. I was never clear on the rainbow at the end of the story, either—did this promise to never kill everyone again mean the unchanging God had changed his mind about something? Surely he could have foreseen it was a bad idea before popping that Earth-coating water balloon?

Rosenhouse writes at the end of the section, relaying his visit to the Creation Museum:

> What would you have me do at this point? ... Should I rant and yell? Find some especially clever put-down for the whole thing? Maybe I should wax eloquent about all of the better uses to which twenty-seven

million dollars could have been put. . . . I *could* do all of those things. At various times I *have* done all of those things. But at that particular moment I was not in the mood. My feelings were not so much anger but more like defeated helplessness. It's like the feeling you get when you see an ant on your kitchen counter and think, "That's not so terrible," until you open your cabinets and see dozens more.

♥ † ♥

The strange thing is creationism appears to be profitable, or at least to have been profitable in the 2000s. How else could Answers in Genesis have funded their $27-million park?

They're not the only ones. In 2001, a Christian fundamentalist named Kent Hovind opened Dinosaur Adventure Land in Pensacola, Florida. Hovind had previously worked as a pastor and a teacher at several private Christian schools (including one he founded), with only the credentials of a bachelor's in religious education from an unaccredited Bible college and an MA and PhD in Christian education from a correspondence college called Patriot University—which, if you can't tell from the name, is also unaccredited and has been accused of being a diploma mill. In the late '90s, Hovind parlayed this expertise into a website called Dr. Dino, where he shared his creationist viewpoints.

I bring this up because Hovind reportedly pulled in $50,000 a year for speaking engagements and sold upwards of $1.8 million in self-produced books and video tapes in a single year (2002). Along with this, Dinosaur Adventure Land reportedly drew 38,000 visitors per year, despite the fact that Wikipedia describes one of the park's "rides," the Jumpasaurus, as "a trampoline next to a basketball hoop; children would have one minute to make as many baskets as they could, and the message was that one had to be coordinated to do more for Jesus."

The other Young Earth creationists don't really claim Hovind; even Answers in Genesis has criticized him for using bad science and poor arguments, which is quite a claim to fame. Along with being a religious fundamentalist and conspiracy theorist,* Hovind is a tax protester and has declared himself a sovereign nation in an attempt to avoid paying taxes to the U.S. government. This gambit ultimately landed him a ten-year sentence in 2007 for owing more than $500,000 in back taxes, from which he has emerged, unreformed.**

While Hovind is certainly a fringe case, having been denounced even by other creationists, it's incredible to realize how much money he was able to pull in with his Dr. Dino merch—that $1.8 million figure gives me much the same feeling as Rosenhouse describes as seeing the ants in the cabinet.

Hovind, too, propagates a fairly common line of argument for creationists: casting evolution—or as they call it, "evolutionism"—as a religion in itself; another way to believe. Of course, this is a false dichotomy—there is no coherent dogma or ideology that defines a "belief" in evolution, nor is it really a belief so much as the sum of several centuries of scientific inquiry. Still, creationists like Hovind need there to be a perceived equality between the claims of creation and evolution. To maintain this perception, Hovind essentially spent the '90s and 2000s challenging various prominent scientists to debate him. (Very few responded.) He also publicized a "standing offer" of $250,000 which he would give to "anyone who can give any empirical evidence (scientific proof) for evolution." The money went unclaimed for years, which was

---

* He's into everything from the New World Order to 9/11 and Oklahoma City bombing conspiracies to UFO sightings, according to Wikipedia.

** The sad footnote to Kent Hovind's saga is that, after serving his prison sentence, he opened a new creationism park in Alabama, which is still open today. The park is free to enter, relying on donations, and operates without liability insurance, which is even more troubling in light of the fact that in March 2020, a seven-year-old boy drowned in a pool in the park. The boy's parents reportedly forgave Hovind, and Hovind was also reported to have spent his time at the hospital with the family handing out his business card to other hospital patrons. He also has had a string of run-ins with the law for domestic abuse of his wives and children. All in all, not a great guy.

supposedly meant to be evidence that no one could do it, until the offer was quietly removed from the Creation Science Evangelism website in 2007.*

Most telling about this gimmick were the qualifications Hovind gave for proving evolutionary theory wrong, in which he defined evolution in a way surely no one else ever has:

> The general theory of evolution . . . believes these five major events took place without God:
>
> 1. Time, space, and matter came into existence by themselves.
> 2. Planets and stars formed from space dust.
> 3. Matter created life by itself.
> 4. Early life-forms learned to reproduce themselves.
> 5. Major changes occurred between these diverse life-forms (i.e., fish changed to amphibians, amphibians changed to reptiles, and reptiles changed to birds or mammals).

One of the big problems with the dichotomy of science and religion is that even the most ardent creationist does not think of themselves as *anti-science*; in fact, they adopt scientific methods and structures of proof to try and put forth their arguments. Their refusal to acknowledge interpretations outside of biblical literalism makes them lean hard into the structures of logic and rationality; they might be stretching those premises to near incoherence, but they are still attempting to do so within a system we regard as scientific. They try to prove the scientists wrong, not disregard science.

---

* Surely a coincidence that this was the same year of his arrest. It also came two years after the website Boing Boing offered $250,000 to anyone who could prove the Flying Spaghetti Monster was not Jesus's father.

Instead, religion versus science is a proxy fight for Christian nationalism versus secularism. The rise of Christian creationism media, books, and theme parks in the 2000s also coincided with a growing trend toward homeschooling and private Christian education in both the U.S. and Canada, as well as a renewed push toward accepting Intelligent Design as a valid theory to be incorporated into school curricula. Evangelicals were on a strangely dualistic mission: to withdraw from a world intent on teaching a corrupt and unfaithful history to their children, while at the same time trying to put their thumb on the scale of public life and make space—even mandatory space—for their own ideas in secular society.

"The front lines of the culture wars are now [North America's] classrooms, where creationists are striding back into the spotlight, flexing their ideological muscles and waging an aggressive new campaign to see their subject taught under a new label: intelligent design," McDonald writes in *The Armageddon Factor*. Indeed, the 2000s saw multiple pushes to incorporate Intelligent Design—the new creationism rebrand—into curricula. In 2004, when a U.S. federal court found it violated a constitutional amendment to teach creationism, a school board in Dover, Pennsylvania, brought a case arguing that Intelligent Design—an entirely different "way of looking at science" that had "nothing to do with the six day Genesis story or religion of any sort"—should be incorporated into the curriculum. The case fell apart when it was determined that the main science textbook the Dover school board wanted to use had been updated from "creationism" to "Intelligent Design" using a simple search-and-replace of the text. A remaining typo—"cdesign proponentsists"—turned out to be the final nail in the coffin.

Brian Alters, at the time a McGill professor and director of the university's Evolution Education Research Centre, acted as an expert witness in the trial. In McDonald's book, he cautions that an increasing push is underway in Canada in the 2000s to teach creationism in school; unlike in America, he points out, Canada has no constitutionally mandated separation between government and religion, meaning there may be few legal options to block the inclusion of creationism in curricula. "In one of Alters's surveys, more than one-third of B.C. science teachers reported pressure from parents to offer some version of creationism," McDonald reports. In several British Columbia school districts, this pressure resulted in under-the-radar creationism teaching, including a secret policy in Abbotsford to discuss "scientific creationism" at students' requests, which went on for 12 years without the provincial minister of education realizing it. Across the country, in Ontario, McDonald adds, "the neo-conservative government of Mike Harris unveiled a new high-school curriculum in 1999 that relegated evolution to the equivalent of a scientific afterthought."

But if these pushes into the public school weren't enough, there were plenty of private evangelical schools, like mine, to choose from—an estimated 1,500 across the country in 2010, according to McDonald. There, teachers were not beholden to the provincial curriculum, and parents could pay thousands of dollars a year for the privilege of keeping such information from their children's ears. This figure may be low, as it didn't account for potentially hundreds of "invisible schools," according to the executive director of the Ontario Alliance of Christian Schools, who told McDonald "some schools that don't want to be recorded" may exist in homes or church basements: "They have a view of the government as being anti-Christian and uncooperative, and they like to stay below the radar."

Others follow the more above-board path of homeschooling their children. At the end of the 2000s, more than two million children in the U.S., and somewhere in the range of 60,000 to 80,000 children in Canada, were being homeschooled by their parents, a move potentially more cost-effective than a private Christian school that still gave parents the chance to remove what they might see as the negative influences and pressures of secular culture.* A 2003 survey showed as much, with 85 percent of Canadian homeschool families indicating that they'd chosen homeschooling to teach their children a particular set of religious and moral beliefs.

Perhaps this shouldn't bother me, but as someone who was educated in this kind of system, it does. I do wish my learning in high school hadn't come with the ideological burden of scriptural inerrancy on the side. I wish that evangelicals' self-removal from the public life was more humble and less recriminatory—that they would stop accusing the secular world of being so depraved and heinous. Perhaps if it were a full withdrawal, I would have less problem with it; but the fundamental belief that the state should be somehow Christian is difficult to square with this. Take, for instance, Patrick Henry College, the Virginia institution founded in 2000 by American pro-homeschooling lawyer Michael Farris,** "an elite training ground for the cream of the Christian homeschooling crop." This college, "Harvard for homeschoolers," was meant to "produce a new breed of crack spiritual warriors who could take over key seats of influence in government, law, business and even Hollywood," Marci McDonald writes. Students at the college "collect academic credits for working on election campaigns—almost all of the toiling for Republicans—and courses use hands-on instruction on how to run a politician's office and interpret polling results." Students are also required to take three-month internships in government, "turning its rolls into a farm team for Washington's right-wing power structure." At one point, in 2004, seven out of

---

* Of course, these statistics speak to the total number of homeschoolers, and not all homeschoolers are evangelical Christians, nor do all Christian homeschooling families choose to do so to keep children from learning about evolution. These numbers do, however, represent a huge spike in prevalence since the 1970s and an increased emphasis on homeschooling in Christian media. Look no further than the Duggar family, of TLC's *19 Kids and Counting*, whose evangelical denomination heavily recommended homeschooling, even producing its own curricula.

** Famed for founding the U.S.-based Home School Legal Defense Association and, more recently, working to attempt to overturn the 2020 election results.

one hundred interns in the Bush White House were from this tiny Virginia college. Up north, Trinity Western University in Langley, B.C., has functioned in a similar fashion. The private Christian university launched its Laurentian Leadership Centre in 2001, and the first class of students found internship positions "in almost every government department and key capital power centres like the *Ottawa Citizen* and the Royal Canadian Mounted Police," or on the staff of MPs like Stephen Harper and Stockwell Day, McDonald writes.

Writing from the front lines on a visit to Laurentian Leadership Centre, McDonald says: "If this is history filtered through a biblical worldview, it is a version that seems hopelessly skewed by conservative bias and a marked disregard for the facts. When students refer to the *Toronto Star* as 'the Red Star' and deride Canada as a 'welfare state,' I feel as if I've stumbled into the ornate clubhouse of some fresh-faced relics from the Reagan era." Meanwhile, in the U.S., prominent homeschooling advocates like Jim Bob Duggar and Mike Huckabee have parlayed their media fame into political office.

One can shelter not only for protection but for cultivation. While religious groups like the Amish may choose to remove their children from wider public society, they don't then attempt to give them political talking points and media training and then send them back in. It's this particular duality of exodus and influence that I find so strange about the trends in evangelical education in North America.

The only explanation for it, of course, is Christian Nationalism, the belief that the government should be run according to so-called Christian principles. Just like it is not enough that evolution be seen as untrue but also fundamentally morally destructive, secular society cannot just be left alone. It is all part of the grander evangelical project of building society in their own image.

Part of the aim of collapsing the definitional difference between science and religion is political. Rosenhouse writes:

> Anti-evolutionists of all stripes are entirely sincere in their belief that evolution has profoundly negative consequences for the spiritual lives of students . . . They want to mitigate this harm by teaching their contrary ideas. It is unconstitutional to teach religion, but science that happens to have religious implications is allowable. Describing [Intelligent Design] as good science is thus a political strategy for inserting it into science curricula, thus making use of public resources to promote their particular religious ideas.

Certainly, as Rosenhouse notes, creationists are not being *nefarious* in their dealings here. The deceptive and calculated means with which they have attempted to work creationism into education are, as he says, in support of a genuinely held belief. But as someone who was captive to those beliefs for so many years, it feels beyond stifling. There's a hubris to it all, a refusal to look anything in the eye: facts, other people's belief systems, other people's feelings, what's best for children in general.

At another conference session, Rosenhouse hears a speaker with a common testimony, one I heard many times growing up—a man who believed in evolution, but, when he went to check out the scientific evidence, was converted by the sheer amount of proof that the world was, in fact, created by a designer, God.

"The major themes [of these kinds of stories] are always the same: Acceptance of evolution is equated with rebellion against God. Christian missionaries are models of wisdom and patience, while the evolutionists are smug and arrogant. An honest and open-minded consideration of the evidence, not religious concerns, leads to a rejection of evolution." Yet, Rosenhouse adds, "These stories never include the logical next step. I refer to the part where, after hearing the church's version of the evidence, the protagonist then seeks out a reply from someone knowledgeable about evolution. The possibility that it is the anti-evolutionists who are presenting a skewed and biased version of things never seems to occur to them."

In my Christian school, we were taught—that is, our teachers verbally told us—that it was important we test our own beliefs and find out things for ourselves. A Jewish group called the Bereans, referenced in the Bible, were held in high regard for this—I often heard teachers and pastors quote a New Testament verse that says the Bereans "were of more noble character . . . for they received the message with great eagerness and examined the Scriptures every day to see if what Paul said was true." Yet, in practice, this was neither required, encouraged, nor modelled for us students. My science and Bible teachers never introduced us to pro-evolution material, not even to try to prove it faulty. We were rarely taught alternative ways of thinking about anything. In some areas, our ability to learn was actively restricted, as evidenced by the narrow band of fiction we were allowed to read and study in English class. Things were constantly being censored: the page of our French textbooks that was glued shut because it contained an illustration of a witch, the Scholastic book order forms which had been doctored with thick lines of Sharpie to prevent kids from ordering Harry Potter books.

Again, it all seemed to stem from fear. Fear that exposure to certain things would instantly and irredeemably corrupt us; fear that our supposedly empirically provable beliefs wouldn't stand up to scrutiny after all.

♥ † ♥

I remember one day, when I was shortly out of high school—maybe 18 years old—being on a phone call with one of my best friends, with whom I'd gone to Christian school. She was explaining something she'd learned in a university lecture that was somehow related to evolution.

"Of course, there's macroevolution and microevolution, which is like the small adaptations animals make to their environment," she said, referring to a popular creationist talking point, which allows for the plainly discernible-to-the-layman evolutions that take place all the time in our world while distinguishing them from natural selection and genetic drift. "I mean, of course I believe in microevolution."

"Right," I replied.

I remember there was a long, nervous beat, a silence while we each calibrated and recalibrated how we were going to proceed in the conversation.

"And, well," she added, "I kind of actually believe in macroevolution, also."

I remember a weird rush of a feeling, like I had released a held breath.

"Me too!" I said.

"Really?"

"Yeah."

"Right?"

"Right."

♥ † ♥

I am writing this in my backyard, surrounded by the glory of nature, in a way. Maybe someone like my grandfather, who built his own house in the bush and is less than enthused about cities, would disagree. But my laptop is dappled in sun and shade, birds are tweeting loudly to be heard above the noise of trundling streetcars. Squirrels are chasing each other through the treetops. The vine curling around my neighbour's fence reaches its feelers straight out into the air, as if it's trying to tap me on the shoulder. The world's roundest bumblebee trundles lazily through my herb garden.

At 32, I understand more than I did as a teenager what people found so spiritually compelling about the natural world. I am more likely now to marvel at a sunset or the propagation of a plant, roots growing out as if from nowhere. I do long to feel more connected to the earth—especially as I see it struggling, as the climate crisis destroys more and more of this planet, as the beautiful sunsets get hazed out by wildfire smoke and my plants shrivel in unseasonable warmth and climate refugees evacuate and heat waves crush Europe and on and on and on.

But would I figure any of this as "evidence" of a higher power?

The intervening years since I graduated from Christian school have taught me to, if anything, be more invested in the idea that this is not just a benign issue on which we can agree to disagree—strangely, I now find myself agreeing with the creationists on that particular point. There are not merely two equally interested parties in ideological opposition. There is scientific consensus and then a group of people with specific political aims that reject it. It's not just that the Young Earth creationists believe Earth is six thousand years old, it's that that belief is tightly tied to harmful projects like Christian nationalism; that the homeschoolers taught about the "lie" of evolution are also funnelled into colleges and training programs designed to place them in positions of power in conservative politics. The belief doesn't happen in a vacuum. Instead, believing that humans walked with the dinosaurs also equates to a belief in conservative, right-wing policy, the stripping of rights from queer communities, defunding of public education, restriction of access to women's and trans people's healthcare, and more. Whether the universe came into being in the dense eruption of a swirling cosmic mass or on the tip of God's tongue may have no tangible effect on my day-to-day life, but these other issues clearly do.

♥ † ♥

Even though I don't have the same vice-like grip on Christian faith that I used to, thinking back to all these supposed arguments for the veracity of the Bible and the origins of the universe returns me to that same familiar tension, that fear in the pit of the stomach, existential spiralling.

Jason Rosenhouse's book was a salve because, as an atheist, he validated these feelings. *You're not wrong to question*, he says, *because what they're proposing is not scientifically sound.*

But then he began talking about Intelligent Design, and strangely, I started panicking again. I guess for a long time I was able to reconcile faith because I didn't think it had to be reconciled. You don't have to believe in a God that literally created the universe to believe in something like "God," I had always thought. In that way, I'd never really been moved in either direction by the rationalistic arguments, whether for or against religion. Religion just seemed like something different than rationality.

But Rosenhouse points out that there actually is a conflict between religion and science, and I was surprised that he saved his harshest critique not for the Young Earth creationists—who apply the scientific method erroneously and just refuse to be corrected—but the Intelligent Designers, who try to incorporate God into any proved theory of the universe.

If your religious belief rests on supposed rationality, he points out at several points, even if one can prove the historical fact of a belief like Intelligent Design, there are still rational arguments to overcome—why would God choose such a convoluted method to express himself, for instance? If the fossil record had instead confirmed the instantaneous creation of humans and all types of animals, if coherent proof had been found for creationism, he asks, "Would anyone today be arguing that Genesis *obviously* was not meant to be taken literally or to instruct us in science?"

Maybe it was wrong for me to gloss over the conflict in my beliefs. In fact, hadn't I, all those years ago, been doing the same things the creationists were doing? Starting with a fundamental invariable—*I have to maintain my Christianity*—and then finding ways to fit the facts to suit? Maybe I should, actually, give some thought to what I believe.

♥ † ♥

I was having dinner with a friend when I told her I was writing this book. When I explained the premise, she asked, "And are you still a Christian?"

"No," I said. And then I said, "Well—" and then launched into a long, convoluted answer. I still have faith, I guess, I said, but in a very different way than what I grew up with, and I connect more with certain elements than others, and I like thinking of myself as culturally Mennonite, and I'm trying to become more comfortable with not having to have an answer to certain things—

After listening to me ramble, she said, kindly, "You should probably figure that out if you're going to write a book about it."

Maybe the politics of refusal, the sitting in-betweenness I've been cultivating in the last few years, has actually been avoidance. But it's hard to think definitively about something like faith when you have the kind of long and tense relationship with it that I feel I've had—something that's brought trauma and joy in what feels like equal amounts. Something you can credit with some of the best things in your life and some of the worst.

I did finally give up the ghost on the label *Christian*, a category that includes some of the people that love me the most in this world and also some people who would literally be happy if I died. For a while, I felt like being a queer leftist Christian woman was an important thing, like I had to prove it was possible, mostly to the other people who claimed the word *Christian*. But eventually, you realize what seems like a noble cause can really just be a chip on your shoulder. Christians aren't my community, I realized. Why not invest your time and love and energy into the people that accept you and love you back?

I do, however, connect very strongly with Rosenhouse's writing on the beauty of being culturally Jewish. He waxes poetically about the power of a cultural community that doesn't necessitate adherence to certain religious dogma. That's how I've felt for a long time about my Mennonite heritage. There are certainly problems, historical and current alike, within Mennonite-ism, the same as in Christianity, but I feel those problematic legacies are *mine* in a way that I don't feel about Christianity as a whole. And I do feel something blessed about pacifism, about resilience, about being low to the earth, about repentance and humility and sacrificial love. I just don't need to wear a bonnet or believe anyone is going to hell.

My former teacher would likely have called this *cherry-picking* and would have claimed that if I threw out any part of the Bible, I was throwing out all of it. But to him, I can finally say, *Who the fuck cares?*

♥ † ♥

Rosenhouse writes:

> Physicists have been ingenious at unraveling the history of the universe, right back to the first moments after the Big Bang—but then our data runs out, and we are left with fundamental mysteries that might never be resolved . . . Many of the usual concepts with which physicists deal, like causality, time, and matter—ideas which seem so simple and straightforward in our daily lives—become very confusing when pushed to the frontiers of existence.

It is precisely there, at our moment of maximum ignorance, that ID [Intelligent Design] proponents insert their most audacious conclusion. Just when the only dignified response is a shrug of the shoulders and a mumbled "Who knows?" they speak with complete confidence. They have everything backward. When biologists summon forth the massive evidence for evolution, drawn from every relevant branch of the physical and life sciences, the ID folks fight them tooth and nail and accuse them of arrogance and dogmatism. When the evidence runs out and we really should be humble and circumspect in our conclusions, they claim instead to have established the most dramatic and momentous facts regarding the nature of existence.

In sixth grade, my class did a lot of learning about the Indigenous peoples that lived pre-contact on this land. One of the units in this curriculum was about creation stories. We spent an entire lesson reading the creation myths of different Indigenous nations: the falling woman, the muskrat who pulled up the handful of earth from the water. At the end of the lesson, my teacher reminded us brusquely that these were just myths. "These things didn't actually happen," she said. "None of us believe in that." As if it would be crazy—not like believing two nudists in a garden got lured by a snake into eating an apple that destroyed the whole world.

CHAPTER SEVEN

THE ROOT OF ALL EVIL

THE STRANGE RELATIONSHIP BETWEEN CHRISTIANS AND MONEY, AS TOLD IN TWO MOVEMENTS

Part One: Health and Wealth
"For the love of money is the root of all evil"

On Minister Creflo Dollar's website, you can buy a one-ounce bottle of Frankincense "anointing oil" for $30.30 USD. Or, if that's too strong a scent or too steep a price, there's also a $13.77 sugar-cookie-scented candle, in a jar that reads, *Trust, REST, relax, Hebrews 4:1*. Pastor Joel Osteen offers no aromatic products but plenty of wall hangings and signs printed with words plucked from Bible verses ("abundant life," "favour follows you"), a set of plain grey linen desk organizers ($10) and a "scripture-inscribed mail shelf & key holder" ($15), the photo of which is too small and low-res to read. I guess the selected inscribed scripture is a surprise.

Love of money is the root of all evil, the Bible says. Except when it isn't. Except when loving money gets you something *good*. Then, suddenly, it becomes God-ordained.

I was browsing the online stores of Dollar and Osteen because I was thinking about money—specifically, Christian teachings about money. Unlike many of the hot-button issues typically taken up by evangelicals—say, abortion or gay rights, which rarely, if ever, appear in the scriptural source text—money is a near-constant presence in the Bible. Proverb after proverb dispenses financial advice. Jesus's parables are rife with references to coins and payments and treasures. Old Testament figures are constantly cheating each other out of material wealth. In the book of Acts, a couple even gets struck dead, clear out of the sky, for lying about their donation plate contribution.

♥ † ♥

The rise of a mainstream evangelical pop culture that hit its economic apex in the 2000s meant that Christianity was, more than ever, an economic force, associated with cottage industries like Christian publishing and broadcasting. It was also a major economic power in the United States and Canada: Megachurches (defined as churches with more than two thousand members on their rolls) were cropping up across the continent, tax laws and government subsidies were shifting, and people in the pews were not only making the customary 10 percent tithes to their own church but pouring money into auxiliary products, "parachurch organizations" (Christian nonprofits), and fundraising efforts.

Yet within different segments of evangelicalism, there were wildly different ideas about what money was meant to mean to Christians. Maybe this is the natural effect of a religion colliding head-on with capitalism—the results are going to be messy. For some, the Bible's repeated use of wealth, treasure, and reward as symbolic of the good Christian life was definitive proof that God's favour would come in the form of financial blessing. For others, the itinerant figures of Jesus and his followers, who scorned material goods and talked about responsibility and stewardship, were proof that money was yet another thing that needed to be sacrificed in order to follow God.

Looking back, I see these two mindsets—the prosperity gospel and the young radicals—as two parallel movements competing for dominance within evangelical culture during that time. Did God want us to forsake everything in His name? Or did He want to bless us beyond our wildest dreams?

"For everyone who asketh receiveth"

The prosperity gospel is a theological framework that essentially promises physical and financial blessing, "health and wealth," in exchange for faith in God. Boiled down to its essential components, it's the belief that God wants to bless Christians with health, happiness, and riches—all you have to do is pray for those blessings. "Ask and you shall receive; seek, and you shall find," Jesus said.

Well, maybe that's not all you have to do. Most prosperity gospel preachers and "ministries" function by soliciting donations and selling products. That's why Joel Osteen and Creflo Dollar each have web stores linked to their sites, something you wouldn't find on the web page of a traditional community church.

Often, donations are not framed as direct payment for God's blessings. There's no menu of blessings and prices—$20 for God to cure your cold, $400 to get you that job interview, $2,000 for Him to magically grant you your brand-new dream car. Gifts—or *love offerings* as they are sometimes termed—are meant to signal an outpouring of generosity that breeds reciprocity from the Lord.

Kenneth Copeland, a longstanding prosperity preacher and televangelist, whose ministry holdings include six international offices, a 33-acre Texas campus, and four private planes, explains the return on investment this way:

> The whole kingdom of God operates according to the principles of planting, seedtime and harvest. The hundredfold return is God's principle of return on your giving. What are you planting into

the kingdom of God? Expect a hundredfold return on whatever you give, whether it be words, faith, money or any other seed you plant.

Churches that preach the prosperity gospel typically encourage, or even require, parishioners to tithe as well. Tithing is the custom (drawn from a commandment in the Old Testament) of donating 10 percent of one's income to the church.

In the 2000s, this prosperity movement counted some of the world's largest denominations and congregations among its ranks. A *Time* poll in 2006 found that 17 percent of Christians specifically identified themselves as following prosperity gospel teachings, and 31 percent agreed with the statement that God increases the riches of those who give; two-thirds of respondents agreed that "God wants people to prosper." According to a Pew Research Center survey, 43 percent of American Christians believed that God grants health and wealth to the faithful. These numbers were particularly high in Latinx and Black American communities, which each have their own cultural strains of these teachings.

In her book *Blessed: A History of the American Prosperity Gospel*, historian Kate Bowler identifies the movement as a particularly American one, tracing its origins back to the "muscular Christianity" of the late 19th and early 20th centuries. Part of the allure, according to Bowler, is the hope and empowerment that such a belief offers. Americans "began to question" the "stony orthodoxy" of European Protestantism, based on self-denial and suffering for Jesus. Instead, she writes, Americans saw in the gospel "abundant promises" of blessings. "The prosperity gospel guaranteed a special form of Christian power to reach into God's treasure trove and pull out a miracle. It represented the triumph of American optimism over the realities of a fickle economy, entrenched racism, pervasive poverty, and theological pessimism that foretold the future as dangling by a thread."

In Bowler's definition, the prosperity gospel centres around "faith as an activator," a supernatural power to be wielded, demonstrated in the faithful's increased health and wealth. "Believers trust that culture holds no political, social, or economic impediment to faith, and no circumstance can stop believers from living in total victory here on earth."

The term *prosperity gospel* is used more often by outsiders to the movement. The preachers themselves tend to call their theology *Word of Faith*, based on the idea that by faith one can speak a truth into existence. Often, there is a component of fake-it-till-you-make-it confidence or strategic denial. Followers are encouraged not to phrase their desires as questions—"God, could you please give me the money to buy a plane?"—but to claim what they want aggressively, confident in the assurance that their wish is as good as granted: "God, I thank you for the plane you are about to bestow upon me!" This school of thought is also sometimes called "name it and claim it."

Bowler calls it "hard prosperity gospel." But she also identifies a watered-down version, a "soft prosperity," as she puts it, that had seeped into mainstream evangelicalism by the turn of the new millennium. This was "a smooth new language and style of persuasion that admirably fit the times," she explains. "It was therapeutic and emotive, a way of speaking that shed its Pentecostal accent for a sweeter and more secular tone." Preachers practicing this soft prosperity gospel might not claim outright that a donation would net you a financial blessing. But they would link psychological and emotional health "to fiscal success, believing that a rightly ordered mind led to rightly ordered finances." Osteen, celebrity pastor of the Houston, Texas, megachurch Lakewood, is a prime example. His teachings keep the mood light and the language positive; he has his congregants make "positive declarations" over their lives, speaking affirmations like *I am blessed. I am prosperous. I am healthy. I am talented. I am creative. I am wise.*

♥ † ♥

If this all sounds a little familiar, it might be because the prosperity gospel wasn't so out of place culturally in the 2000s.

As Bowler traces in her book, the ideas that animate the prosperity gospel are rooted in spiritual teachings that began in the 19th century, called *New Thought* or *Law of Attraction*: a set of "rules" that can be harnessed to unlock the power of the human mind and get what you want simply by wanting it. Secular bestsellers like *Think and Grow Rich* (1937), *The Power of Positive Thinking* (1952), and *You Can Heal Your Life* (1984) popped up every couple of decades to move millions of copies on the promise of this tantalizing proposition.

And then came the new millennium and *The Secret*.

Published in 2006, Rhonda Byrne's book makes the claim that thinking about the things one wants in life—what she calls *manifesting*—will cause those things to appear. By sending positive energy into the universe, one can attract all manner of changes to material circumstances, including, of course, health and wealth. While this was just the latest in a constant repackaging of New Thought ideas, the book's appearance on the *Oprah Winfrey Show* (and Oprah's glowing endorsement) shot sales into the stratosphere. By 2009, the book and accompanying film had grossed $300 million in sales. A 2007 article in *Slate* reports that the book was selling 150,000 copies per week. It was impossible to live in North America in the mid- to late 2000s and not have heard of *The Secret*. Words like *manifesting* and *vision boards* were adopted seamlessly into the cultural lexicon.

It's easy to see the appeal of this way of thinking. It is, after all, a lot less depressing to move through a universe you believe is fundamentally good and interested in your personal well-being than it is to look, clear-eyed, at the often-overwhelming reality of life around you. Manifesting, positive affirmations, and declaring that God has already solved your problems all offer immediate psychic relief, along with the promise that you won't have to actually do anything to try and alleviate a troubled situation. When people find themselves faced with death, grief, injustice, or any other reality, it can be hard to see another way out.

Still, it's hard to ignore the structural issues that such a worldview poses. "Imperfect thoughts are the cause of all humanity's ills, including disease, poverty, and unhappiness," Byrne writes in *The Secret*. You don't have to think long about Byrne's philosophy to discover its dark underside. If we, alone, are responsible for the good in our lives, then we are, too, responsible for every awful thing that happens to us—and the whole world, apparently. Byrne seems to suggest that we might collectively be able to think ourselves out of war, ecological disaster, and poverty. And by the same token, she implies that entrenched systemic forces, like racism and misogyny, are not real, merely the product of a lack of (personal or collective) manifestation.

Prosperity teachers take a similar line. Kenneth Copeland apparently believed that "The gospel to the poor is that Jesus has come and they don't have to be poor anymore!" While markets were collapsing and banks were getting government bailouts in the wave of the financial crash, Joel Osteen declared 2008 "a year of promotion, a year of increase, a year of favor, a year of supernatural opportunities!"

On the one hand, I think it's telling that the people most interested in promoting positive thinking and its ilk, including yacht-owning prosperity preachers and Oprah Winfrey, are those who see it "working" because their lives are on the up and up. And yet, I can't really fault people for being drawn in. In her history of the prosperity gospel, Bowler notes the prevalence of such teachings in the Black Pentecostal tradition and other marginalized segments of Christianity. The message has a lure of potential empowerment for the economically marginalized, a possible end-run around the immovable forces of racism and wealth disparity—if only it were true. "You have the power to change your life" is a hopeful message for anyone.

Still, the more insidious elements are unignorable. And when it comes to Christianity—a powerful segment of the body politic—an ethic that places all responsibility on the individual can have dire social consequences.

As usual, this niche Christian belief can lead to some pretty unhealthy places.

♥ † ♥

The rise of faith healing and revival preachers in the 1930s and 1940s were followed by rapid church expansion in the midcentury's postwar economic boom, and eventually made the leap to broadcast media in the late '70s and early '80s. By the '90s and 2000s, televangelists were well-established figures, many already subject to scandalous rises and falls, and megachurch ministries were thriving, often broadcasting their services via TV, radio, or the young internet.

The idea of the "hundredfold return" meant that conspicuous consumption for these prosperity preachers was not only allowable but kind of necessary to prove their thesis that financial blessing followed a life of faith. Copeland was far from the only one to be jetting about in private planes. Atlanta-based Creflo Dollar has broadcast his sermons since 1995 from a $20-million church called the World Dome; he owns two Rolls-Royces, several multi-million-dollar properties, and once asked his followers to each pledge $300 so that he could buy a $60-million private jet. (Financial transparency organization Ministry Watch has given his organization an F grade.) Then there's Pat Robertson, Jim and Tammy Faye Bakker, Joyce Meyer, and Benny Hinn—prominent televangelists and broadcasters who built their careers in the 1980s through to the 2000s by preaching about wealth and showing off their own: the Bakkers with their Bible theme park, Meyer with (according to a 2007 U.S. Senate investigation into several televangelists' lavish spending) her $23,000 toilet seat.

It's impossible to separate the growth of the prosperity gospel from the rise of broadcast media. Some scholars see the boom in prosperity ministries as a direct result of a 1960 decision by the U.S. Federal Communications Commission that allowed broadcasters to charge religious groups for airtime. "As a result, most American mainline denominations decided to bow out of television . . . but those Pentecostals who saw themselves as the heirs of the old-time revivalists had no hesitation about turning to the new electronic big top of shilling for donations to fund their on-air evangelizing," journalist Marci McDonald writes in her book *The Armageddon Factor*.

One of the most famous examples of this televangelist telethon mentality is Pat Robertson. In 1966, the future Republican strategist broadcast the message that to keep his young religious station on the air, seven hundred viewers needed to mail him $10 each—the auspicious start to *The 700 Club*, which became the Christian Broadcasting Network (CBN)'s flagship show and is still running more than 50 years later.

"The on-air cheerleading of televangelists like Jerry Falwell and Pat Robertson played a pivotal role in making the religious right the dominant voice of the new conservative movement that was unleashed by the Reagan revolution in the 1980s," writes McDonald. These evangelical powerhouses, by soliciting donations from viewers, had also amassed gigantic—and valuable—databases of like-minded contacts that could be used in political organizing.

The same names that filled these databases would be mobilized in the 2000s to cast their votes for George W. Bush; that legacy continues today. In 2024, evangelicals ushered Donald Trump—a congregant and mentee of prosperity preacher Norman Vincent

Peale* and television and radio personality—into the White House for the second time.

Up north, though, harsh on-air spats between religious factions in the 1920s had caused the Canadian government to crack down on religious programming, essentially banning it from the airwaves; this didn't change with the introduction of television.

"The ban on religious broadcasting may be the single most important reason why Canadian evangelicals have lagged behind their American brethren in both numbers and political clout," McDonald writes. The Canadian Radio-television and Telecommunications Commission only began to relent in the late '80s, allowing Vision TV— a multifaith channel that guarantees equal airtime for each religion—a broadcasting licence. By the '90s, the CRTC had loosened its rules, and Christian radio and TV stations proliferated—though by that time, several major pirate stations had been broadcasting evangelical content over the airwaves.

Despite the lag, Canada was not immune to Word of Faith fever, especially since Canadians could access American rebroadcasts. McDonald reports that by 1979, "Canadians were already sending $15 million a year to televangelists, more than half of it to those south of the border."

In McDonald's book, she offers a portrait of two such Canadians: the Thibaults, an Albertan couple who began listening to the Lethbridge-based Miracle Channel—then run by George and Hazel Hill—when it was still a pirate station. According to Tim Thibault, the couple already believed in the prosperity gospel ethos ("sow a seed for your need"), and it was a small push to be told the blessings would roll in with a donation to the channel. They pledged automatic $30 monthly payments to the Miracle Channel from their bank account and sent in extra donations during telethon weeks. A telethon volunteer prayed for Thibault's

---

* "How Positive Thinking, Prosperity Gospel Define Donald Trump's Faith Outlook," NPR.org.

prayer request on air, declaring: "Tim, your company is no longer struggling."

Unfortunately, Thibault's business *was* struggling, almost $50,000 in debt, with credit cards maxed—"but like some compulsive poker addict, he was afraid not to gamble on one more donation: after all, if he wasn't prospering, maybe it was because he hadn't given enough."

This kind of predatory "ministry" is all too common in prosperity gospel spaces, particularly those that found a home on television. Televangelists like Jim and Tammy Fae Bakker, Kenneth Copeland, Robert Tilton and more held telethon-style fundraisers; Church Financial Seminars in the 1990s taught churches "How to Prove Tithing Is in the New Testament," "How to Double the Pastor's Salary," "How to Prove That Non-Tithers Are Robbers" and "How to Setup a Love Offering Program LEGALLY"; prominent prosperity pastors taught their congregations to swap modern medical interventions for prayer; Christian diet and weight loss books (*The Maker's Diet, Lay Aside the Weight,* the Daniel Fast) and Pat Robertson's branded diet shake hit the shelves; and in the aftermath of the 2008 recession, TV preacher Morris Cerullo hawked his "Financial Breakthrough Spiritual Warfare Bible" ($69.95). As an early pioneer of the prosperity movement wrote in 1936, "The Lord is my banker, my credit is good."

In Thibault's case, he came to realize the troubling nature of the ministry he'd been shelling out his money to. Eventually, in 2004, he filed a formal complaint with the CRTC. The commission ruled eventually that the Miracle Channel "had contravened its fundraising guidelines for broadcasts, even daring to suggest 'divine consequences' if viewers failed to send in a donation," McDonald reports.

That, of course, is the implicit flip side of the positive-thinking prosperity gospel message: If God blesses the faithful who give, what does it mean when you are not blessed, if you do not receive?

Under this framework, the mere lack of success—even, the lack of gratuitous wealth—is transformed into an assumed moral failure. The same goes for health and happiness, or the lack thereof.

From the outside, prosperity preachers seem silly. Their opulent lifestyles are infuriating, especially if you're the type of person who tracks carbon emissions from private jets, but their braggadocious consumption habits aren't all that different from, say, social media influencers or certain types of glamorous celebrities.

But as the Thibaults' story shows, this greed spawns further reaching and more harmful effects. It causes direct harm to these teachers' own followers, building their wealth off the hopeful offerings of an audience desperate to improve their own situations.

My father's background is Scottish and my mother's Mennonite. Two cultures known for penny-pinching—I know all the cheapskate jokes.* I was taught by my family to prize things like financial responsibility and living within one's means—and if copious wealth was not in and of itself immoral (dubious), than showing it off certainly was.

In the church we attended on Sundays, the offering plate was passed with a kind of eye-averting embarrassment, donations slipped into envelopes so as not to be visible. Members were asked to give, certainly, though there was little talk of expansion, maybe some building needs. There were fundraisers to pay overseas missionaries and to sponsor refugee families coming to Canada, can drives for food banks, a jar passed around children's Sunday school to collect donations of our parents' spare change.

The first time I flipped past a Sunday morning broadcast from the Crystal Cathedral (a California megachurch that was the largest glass building in the world when constructed in 1981) on Vision

---

* What's the biggest ethical quandary a Mennonite can face? Free dance lessons.

TV, I was shocked. I'd never seen a church like that—not just because of the wild glass ceiling and walls but because it looked like a football stadium, a crowd of roaring fans clamouring for Jesus. I couldn't believe such a giant church asked for viewer donations as if it were PBS. At my friend's Baptist youth group, the church sanctuary—three times the size of my family's church—sported a huge wall banner with the image of a thermometer, on which donations toward a new "campus" were being counted. At another friend's Pentecostal youth group, we played games inside a complex so large I kept getting lost, and then we spent our loonies and toonies at a church-run tuck shop, buying candy bars and chips. All my church had was some watery coffee and the occasional soup-centric potluck.

♥ † ♥

In 2009, on the brink of bankruptcy, the Miracle Channel hired a new CEO, "Manitoba pastor Leon Fontaine, an entrepreneurial whirlwind who has turned Winnipeg's Springs Church into a ten thousand-member megacongregation by preaching the message that God wants nothing more than to reward his faithful with an 'abundant' life," writes Marci McDonald.

2009 was the year I graduated high school. In the preceding years, I'd heard a lot about Fontaine and his church. Springs Church had its own private Christian school, a kind of mirror universe of my own, which was also nestled inside a big suburban church. We were sports rivals. Some of my classmates attended the church—the ones, it seemed to me, who had designer clothes and new phones and other pricey teenage markers of familial wealth. Springs was the rich church, in my mind. It was also one of the few megachurches in Winnipeg, one I sometimes heard spoken about by other Christians as a business success story.

I didn't pay much attention. I didn't know what Leon Fontaine was preaching to draw in the masses to his south-end sanctuary.

I didn't know what the Miracle Channel was, let alone its pirate-radio prosperity past. It wasn't until reading McDonald's book that I knew about this Winnipeg connection.

Curious how Fontaine had fared with the struggling station, I checked in the way anyone who has moved from their hometown does: I googled him.

The first thing that greeted me was news of his death after a sudden diagnosis of late-stage cancer in the fall of 2022. Fontaine's son, Zach, is now the head pastor of the church.

The previous few years had been fraught. During COVID-19 lockdowns in Manitoba, when churches were prohibited from meeting, Springs had pivoted to a drive-in model, with cars parked to watch a projection of the service on a giant screen in the church parking lot. When the government tightened restrictions again, however, now prohibiting the drive-in gatherings as well, the church chose to keep holding the banned services and was fined a total of $20,000 over the course of the lockdowns.

Then came the trucker convoy, the right-wing anti-lockdown protests that took over Ottawa in 2021, for which Fontaine voiced his full-throated support. Fontaine dismissed public health restrictions, to the consternation of many Manitoba-based church leaders, who all signed an open letter critiquing him. He likened COVID-19 measures to the regimes of "Hitler, Stalin, [and] Mao Zedong" and started interviewing far-right figures and conspiracy theorists for his website, Return to Reason. He preached a four-part sermon series called "No Deadly Thing," in which he claimed that nothing could hurt or make sick followers of Jesus and entreated his followers to have "faith over fear."*

It's not hard to see the leap from prosperity preaching to COVID-19 conspiracies by way of anti-vaccination and anti-lockdown beliefs. After all, Fontaine was, like most people in a global pandemic, being directly confronted with an unstoppable

---

* Josiah Neufeld, *The Temple at the End of the Universe*, p. 47.

threat to his health and livelihood—the very things he'd become convinced he could control through divine power.

As Josiah Neufeld notes in his book *The Temple at the End of the Universe*, the pandemic threatened Springs' business model as much as it "challenged the core of [Fontaine's] gospel." Neufeld references an August 2021 article by Jim Hinch in the *Los Angeles Review of Books*, where the writer notes that having "embraced an explicitly business-oriented approach to ministry that has remade Christianity in the image of corporate America," modern-day evangelical churches were perfectly primed to be decimated by the crisis of the pandemic. Lockdowns meant giant, empty mega-sanctuaries, congregations with shrinking tithes as their incomes were threatened, and an audience slipping away as the name-it-and-claim-it method failed to offer the solace or results necessary in the face of such a threat.

In his book, Neufeld recounts a visit to Springs Church in the spring of 2022. Fontaine began an impromptu healing service, announcing that he "didn't need to lay hands on people to heal them. He could simply send healing power out over the crowd with words." Fontaine proceeded to "speak healing" into various body parts of congregants in the room: "I speak healing right now into that pelvic cavity. Brains, receive the touch of the Master. Cancer, I command you to take your hands off the child of God!"

Like a diet founder who dies of a heart attack, any faith healer whose life is cut short by illness is subject to a kind of uneasy scrutiny. After years of hearing someone preach on the power of faith for holy healing, how should a congregant respond to the seeming failure of healing in that teacher? In *Blessed*, Kate Bowler recounts claims by the families and employees of several prominent prosperity preachers that they "chose" their time and place of death, despite evidence to the contrary. After Leon Fontaine passed away, religion writer John Longhurst raised a series of questions in the magazine *Faith Today*:

How will people at Springs respond? His passing might prompt some uncomfortable questions for his followers, such as: Was what he taught wrong? If Fontaine could die young from cancer, a disease he said God would cure people from, was it all a lie? And if it wasn't a lie, here's a troubling thought: Did Fontaine not believe what he preached? Or did he not have enough faith to get his own miracle? If a man so close to God like him couldn't get healed, what hope is there for others?

I am reminded of a charismatic church I attended briefly while participating in a Christian missionary program. I didn't like the theology of the church—there was a lot of prophesying and praying for miracles, which my stuffy Mennonite self was uncomfortable with, and the services stretched for hours, testing the limits of my attention span. Still, I thought the church was full of good people—it was small, everyone knew each other, and it seemed like everyone there really cared about everyone else. One of the congregants had cancer but would show up every week while she struggled through chemo. Sometimes the church would gather around her and pray for her for a long time, asking, begging, pleading with God to make her well again.

I didn't know what to do with it. I was 17. I didn't really believe in miracles, though I wasn't about to tell anyone at the missionary organization that. I wanted to believe; I experimented in believing. I prayed for her, too. But when I heard, months later, that she had passed away, I didn't feel shocked.

Did all that prayer and pleading help or hurt? I feel there's no way to know. As research reviews in the National Library of Medicine show, some studies seem to suggest that prayer and positive thinking can have a positive impact on patients, while others find that beliefs "New Thought" or "Law of Attraction" (à la *The*

Secret) actually worsen patient outcomes. I think that, during those prayer sessions, the woman seemed grateful—from the outside looking in, it seemed like she felt loved and valued by the community that was trying, in their own way, to save her life. But who knows. Would she have felt less suffering if she could be at peace with her prognosis? Did she turn down any medical interventions in favour of divine intervention, and was that a good or a bad decision?

For everyone left behind in these types of scenarios, it seems like there's an extra edge to the pain, the twist of the knife of hopes dashed. Manifesting and prophesying, naming and claiming, all require the language of certainty: You have to speak it and make it so. Don't say, *I wish I had a better job.* Say, *I'm so glad I've been blessed with a wonderful new job*, and eventually that opportunity will knock on your door. But when the opportunity never comes, all you're left with is an advocation of denial.

In his book *Evangelicals Incorporated*, Daniel Vaca argues that evangelicalism itself exemplifies what he terms *commercial religion*.

> Commercial religion involves more than "the commodification of religion," a phrase that both scholars and pundits have used to describe what they have seen as the modern transformation of religions into commodities, which people literally and metaphorically buy and sell. . . . By contrast, I understand religions as forms of social organization and authority that continually take shape through realms of social life that include commodities and their circulation.

While people often argue that commercialization has cheapened evangelicalism, Vaca sees those things as inseparable;

commercialization is both what enabled the religion to grow, and the market forces of its commercial products (particularly books, the focus of his studies) have actually shaped the tenets of evangelical belief.

The Christian bookstore might be the place that most clearly exemplifies 2000s evangelicalism. Moving through the aisles of Jesus fish mugs, colourful Bible carriers, and freshly printed tomes about how to live a Godly life was the first time I saw evangelicalism for what it was: a subculture all of its own. This was different from a church community or a denomination, which gathered around a list of rules and credos. This was Christianity as it was marketed and sold, under an appealing gloss, where the James Dobson's diatribes against liberalism could sit on the shelf next to future Oprah network star Rob Bell's vaguely progressive pontificating. They might even be released, in fact, by the same publisher. There was not much ideological coherence—at least not purposeful coherence.

As Vaca points out, the cultural homogeneity that seems apparent in evangelicalism is in part a function of the Christian book industry. "For most of the twentieth century, evangelical publishers created relatively few books written by or intended for nonwhite consumers, and even fewer books that drew explicit attention to ethnicity and race. Publishers worried that significant attention to those issues might alienate members of the mass market that their companies prioritized." Even the whiteness of Christian culture was a result of the market and the money. It wasn't God that dictated what was written and what sold well, it was the customers who were willing to buy.

And customers wanted to buy the prosperity gospel, with thousands of readers picking up copies of *The Prayer of Jabez* and *He Touched Me* (televangelist Benny Hinn's unfortunately-named autobiography) at their local Christian bookstore. The 2000s marked the peak and the slide-down of this booming industry. By 1994, major Christian publishing conglomerate Zondervan (which published *The Prayer of Jabez*) owned 153 Christian bookstores in 27 states, becoming one of the largest bookselling chains in the U.S. The bookstores reported more than $110 million in revenue in 1993 (more than the brand's publishing division). Christian bookstores accounted for as much as 66 percent of industry sales in the 2000s. But less than 20 years later, most Christian bookstores have shut down or closed brick-and-mortar outlets. Between 2000 and 2007, one chain's sales fell from $1.25 million per year to $800,000.

But let's not look ahead to the dark times of the collapsing publishing industry. The year is 2006, and publishers still have hope. And Zondervan, that major Christian publisher, puts out a book by a dreadlocked white Tennessee boy named Shane Claiborne.

This was the answer to the prosperity gospel, to the megachurches, the consumerist sheen of American-style evangelicalism. This book was called *The Irresistible Revolution*, and it would launch a thousand keen alt-Christians with poorly planned community houses.

Part Two: The Young and the Radical
"You cannot serve both God and money"

The mid-2000s were something of a turning point for millennial evangelicals. As post-9/11 patriotism curdled in the United States, and young people raised on Christianity felt themselves pulled away from the political conservatism of their parents, a looser, more social justice–focused varietal of evangelicalism began to spring up—a subculture to the subculture, an alternative not only in aesthetic but in practice.

Claiborne's *Irresistible Revolution* was part of a movement that aimed to offer a solution to the cognitive dissonance that came from comparing the teachings of the Bible to the suburban comfort in which many American evangelicals lived. The solution offered was not to reconcile them but to find a new way, to reenvision the project of Christianity as *radical*, as *anti-establishment*.

Claiborne and a group of friends founded The Simple Way in Philadelphia, Pennsylvania, in 1998. Now an official non-profit organization, it was first an "intentional community" house, a group of like-minded Christians who shared a passion for social justice causes and inspiration from early Christian monastic movements and organizations like the Catholic Worker. Rather than founding a church, they decided to move into an impoverished neighbourhood and provide support in the form of community gardens, housing advocacy, a community storefront, and other similar initiatives. These included protest actions, like an encampment of displaced families inside a church (recounted in his book) and protesting a law that prohibited handing out food on the streets by blessing the food and calling it a Eucharist.[*]

In 2004, some of the main players of this new community-centred way of living Christian lives met in Durham, North Carolina, for a conference and solidified a name for what they were doing: *New Monasticism*, an attempt to revive the monastic tradition as modern-day Protestants, not Medieval monks. The concept and term were drawn from the work of writer Jonathan R. Wilson and his daughter and son-in-law, Leah and Jonathan Wilson-Hartgrove, founding organizers who went on to write books and go on speaking tours themselves. At this conference, the group nailed down "12 marks" of New Monasticism, a list inspired by monastery rules of life.

Like prosperity gospel churches, these were a loose collection of like-minded communities, not a denomination, and the marks were descriptive, not binding. "There are literally dozens of

---

[*] All actions displayed an admirable commitment to helping others, though not without the troubling politics of "moving in" to a neighbourhood selected for its poverty or the Bible-based rhetoric that often labels others "the least of these," "broken people," or other similarly patronizing titles.

communities that I could consider part of the new monasticism," Claiborne, who was at the conference, told *Christianity Today*.

Along with those who chose to revamp the traditions of monks and live communally were other young radicals trying to find different outlets for their dissatisfaction with the system they found themselves in. Some turned to experiments.

A year before *The Irresistible Revolution*, another Christian trying to do something revolutionary for the Lord published a book: *Under the Overpass*, Mike Yankoski's 2005 account of the five months he spent "living as a homeless man." He and a friend, Sam, spent one month each in five different cities across America, sleeping on the streets or occasionally in shelters, eating at soup kitchens, and busking for change by playing church worship songs on guitar.

The book is in line with similar "social experiment" books, which time has not looked kindly on. The author specifically cites John Howard Griffin's *Black Like Me* as inspiration, and I couldn't help remembering supermodel Tyra Banks's 2000s-era experiment where she donned a padded bodysuit and went out to experience what life was like for a fat person. As one Amazon reviewer said of the book, "I do think there must be better ways to learn the actions we can take to do better than by basically impersonating the homeless for a year."

Much of Yankoski's takeaway from his experiment is rather focused on the treatment he received from churches and other Christians while living unhoused in major cities. He and his companion were sometimes invited in, sometimes given food, money, or help, but most often chased away from church doorsteps or avoided by congregants troubled by their smell after weeks unable to shower. Meanwhile, he waxes poetic when he meets someone else living on the street who expresses a Christian faith, especially if they share some meagre morsel of food or spare change.

It's troubling that the author never bothers to look beyond the individual to the systemic, pondering neither the broad structural causes or big picture solutions to homelessness. Like the prosperity gospel, his vision of Christian generosity seems troublingly individualistic, albeit in another direction.

At one point, while panhandling in Berkeley, California, Yankoski and his friend ask a university student carrying a half-empty pizza box if he can have his pizza. When the guy gives it to them, they loudly exclaim their thanks to God and devour the pizza. After pondering their good luck for a moment, Yankoski starts comparing himself and his travelling companion to the Israelites in the book of Exodus, who were saved from starving by God's gift of manna from heaven. "Don't you think they would have starved if they never actually went out and picked the manna off the ground?" Yankoski asks. "We prayed for God's provision, right? We prayed that He would bless us and give us what we need. But then when it walked by, we had to make our move. Asking and receiving means different things out here on the streets than back home. But the idea is the same."

Justice for the poor, generous kid who gave up half a pizza only to be eclipsed as a mere messenger of God's provision. Aside from the erasure of the actual agent of this gift, this mindset also hints at a troubling sense of what might be called *personal responsibility*—after all, is this to suggest that sustenance is just there for the taking should any unhoused person simply ask God for it and "make their move"?

It all sounds strangely close to the prosperity gospel. Ignoring the human (or natural) element of any interaction, the *Under the Overpass* pair look for signs of God everywhere. After all, this was the reasoning behind the experiment—not just to gain empathy for those who have to sleep on the streets, or understand why people are unhoused, but to strengthen their faith. "I claimed Christ was my stronghold, my peace, my sustenance, my joy. But I did all that from the safety of my comfortable upper-middle-class life. I never really had to put my claims to the test," Yankoski says, when he has this revelation sitting in church one Sunday.

"What if I stepped out of my comfortable life with nothing but God and put my faith to the test alongside those who live with nothing every day?"

Perhaps it's obvious from the previous sentence, but Yankoski never bothers, throughout his journey, to learn about the root causes of homelessness, providing only asides like, "Most of the homeless [in Washington, D.C.] were war veterans. Maybe they had arrived in town long ago to protest on one issue or another and just never left." Brushing aside anything "political," he refuses to understand why people are unhoused and what might be done to alleviate suffering more widely beyond some Christians bringing sack lunches to the park every so often.

Worse, despite living as an unhoused person, Yankoski never seems to fully consider himself a part of the community on the streets of any of his temporary homes. He uses words like *forgotten*, *ruined*, and *broken* to describe people—as well as commenting near constantly on how badly everyone smells. While he complains about the "dehumanizing" feeling of being passed by while panhandling without so much as eye contact from commuters hurrying by, he continues to use language I would only call *dehumanizing* to describe the others sharing shelter bunks and street corners with him.

And then, of course, are the moments when, confronted with a clear opportunity to save another person, he and his companion simply choose . . . not to. While they wait for miracles from heaven in the form of spare change from strangers, moments when they could be the agent of a miracle seem to pass them right by, with so little recognition that the author simply chirpingly recounts what happened. The first takes place at the very beginning of the book, a kind of action-packed scene to hook the reader—only the action is a man being brutally beaten inside Golden Gate Park. Not only do our Christian heroes not step in to try and deescalate the violence, they don't even alert anyone. In fact, they run. In another scene, a new acquaintance watches his friend get harassed and arrested by the police. The man being arrested slips away and jumps into the ocean, still wearing handcuffs. The boys' new friend, Doug, screams that the man is going to drown and runs into the water to save him. Again, the Christians stand dumbly by. When Doug comes back from saving the man's life, panting and drying himself "with a filthy towel from his backpack," Yankoski offers him a tortilla and Sam says, "You did really well, Doug."

How these moments seemingly function as a splash of colour in the narration, while the reluctant gift of a stranger's pizza results in a two-page musing on the nature of God's generosity, I can't fathom.

♥ † ♥

My own radicalization happened in math class. Even though the subject was pre-calculus, in a Christian school, the curriculum afforded a fair amount of latitude, which meant assignments tenuously connected to the subject but reliant on some kind of faith-based teaching were fairly common.

My teacher was passionate about teaching us personal finance skills, and from what I remember, once spent a large portion of a class statistically proving that it was not a good idea to buy lottery tickets. So, it didn't seem that strange when he revealed his big assignment for the year: a piece of paper printed with a long list of Bible verse citations.

The list contained every mention of money in the Bible, Old and New Testament. For our assignment, we were meant to read every reference and write a paper on what we thought the Bible had to teach us about money.

Ever an obedient student, I set to work. But the more I read, the less comfortable I felt with what I found.

I got the impression that the assignment was most interested drawing our attention to the kinds of proverbs that would make us into law-abiding, responsible adults. I'm not sure if what I took from it was the desired outcome, which was that Jesus was a radical communist, and that it seemed entirely possible we were all going to hell for not giving away all our money. For instance, Jesus famously tells a rich young man that it is "easier for a camel to go through the eye of a needle" than for a rich person to "enter the kingdom of God." The rich guy leaves, dejected, because he doesn't want to give away all his possessions. But, I'd been told in school I was in a country and a demographic that made up the global 1 percent—the very definition of the rich young man in modern times, surely?

What were we all doing there, our parents paying thousands of dollars a year, when we should have all been dropping out of school and going to preach or heal people or whatever it was that Jesus wanted us to do?

That same year, everyone in my high school was required to participate in a Day of Service, where we were shuttled off to different charitable (Christian) nonprofits around the city for the day. I spent the day bagging dried goods at a food bank; others sorted clothing donations at an emergency shelter (a friend told me that this involved sorting the clothes into piles—one clean and relatively unworn to give away at the shelter, the other ripped or soiled stuff which would be sent to Africa), or served food at a soup kitchen. Upon our return to school, we were subjected to a lecture (sorry, *sermon*) about the importance of doing this kind of service, how God required it. I remember a heavy depression settling over me. Isn't this what we should have been doing at all times, devoting our lives to it, if we really lived the way the scriptures dictated?

All of this trickled into my world, in my teen years, through the same evangelical media outlets I was used to. I read books like Donald Miller's *Blue Like Jazz* and *Through Painted Deserts* (put out by mainstream evangelical publishers) and wanted to live in a community house and take soul-searching trips to find my spirituality. I read *Relevant*, a "cool" Christian magazine that ran articles about social justice next to cover stories about which Hollywood celebrities are secretly Christian. Representatives from Christian organizations came to my school and pitched missions trips and Bible schools that would take me to far-flung places to "serve" those less fortunate than me. My youth group attended a Christian conference where I sat in on a speaker telling stories about his work in the dangerous "inner city," which included a memorable story about how he threw himself in the middle of a knife fight, knowing his body would be protected by God.

At the time, all this seemed admirable.

Though it had been years since I was the New Girl in class, fresh from living overseas with no idea what Christian music was, in high school, I still hadn't shaken the sense that I didn't belong—in my school, with my peers, even in my faith. I often felt deeply at odds with the concepts I was being taught in school. When a social studies teacher asked the class to line up along a left-right spectrum, visually placing ourselves based on our political leanings on different topics, I found myself all alone, wedged against the lefthand wall. When our Bible studies teacher introduced material that was meant to prove our Christian faith to be unimpeachably, rationally true, I felt myself spinning out into an existential crisis. When touching another girl's hand sent a rush of butterflies into my stomach, I spiralled into panic. When I heard others talking about "God's plan" for their life, citing things like having babies and getting married, I felt like an alien. I wasn't sure I wanted any of those things, let alone feel a heavenly prompting in that direction.

But I also didn't want to divorce myself from this religion that had become my whole life. All my friends were Christian, from school or church. My family was Christian. And when I tried, when I leaned into praying and singing church worship songs and reading my Bible, I thought I could feel something there—sometimes a sense of purpose, of spiritual fulfillment, a temporary balm to my always-sky-high anxiety.

I came from a family that worshipped in house churches and community gatherings; my parents took us to a small neighbourhood church and found community in small Bible studies. My family was more liberal than most of the Christians around me at school—it was my mom who subscribed me to *Relevant*, the *cool, alternative* Christian magazine, after all. But despite all this, my day-to-day at school took place in the world of suburban Christianity, the world of two-car garages, where being a Christian meant marrying young and voting Conservative. When I tried to imagine how I could be as a young adult, how I could fit into the world I was going into, I saw that future looming. Like any good angsty teen, I wanted to swing the pendulum as far in the other direction as possible. So when I realized there were people my age promoting another way to be a Christian, it felt like, well, a godsend. These were churches that met in living rooms and people who lived in communal houses where they pooled their money and possessions. These were Christians who didn't believe in corporal punishment or anti-2SLGBTQIA+ legislation. These were Christians who read the Old Testament figuratively—and took Jesus literally when he said all that stuff about giving up your money and following him.

In my late teens and early 20s, I'd heard Claiborne speak, participated in a study group that used his material, and been a part of churches inspired by the format of his community, The Simple Way. I had a cursory knowledge of what he was all about, knew he preached a kind of social justice- and service-oriented Christianity that I was drawn to, that he was maybe a little more conservative, a little more evangelical, than I was comfortable with. Overall, I had categorized him the way the Christian bookstore did: as a "radical." Or in his own language, an "ordinary radical," someone who had chosen to live as close to Jesus's teachings of having nothing and spreading the Good News as modern-day society would tolerate.

But I had never read the book that had started the Shane Claiborne–fever. *The Irresistible Revolution,* Claiborne's wave-making manifesto, was published in 2006 and kicked off the popularity of New Monasticism and associated movements. I decided to go back to the source text.

As expected, the book detailed Claiborne's ideas about how to live an "ordinary radical" life for Jesus, decried the consumerism and capital excess of modern-day American Christianity, and delved into his origin story of working with Mother Teresa's mission in Calcutta. But then, in chapter four, Claiborne returns to the United States to attend seminary at Wheaton College. And starts a one-year internship at Willow Creek Community Church.

Willow Creek was one of the largest megachurches in the United States, and I had been there on a school trip to Chicago. Set on a 155-acre plot, with a 7,200-seat auditorium, I remember it feeling like the campus of a university, its massive concourse housing a bookstore, coffee shop, and food court. TV screens advertised different youth and community groups congregants could join. It felt not unlike the Medieval Times Dinner & Tournament my class had visited the night previous. Certain details made me go wide-eyed: Our seats were up on a massive balcony (there were two!); the worship team performed with Britney Spears-style headset mics; the church bulletin—just like my home church— listed the YTD budget; but—unlike my home church—the figure was in the millions of dollars. High on my horse, a know-it-all teen, I could only *tsk* and mutter about that Bible story where Jesus drives the money-changers out of the temple.

It was strange to read about the megachurch that had so disgusted me then through the eyes of another. In truth, I was waiting for Claiborne to rip them a new one. Instead, he made a brief note of the culture shock of returning from a leper colony in Calcutta to a megachurch with a food court inside it before expounding on Willow Creek's virtues.

> I had heard the beautiful story of Willow Creek's beginnings as a bunch of young people who were pretty disillusioned with the church. . . . Rooted in the vision of the early church and with the book of Acts on their lips, they started—small, sloppy, passionate. Now some thirty years later, they are one of the nation's largest congregations, with over twenty thousand folks coming onto the 150-acre campus each week.

Despite quoting Mother Teresa, who he calls *Momma T,* "it is among the wealthy that we can find the most terrible poverty of all—loneliness," Claiborne seems fairly easily won over by the excess of Willow Creek. "I would be eating in Willow Creek's food court, still digesting my time with Calcutta's starving orphans," Claiborne writes. "Sometimes I was incredibly frustrated and angry, wondering how these extremes could exist in the same world, let alone in the same church. . . . But it was hard to stay cynical, as I met more and more beautiful people."

His friendship with the congregants and leaders at the megachurch prevents him from castigating them. And as he learns about the ministries they offer—letting unhoused people sleep in the building during cold snaps, donating cars to people who need them, facilitating donated labour from auto mechanics for single mothers, and donating the profits from the food court to world hunger relief—he sees their ministry as valuable. "I learned not to be so quick to judge," he writes.

Yet merely one page later, Claiborne is recounting the biblical story of the Rich Young Ruler, telling us that Jesus is asking everyone to give up everything, to give up their wealth. "Jesus doesn't tell the man to be a better steward, or to treat his workers fairly, or not to make money an idol. He tells this highly educated and devoutly religious young man that he lacks one thing: giving up everything he owns to give to the poor."

This apparent friction doesn't seem resolved in the text. Claiborne talks about the good work Willow Creek was doing and in the next breath complains about the church's suburban insularity, or the fact that they don't have any crosses hanging in the church. (He finds their brand of "seeker-sensitive" church coddling and wants them to present the harsh necessities of being a Christian.) He also seems impressed by the size of the church and its coffers, in a way that still seems to prioritize financial success as a marker of spiritual success. Reading *Irresistible Revolution*, I felt an oppressive sense that money had its claws in everything—that capitalism's inescapability had made it impossible to divorce the essence of Christianity from the business of Christianity.

In general, returning to Claiborne's writing now feels a little disappointing. Not as bad as googling prosperity preachers, but certainly not the radical, world-changing ideas I thought they were back when I was a teen. For the most part, his advocacy seems more on the helpful than hurtful end of the spectrum, and I admire his commitment to certain ideals, especially around money—for instance, he pledges the entire profit from the book to a charitable organization, including his advance and ongoing royalties, and seems to have some qualms about publishing the book through Zondervan.

Instead, I found Claiborne's motivations were what left me cold. By rooting his activism and justice initiatives so entirely in religion, he seems to be trying to promote an apoliticism that I simply don't believe is possible. He declares himself a political independent, neither Democrat nor Republican, and spends sections of the book downplaying the work that can be done by charitable or activist organizations—secular *or* faith-based—or through political organizing and government support. What is left, then? In his view, only "red-letter Christians," what he calls the Christians whose beliefs are similar to his own—should be in charge of maintaining any positive help in society. Jesus did not set up any programs, "organizational establishments or structural systems," he argues (I guess the disciples were never incorporated) and proudly touts a quote from a colleague: "When we truly discover love, capitalism will not be possible and Marxism will not be necessary." For what system, then, is he actually advocating?

What bothered me most were the vagueness of terms. The above quote, not even original to Claiborne, is the only by-name mention of any definable political ideology. When defining his own beliefs, Claiborne clings to a gotcha-vibe of rhetorical quips, as though he's playing defense against the bad press engendered by the groups with which he aligns himself: evangelicals, pro-lifers. He explains, for instance, that he identifies as an evangelical under his own definition which prioritizes "evangelizing" through charitable actions that demonstrate what he views as the personality of Jesus, rather than by preaching directly. Would this subtle distinction mean anything to those outside of evangelicalism? He is pro-life, he explains—but not like those *other* pro-lifers. He's not merely anti-abortion, he's against the ending of life in any manner—anti-war, anti-death penalty. Still, he never explains his anti-abortion stance, and it's unclear if he's given serious thought to women's health, autonomy, and general welfare.

When it comes to what he's opposing, there is little to no definition. He refers negatively to "systems" that are never defined—is he railing against capitalism? Patriarchy? The prison-industrial complex? It's unclear. It may just be that in his conception of the world, he is simply railing against secularism, similar to the evangelical belief in a "fallen world" dominated by "sin." But all of this is implied, not stated.

Instead, he aims to reject politics entirely. He writes:

> Many of us find ourselves estranged from the narrow issues that define conservatives and from the shallow spirituality that marks liberals . . . We are thirsty for social justice and peace but have a hard time finding a faith community that is consistently pro-life or that recognizes that there are "moral issues" other than homosexuality and abortion, moral issues like war and poverty. So some folks just end up trying to save individual souls from their sins, and others end up trying to save the world from "the system." But rarely do we see that the sickness of our world has infected each of us, and that the healing of our world not only begins within us but does not end with us. . . . A "silent majority" is developing as a growing number of folks are deliberately distancing themselves from the noise and arrogance that have come to mark both evangelical Christianity and secular activism.

Claiborne places his philosophy squarely in the middle of this false dichotomy. Eager for some both-sides-ism, the book clings to weird stereotypes about "legalistic" conservatives and flighty liberals, providing no solid evidence of either experience, whether anecdotal or statistical. The specifics of how to walk this spurious middle ground are never quite elucidated.*

---

* In yet another example of his inscrutable politics, Claiborne notes he is "a big fan of being radically inclusive, whether that means not turning off transsexuals [sic] or folks who drive SUVs." Aside from the truly wild choice to equate those two demographics, this again gives no indication of what Claiborne believes about a very pressing and politically-charged issue, the church's castigation of gender-nonconforming people, instead sidestepping the issue entirely.

As previously mentioned, Claiborne's book is published by Zondervan, the major Christian publisher which also put out the prosperity gospel bestseller *Prayer of Jabez* and dozens of other titles that would directly contradict Claiborne's theological ideas. Daniel Vaca explains in *Evangelicals Incorporated* that constant "horizontal mergers" in Christian publishing, coupled with different imprints that cater to different strains of Christianity, followed the secular conglomerate publishing model so popular in the '90s and 2000s. This allowed for a "greater variety of consumers, with diverse interests and media consumption habits." According to a former Zondervan executive, by the early 2000s, the company had abandoned an acquisition ethic based on "pure ministry" and instead required every book acquired to be profitable. "I told my editorial staff to think of themselves as mutual fund managers," the executive told Vaca.

Sounding starry-eyed to the point of naivete, Claiborne writes that he "truly believe[s] that when the poor meet the rich, riches will have no meaning. And when the rich meet the poor, we will see poverty come to an end," as though income inequality is the mere product of a lack of proximity. Perhaps this is what is behind his decision to disseminate his ideas through a capitalist outlet like Zondervan. But like his foray into Willow Church,[*] it seems more likely to water down his already mealy message than inspire radical change in the wealth class.

"Whoever loves money will never have enough"

While I now distrust both ends of this spectrum, I can understand the appeal of each. We all want to feel we have some control,

---

[*] Founder and pastor of Willow Creek Bill Hybels stepped down in 2018 amid numerous sexual misconduct allegations, reported in the New York Times. According to Christian media outlet The Roys Report, the church announced in 2024 it would be selling one of its Chicago campuses, saying it was facing an "unsustainable financial scenario."

whether that's over how we are able to survive financially or how we can end the world's suffering. It's tempting to take positive anecdotes from the *Under the Overpass* guys and Joel Osteen alike, and say, well, it worked for them. So, what's the harm?

But it's precisely this assumption that a positive-seeming outcome justifies the belief that I find troubling. When your framework begins and ends with an active and yet unimpeachably moral God, then all logic is backward and circular. It's like the friend I had who told me her migraine was cured the moment she prayed and forgave a family member who had wronged her. But she didn't stop having migraines. The next time, the same method didn't work—so it must have stood to reason God was trying to teach her something else through *that* migraine.

I think of a favourite joke from the sitcom *30 Rock:* Kenneth the page repeats the worn axiom that "God gave us two ears and one mouth because He wants us to listen twice as much as we speak." Then he looks down, and his eyes widen. "But he gave us *ten* fingers. He must really want us to poke things!"

All of this is about money. But it's also, fundamentally, about trying to order the universe. It's about trying to justify the existence of the haves and the have-nots in a world you've been taught was created by a just and all-powerful being. It's about reckoning with the randomness of life—why was I born into relative safety, into privilege, into wealth? Why was I given what I've been given? Why have I been denied what I've been denied? When you start asking these questions, Godly answers start appearing—when you start looking for signs, you start seeing them, and God, everywhere.

My feelings about money have, at different points in my faith, made me feel spoiled, ineffectual, guilty, superior, privileged, thankful, miraculous, utterly quotidian. Money has always seemed fundamentally unfair. And I guess, at the root of it, that's my problem with both sides of the Christian coin when it comes to money miracles. It's always been about making sense of—or accumulating—something that just doesn't make sense.

CHAPTER EIGHT

CLEAN COMEDY

CHRISTIANS, COMEDY, AND CANCEL CULTURE

When I was a kid, my parents took me to see an improv troupe that one of their church friends was in. It was a Christian comedy troupe and promised *clean comedy*—no swearing or sexual innuendoes, no nudity, no touchy subjects.

I don't know if it's fair to judge an amateur improv show's quality, or to equate that quality with it being Christian. I do remember finding the whole thing not very funny and a little bit, somehow, embarrassing. (Again, not saying I wouldn't feel the same way about a non-Christian improv show.) But at the time, it lodged in my child-brain as an example of something I was starting to have a big problem with. Namely: Christians were not funny.

My family was a humour family, a funny family. We communicated with each other through jokes, showed our love by teasing each other. All of the legendary family stories and quotations that were passed along through the years in my extended family were *funny* stories. I've been around other families who tell stories about their ancestors and family members' accomplishments, wealth, bravery, heroism, whatever. In my family, the stories were about people having to go to the hospital because they got food stuck up their nose or something. There was a whole sub-genre of Grandpa

Playing Board Games stories, centred around his flailing attempts at Taboo and Balderdash. And of course, Embarrassing Childhood Stories, a constant favourite. My dad was the king of this kind of story: He had a compendium of tales from his childhood, often involving him and his three siblings running wild and unsupervised on their parents' farm. (The Time He Got Charged by a Cow continues to be a huge hit with his grandchildren.)

My family likes to do it for the bit. One exemplary family story: My brother once lost marks on a science test for his answer to the question, *Looking at the population graphs below, describe the relationship between the rabbits and the wolves.* He wrote, "Strained."

I remember him sharing this at the dining room table, over dinner. My parents and I laughed into our mashed potatoes, and then one of us asked, "But did you know the real answer?"

"Sure," he said. "But that's not funny."

♥ † ♥

I always knew that I wanted to be a writer. In particular, as a kid, I wanted to write novels. But this presented its own conundrum: How does a Christian write novels—do they have to be Christian novels? It was the same question, in a way, that illustrated what I felt was the irreconcilable gap between the kind of Christian life laid out in Gospel stories—the life where Jesus yelled at you while you were on your fishing boat and you dropped everything and lived as an impoverished, transient nomad for the rest of your life until you were violently killed for your faith—and the comfortable, middle-class lives the Christians around me were living, where everything that populated your reality was just a Christian version of the "regular" thing. Christian music, Christian books, Christian improv shows, Christian fashions, Christian magazines, Christian school, and church on Sunday.

The novels I admired had a spark of irreverence that I didn't think I'd be allowed to emulate if I were a Christian Writer. I'd read a few Christian novels; there was a lot of praying in them, and someone usually got saved by the book's end. Sometimes there was a chaste romance, or a science-fiction-like plot that was actually supernatural. But how would you write about the human experience, in a *real* way, I wondered, if you couldn't write about anything *sinful*?

Was that also the problem with Christian comedy? Was there something about *sin* that made things more exciting, more fun? Like other Christian media, Christian comedy is more often about what it restricts than what it adds. Christian stand-ups usually operate as "clean comedians," staying away from humour that would be deemed inappropriate for any God-fearing evangelical. This precludes a sense of safety for the audience, not just that they won't hear any "bad words," but that they can rest assured that their lifestyle, their religion, their God, none of it will come under fire.

I wondered if, as a kid, I had cared about finding enjoyable Christian literature only because I was interested in being a writer. After all, I didn't have the same feelings about music or movies—there I veered definitively secular in my preferences. But while talking about this recently with my partner on a walk one day, they recalled feeling the same way about Christian media. They wanted it to be good—not just in spite of being Christian but *because* it was Christian. There was a prevailing sense among their Christian peer group, they recalled, that Christians, by dint of having God and goodness on their side, should be the best at everything.

In my anxious childhood mind, I believe I had a slightly different motivation. I just wanted to make sure I could stand being around other Christians, particularly if I was going to be sentenced to spending all of eternity with them. If Christians got into heaven, and Christians weren't funny, what was I going to do up there, forever and ever amen? It was bad enough that we probably weren't going to be able to watch *The Simpsons* in the afterlife. (Maybe that was why I spent so many hours of my one wild and precious life slumped over my parents' couch watching reruns.) What if the Christian improv troupe was a forecast of eternity to come?

♥ † ♥

1. Meet the really-not-ready-for-primetime players

> **Mike Warnke:** I'm a Christian because of what happened in my heart, not what happened in my hair. The Lord didn't come to change my shirt, he came to change my life. And he did that because I accepted him as my personal saviour.

The history of Christian stand-up comedy is a strange one, mostly for the figure that pioneered it. Mike Warnke, largely recognized as the first major Christian stand-up comedian, got his start telling the story of his life on stage, peppered with jokes. The story of his life was that he was a former Satanic priest.

In his book *The Satan Seller*, published in 1972, Warnke details his journey from hippie-burn-out to Satan-worshipper, explaining how he rose through the ranks to become a Satanic high priest in this secret community proliferating right under the noses of clueless Americans.

If you can't imagine how this translates into a tight-five, well, you'll be left wondering, even after watching Warnke's comedy albums and clips from his 1980s shows, available on YouTube. In these videos, he takes the stage in colourful button-up shirts, curly mullet spilling gloriously from his back collar, decked out in Weird Al glasses and a single earring glinting in one lobe. His material doesn't exactly read as comedy to me; his stories are meandering and only funny in the general sense. There are no real punchlines. It's more like watching a sermon by a goofy pastor.

Still, Warnke was charting a strange, specific path. It wasn't just that his comedy was Christian because it was "clean," or because he riffed on religious topics, it was rooted in a particular evangelical mission: He was actively working to dismantle Satanism and the occult.

One major problem with this mission, as it turned out, was that he'd made it all up. A 1992 investigation by journalists at the Christian magazine *Crossroads* blew his story open—the in-depth article drew from interviews with more than one hundred people who knew Warnke throughout his life, fact-checked just about every claim made in *The Satan Seller*, and found that nearly all of them were fraudulent. He'd never been a Satanist or drug addict, as he'd claimed; he hadn't really even been a hippie. Even the book's descriptions of his long hair were fabricated. And most of the "love offerings" he'd collected for his ministry instead, the article alleged, went straight into his pocket.

But by that time, Christian stand-up was starting to find its footing as a genre, and it continued beyond its truth-allergic founding father. By the Y2K era, there were several stand-up comedians of note operating in the Christian mainstream.

Chonda Pierce: The Lord gave us two things in this world: chocolate and epidurals.

The most popular, the one on the cutting edge of Christian comedy, was Brad Stine. At least, that is how he's painted in a 2004 *New Yorker* profile entitled "Stand Up for the Lord." "The big names in Christian comedy today . . . look like the churchgoing suburban moms and dads that they are," the profile says. "Their old-fashioned humor, which consists of mild gibes at Christian family life, musical spoofs, funny props, and inspirational testimony, carries a lingering whiff of the fellowship hall and the worship-center rec room." By contrast, Stine performs "contemporary-style" humour, considering himself "less as a Christian comedian than as a comedian who happens to be Christian," and one "to whom conservative, Bible-believing Americans, who 'have never had their own George Carlin,' can point with pride."

But elsewhere in the article, Stine's references to his audience seem laced less with pride than contempt—or at least a sense that they are not the most cosmopolitan in their comedy taste. After all, Stine had, by his own account, been trying to break into the secular media industry (first as a magician, then as a clean but not explicitly faith-based comedian) for years before he found his niche performing the church circuit. He tells the writer: "What these churches are becoming, as venues, is sort of what those comedy clubs were in the seventies and eighties . . . It's this gigantic market of people who literally have never had this before. I've been stinkin' digging for years in this mine, and suddenly it's like—oh-ho-ho-ho—I've struck the mother lode."

If Stine represents the cutting edge, Southern belle Chonda Pierce, who also gained a following in the 2000s, with her squeaky-voiced charm and goofy specials, is the solid middle; the safe choice for some gentle chuckles for families who want to hear some God-fearing comedy. Chonda Pierce's comedy feels more familiar to what I would have experienced in the church sanctuaries and youth group conferences of my youth. In her 2002 special, *Be Afraid . . . Be Very Afraid* (available via stretched-out VHS rip on YouTube), stand-up is interspersed with parody songs (like "I'm Satisfied," a Gloria Gaynor number about quitting her diet), skits, and pre-taped commercial parodies. A cooking segment features oh-so-evangelical jokes about having your pastor over for dinner and childhood corporal punishment (holding up a rolling pin: "My grandmother used one of these often . . . on me."). All of this made her popular enough to start going by the title "the Queen of Clean."

Brad Stine: I knew we were getting lazy in this country when we started putting handles on our Bibles!

Brad Stine's comedy is explicitly drawn around community lines. It's for Christians, conservative Christians, and it's—mostly—about making fun of people who are not.

At the time of the *New Yorker* profile, his special *Put a Helmet On!*, which Stine had taped in the auditorium of Jerry Falwell's church (with the notorious right-wing pastor's blessing) and distributed on his own label, had sold about 40,000 copies. He had also expanded his audience by partnering with Promise Keepers, the "men's ministry" that ran conferences for Christian men on how to be good fathers and husbands, performing and selling his merch at their events.

Still, Stine told the *New Yorker* reporter that mainstream success was elusive, that despite his ultimate dreams of performing on *The Tonight Show*, it would be an uphill battle:

"As Stine told me many times, he is battling a 'liberal-biased media-entertainment structure.' He figured that after having proved himself as a standup for nearly two decades, the only conclusion he could draw from his not being asked onto the 'Tonight Show' was that the powers that be were determined not to give airtime to anyone with a conservative or Christian message." The writer adds, "I noted that for most of those years Stine had kept his religious and political views to himself." Stine doesn't seem to pick up on this.

Surprisingly—or maybe not—Stine's complaint about the strictures he faces from the likes of the liberal, the sensitive, and the politically correct moves from meta-textual to textual halfway through *Put a Helmet On!* After a long, racist joke about chopsticks, Stine stops the act to talk about the very joke he'd just finished telling: or rather, about how said joke got him fired from doing gigs at Pepperdine University.

As he continues his story, the frequency of punchlines drops away, until what he is performing is less a comedy routine and more of a rant aimed at the university. "I don't call that sensitivity, I call that censorship," he says. He is just sad, really, for all those kids who would have been so enriched and moved by his comedy, who now don't get to see it. "Shame on you!" he cries at the end of this diatribe. (Indeed. How will this small Christian college ever find another comedian willing to perform?)

Stine's railing against political correctness felt familiar to me. In the years since his special, the complaints haven't changed, though the name has: Today, *cancel culture* is the phrase at which conservatives and comedians, and especially conservative comedians like Stine, focus their ire. While the definition is kind of nebulous, what people usually mean by cancel culture is a social climate in which people are ostracized, boycotted, or otherwise shut down for any perceived moral misstep. (The term's ascendancy around 2019, just when the backlash to the #MeToo movement was doing its lashing back, is not exactly a coincidence.) Cancel culture is more of a feeling than an observable fact—as exemplified by the likes of comedians who routinely complain about it and the tally of their bank accounts.

2. The way things are going, they're gonna crucify me

Mike Warnke: Someone says, "Don't you think you're rather closed-minded?" I say, "Yeah, but I can afford to be—I'm right."

In the year 2000, less than ten years after the expose that revealed his many lies, Mike Warnke was granting an interview to *The Oklahoman* newspaper. "Laughs stopped for Christian comic," the headline proclaims. "Mike Warnke offers fans new outlook after ministry's crash."

"In 1982, Mike Warnke flew in a private plane to perform for thousands in Oklahoma City's Myriad Convention Center," the story begins. "Limousines ushered him around town, guards pushed fans back to a respectable distance of 6 feet, and one staff member kept her job secure by knowing the precise moment to place a perfectly chilled Diet Pepsi into his cupped hand before and after he spoke."

On the not-so-triumphant occasion of his return to Oklahoma, by contrast, "The man who was once billed as the nation's top Christian comedian now settles for drinks from public water fountains in small church foyers when he gets thirsty. The limousines are gone, too, replaced by compact rental cars. If he's chauffeured around town, it's by a local minister in a pickup."

Warnke had been cancelled. Yet, despite the colourful opening, it becomes clear throughout the piece that he is still performing, and that the wholesale takedown of his assumed persona has not, in fact, derailed his career. This trajectory is surely familiar to anyone who's heard the recent protests of cancel culture from modern-day comedians and then turned around to read about a Louis C.K. stand-up show or Dave Chappelle Netflix deal or see Shane Gillis host *Saturday Night Live*. In fact, those comedians could probably learn a thing or two from Warnke's repentance tour, which reportedly included "assembl[ing] a tribunal of elders and submit[ting] himself to them for discipline and direction," apologizing to "fans and believers," and offering "repayment of back taxes to the government."*

Reading about Warnke and watching Brad Stine reminded me of so many other supposedly hot-button "takes" from secular comedians over recent years, of how the genre was plagued by these tiresome ideas about political correctness and censorship. Christopher Hitchens saying women aren't funny; Ricky Gervais and Dave Chappelle calling audiences oversensitive for critiquing their transphobic jokes; director Todd Phillips claiming comedy

---

* Yet Warnke continued to sell, and I assume, profit from his entirely fabricated memoir and related merchandise, the article notes.

films no longer "work" in "this woke culture." Brad Stine, it turns out, was perfectly at pace with his secular counterparts in whining about the deficits of his audience and America at large. It's mainstream, now as then, for comedians to complain about their audiences getting soft, being too sensitive.*

Unlike the secular examples above, though, Stine's position has an odd fold in it. The usual line is something to the effect of, *Comedy is about pushing boundaries, comedians should be able to say whatever they want, chasing a pure laugh, no matter if that thing is shocking or wouldn't hold up in a regular conversation.* They are exempt because *it's just a joke.* This logic is far from impenetrable, but it seems much more straightforward than the alternative when you consider that the Christian comedians pushing the anti-censorship line are *clean comedians.*

Stine, who devotes an entire segment of his special to his outrage at being censored by Pepperdine University, is in essence performing an entire act based on self-censorship. He's enabling a public that will only take in content that meets certain bounds in topic and language. He should be allowed to make racist jokes, he is arguing, but by no means be able to say the work *fuck* on stage.

Brad Stine: If I'd worn a helmet when I was learning to ride a bike, my friends would have beaten me up. AND THEY SHOULD HAVE!

Taboos, the words we don't say or things we don't talk about in normal, polite, conversation, can make for some of the most fertile areas for comedic exploration, and comedians are often crossing these lines in strange and exciting ways. But as critic

---

* In his book *Outrageous*, historian Kliph Nesteroff traces this comedic complaint as far back as the 19th century, in the riotous backlash to complaints against vaudeville and minstrel shows.

Jesse David Fox argues, in the conception of comedian-as-truth-teller, political correctness is actually an important part of the equation: "Political correctness is great because it makes the line clearer, if the comedian cares to look, better allowing them to twist and turn the audience around it." He argues that if a comedian's goal is to be "edgy," they should welcome offense, not complain about it: "If you are saying supposedly offensive things and the audience is instantly all on board, it is not a comedy show, it's a rally."

It's true that, historically, comedy has been subject to legal prohibitions—more than most forms of entertainment, one could argue. But as critics for the *New Yorker* podcast *Critics at Large* noted in their 2024 episode "What Is the Comic For?", comedians and discourse about comedians can fall into the trap of conflating two different types of prohibition: official censorship (e.g., decency laws) and threats to social standing (e.g., being "cancelled"). While George Carlin railed against the "seven words you can't say on television," he was making a point about a legal prohibition against his speech; when Dave Chappelle uses transphobic slurs, he doesn't face a network fine (quite the contrary, he is able to so on Netflix specials for which he was paid $20 million) but is subject only to criticism from below, rather than above, so to speak—an audience reaction which has only the soft power of his social perception and potential economic viability. The critics further delineate this distinction as one between depiction and denigration: one regulates what can be shown, and the other denotes how your subject perceives themself as shown—two very different pressures.

The *New Yorker* critics mention George Carlin as a kind of framework for comedian-as-social-critic, and I could see this at work in Brad Stine's mimicry of Carlin's style. It's clear Stine is going for the "angry prophet" style of excoriation that Carlin was doing, if from a different angle. Carlin was famous for his diatribes against American complacency and consumerism; Stine goes after atheists. But I think Stine's schtick falls flat not only for a lack of panache but because his premise is flawed. The picture of America that he paints is not rooted in the reality of how things are, and if his set-up is erroneous, how can his punchline work? He isn't dismantling a system upheld by the mainstream, in fact, he is simply railing against the efforts of the people who are. As critic Alexandra Schwartz notes, if a comedian paints themself as a taboo-breaker but ends up just upholding a majority belief, "you're not turning anything on its head, you're just participating in it."

Writing for *The Walrus* in 2020, Erika Thorkelson defines the mainstream cultural shift in what's acceptable in comedy: "It's no longer possible to pretend we're not in the room," she writes, referring to marginalized members of the audience as well as other comedians. This is part of a move away from what comedian Marc Maron called, in an episode of his podcast, *WTF*, "shamelessly punching down for the sheer joy of hurting people, for the sheer excitement and laughter that some people get from causing people pain, from making people uncomfortable, from making people feel excluded." Thorkelson pulls on the thread of this idea of exclusion, noting that the cultural recognition of this phenomenon gives rise to new forms of media—podcasting, streaming, social platforms—that allow for both highly niche content to thrive and for wider audiences than ever to get their eyes on any particular joke.

But as Fox notes, there's a big difference between the consequences of so-called *cancel culture* and an actual muzzling of expression; Carlin's routine, for instance, got him thrown in jail seven different times. A few years before Brad Stine's special, Mel Brooks could be found complaining that his 1974 film *Blazing Saddles* couldn't have been made in the 2000s because of the sensitivity of audiences (the film contains instances of the N-word, along with other racially questionable depictions). But the same year *Blazing Saddles* was released, Fox writes, "its cowriter Richard Pryor was arrested in Richard, Virginia, for using the same sort of 'obscene' language he wrote into the film."

"Today, the people who say they can't say anything anymore are often found saying it during a performance they earned tens of thousands of dollars for, on their podcast they make hundreds of thousands a year on, or the special they got paid millions for," Fox writes. "Unlike Carlin, unlike Pryor, you know where they aren't saying it? A jail cell."

♥ † ♥

>   **YouTube comment:** Why have I never heard of this brilliant man before? He's not telling dirty jokes, he's funny, and he's unafraid to teach the truth about God! Now I know why I haven't heard of him. He's not telling dirty jokes, he's funny, and he's unafraid to teach the truth about God! . . . We must spread this video like wildfire before they try to cancel him.

Like the self-censoring clean comedian who cries free speech, Christian comedians are in a strange double bind; they are somehow trying to alienate and invite people in at the same time. If the goal is ultimately to evangelize, to win more people to Christianity, there can be no self-deprecating of the religion in the act. But if you can't make fun of yourself, who to go after? (The short answer seems to be Angry Vegan Feminists.)

Thinking about all this, and how worried I felt about not finding Christians funny as a kid, I realized back then I'd been ruminating on the wrong question. It isn't a question of Christians being funny *in general*. The real question was why *didn't* I find them funny?

Humour doesn't happen in a vacuum; that's why comedians obsess over tough crowds and warming up the audience. That's why we have concepts for jokes that don't land because of the context—*too soon, read the room, wrong crowd.*

"Comedians are in the business of creating the feeling of 'it's safe to laugh' that people get naturally from our friends and family, so if the audience similarly trusts them, they offer them a similar grace," Fox writes. He adds, "There is no bigger factor in offense than your relationship to the person telling the joke." In-jokes about cultural stereotypes between people from that culture kill; the same joke told with sneering contempt by an outsider would, obviously, be less welcome.

It was me who didn't find Christians funny, then or now. The atmosphere of "safe to laugh," was never one I felt had been cultivated. As a kid, I buzzed with anxiety when I encountered Christian comedy: Sometimes I was worried the performers were going to embarrass me, make me feel like a joke for participating in this religion that now seemed so corny. But on a deeper level, I was scared that I would somehow be castigated. That I would be the butt of the joke, the person at which they were taking cruel aim—that someone would yell at me to put a helmet on. I knew, intrinsically, that they were not on my side, that I was on the other side of this excluding line they were drawing around themselves.

The essential set-up of a joke—premise and punchline—is a trust fall. The same twist of expectations that makes us laugh is a tiny threat: The audience depends on the comedian to carry them through whatever turn or reversal is coming.

3. Me talk Christian one day

> **Donald Miller:** Reality is like a fine wine . . . It will not appeal to children.

When I try to recall an example of Christian pop culture that I thought was genuinely funny, my memory skips past the comedians and improv shows and church skits and lands on a memory of a book.

When I was a young high schooler, my favourite English teacher read us a chapter of Donald Miller's memoir *Searching for God Knows What*. In the section he read, the author relayed a story from his childhood: On a trip to the mall to sit on Santa's lap, he went to the washroom and found himself at the urinal next to Santa Claus himself. When Santa hiked up his red pants and left with a *Merry Christmas,* the kid was horrified to learn that Santa didn't wash his hands.

I laughed—for real. Out loud and everything. I sat back in my green plastic school chair and marvelled. This was a *funny book*—*a funny* Christian *book*. It was real. It existed. I set out to read everything Donald Miller had written.

♥ † ♥

Donald Miller: I always thought the Bible was more of a salad thing, you know, but it isn't. It's a chocolate thing.

In 2003, Nashville-based Thomas Nelson—one of America's largest and oldest Christian publishers[*]—published *Blue Like Jazz: Nonreligious Thoughts on Christian Spirituality* by then-fledgling author Donald Miller. Miller had published one other book (*Prayer and the Art of Volkswagen Maintenance,* a reflective memoir about a road trip through the desert) with a smaller Christian press. But it was *Blue Like Jazz* that took off, landing on the *New York Times* bestseller list and topping one million sales four years after its release.

Blue Like Jazz struck a chord. As might be obvious from the subtitle, Miller's free-floating style broke from the typical Christian nonfiction "voice"—somewhere between scolding schoolmarm

---

[*] The company was acquired by HarperCollins in 2012.

and self-help huckster—and took on a more explicitly memoir-ish tone, tackling subjects such as grace, going to church, spending money wisely, romantic relationships, and community, not with theological rigor but with musings drawn from his experiences and coterie of Portland Christian–hipster friends, many of whom he appended with twee, capitalized titles: Tony the Beat Poet,[*] Andrew the Protester, Mark the Cussing Pastor.[**] It was also indicative of a kind of evangelicalism that was rising parallel at the same time the James Dobsons of the world made their ascendance—a kind less aligned with the whims of the GOP, more willing to integrate and even tolerate secular society, more focused on social justice ministry than piety. This movement would come to be labelled the *Emerging Church*, and though Miller was never explicitly affiliated, his brand of sensitive, artistic, politically centrist "Christian spirituality" (he refused the term *Christian* in the book and instead adopted *Christian spiritualist*) was right in line with the writings and teachings of the movement's leaders.

In a Christian media landscape that—in the 2000s as it is now—skewed so heavily conservative, Miller was a breath of fresh air to nascent progressives like my young self. He went on to stump for then-Democratic candidate Barack Obama and gave the benediction at the 2008 Democratic National Convention. His books were self-searching and non-judgmental. A major throughline in *Blue Like Jazz*, in fact, was his experience auditing courses at the liberal, atheist-hotbed Reed College in Portland, Oregon, where Miller collects ragtag groups of anarchist friends and has deep conversations with them about whether or not God exists. Amid the Christian books, movies, speakers, and comedians constantly bemoaning and vilifying atheists on college campuses—painting them as ravenous and

---

[*] He is not actually a poet but simply likes to wear "loose European shirts" that remind Donald Miller of beat poets, for some reason.

[**] Though only identified in the book by first name, this is Mark Driscoll, pastor of Seattle's Mars Hill church—for more on him, see chapter two.

ready to tear Christians limb from limb like the lions in the colosseum—*Blue Like Jazz* felt real, and human, to me. It made me less scared of the world outside my Christian school bubble—made me excited, in fact, to get out there. It stirred and tickled my 14-year-old self, making me laugh with his punchy writing style, moving me with reflections on loneliness and the bigness of the universe.

And then, 20 years after that trendy blue cover with its outline of a suspension bridge hit bookshelf stores, I pulled it from a stack of books mounded next to my office desk.

Through all the phases of my life, as my sense of self and religious identification has shifted, as I've moved apartments and cities, there have been many bookshelf culls, but *Blue Like Jazz* had managed to survive them all. I had only read it once, at 14, but my memory of that reading experience and the feelings I harboured toward it were tender enough to keep me from dumping it in the *TO THRIFT STORE* box with my copies of *The Message* and *The Shack* or into the trash with my Francis Chan books. Now, I pulled it out happily, inhaled the scent of its time-yellowed pages, eager to—after hours of Brad Stine and Chonda Price chirping and yelling in my ear—crack open a book I actually remembered fondly.

It was not funny.

Worse than that—it was *bad*. I didn't like it.

What had seemed so profound at the time had somehow been transformed into flaky platitudes. The open-mindedness I remembered was gone, replaced by thinly veiled cruelty. Simplistic observations were treated as undeniable truths. Conservative ideology went unexamined. Important issues were brushed aside. The women in the book were thin caricatures. The men had their strange, capitalized titles. Miller took every possible opportunity to remind the reader that he rides a motorcycle.

I could trace the lineage of Miller's style in a way I couldn't when I was 14. At that time, I'd never read a Christian memoir—

I probably had read very few non-Christian memoirs, now that I think of it. Online, it's easy to find interviews with Miller where he sings the praises of Anne Lamott, citing *Traveling Mercies* as one of his favourite books, but you could guess as much from reading *Blue Like Jazz*, which pretty much lifts her style wholesale. Reading the book now felt like listening to one of those Christian bands mimicking a secular style—this was a humour-laced memoir in the popular style of the time, only made Christian, something which I hadn't recognized then. This is even more true of the follow-up, *Searching for God Knows What*, of the famed Santa story. I can imagine these books on a shelf in a Christian bookstore with a sign: *If you like David Sedaris, you'll like . . . Donald Miller*. It's also abundantly clear that Miller, like me and so many other poor, book-loving souls, shared a youthful obsession with J.D. Salinger; I can't imagine it was actually typical for 20-somethings in Portland in 2002 to be ending their sentences with "if you want to know the truth." My copy of *Blue Like Jazz* soon became overrun with scribbles of *OKAY HOLDEN* in the margins, among other notes. I couldn't help myself, even though this was the very same copy that I had loved, happily turned the pages of in my parents' living room, fondly packed away in a box to ship across the country when I moved.

Of course, the book hadn't changed. I had changed.

4. Humourless

> **Mike Warnke:** Christians don't gossip, they "share"; and when they get really mean they "share in love." If a Christian comes up to you and says, "I'm going to share this with you in love," watch out.

Conservative comedians—not just Christian ones—like to paint left-wing or progressive groups as humourless. This figures heavily in the flustered griping about political correctness "killing" comedy, the idea that young people, college students, feminists, whoever, are somehow these grim and militant forces trying to quash the funny.

Before their death in 2021, cultural theorist Lauren Berlant was writing about the question of humourlessness, or to be more precise, the question of who is *allowed* to be humourless. "If you already have structural power, humourlessness increases your value," Berlant told an interviewer. But "the privileged demand that the less privileged not be humourless." Being able to laugh at oneself is a value prized more highly by a society that is already laughing at you, and by the same token, offense is only taken seriously if the offended subject is at the top of the heap.

Christian comedians like to deny their own social power, convinced they are marginalized because their religious beliefs have barred them from secular success or major opportunities. I see a humourlessness in Brad Stine talking about his exile from Pepperdine University: In theory, he's turning this slight into a humourous anecdote, but the humour isn't really there. It's not really a joke. You can see how angry he is, for one, and there are no surprising turns that might take the performance from the realm of "rant" to "joke." It's not constructed like a joke. The offended parties are meant to have a sense of humour about themselves—meant to see that their culture has quirks that others can pillory and spoof—and yet he is not required to. Thousands of years of Chinese culture is up for grabs joke-wise, but don't you dare tease a Christian. A joke would turn something on its head: upend an expectation, create an incongruity, create and release a sense of tension. Instead, he is just telling the audience that he's been wronged.

Brad Stine: And then the pièce de résistance, the *anti-bacterial wipe*... No wonder we have a multi-billion-dollar antibiotics industry, we won't let a single germ get inside us so the body can fight it off the way God designed it to do!

On Donald Miller's progressive campus, the Christians staged an event. During Reed College's annual Renn Fayre, Miller and his ragtag group of Christian spiritualist friends built a confession booth, with a sign saying, "Confess your sins." The twist was, when people got into the booth, they would be *receiving* the confession, not giving one.

Miller's friend Tony (the non-beat poet) says:

> We are not actually going to accept confessions... We are going to confess to them. We are going to confess that, as followers of Jesus, we have not been very loving; we have been bitter, and for that we are sorry. We will apologize for the Crusades, we will apologize for televangelists, we will apologize for neglecting the poor and the lonely, we will ask them to forgive us, and we will tell them that in our selfishness, we have misrepresented Jesus on this campus. We will tell people who come into the booth that Jesus loves them.

His idea is greeted with stunned silence, recognition that it is, Miller says, "beautiful and true." And so, they do it. They build their booth, they humble themselves and begin confessing—that is, apologizing for the Crusades and their own sins. The man in Donald Miller's booth cries in response. A line forms, and Tony takes overflow at a picnic table nearby. "I think that night was the beginning of change for all of us," Miller muses.

Rereading this section, I can feel how edgy this idea was supposed to be. And surely, compared to the other Christian media

I have consumed from the time, it was. I certainly can't imagine Brad Stine humbling himself to apologize to any atheists on a college campus. He wouldn't even apologize to the students he offended with his dumb chopsticks joke. Yet my instinctive reaction was distaste.

The first time I read the book, I identified myself with Miller. I imagined what it would be like to apologize for the harms of my religion—how uncomfortable it might make me feel, but how necessary, how Jesus-like, it really was. I imagined that it might make me feel, like Miller, "very peaceful . . . very connected to God." Years later, I would attend a church that got press for its involvement with a campaign that made apologies to the 2SLGBTQIA+ community for Christianity's historical and modern-day treatment. What I didn't recognize at the time was how many of us in that church were awkwardly situated on both sides of the apology. Can you apologize to yourself on behalf of your own religion?

Coming to this book in my early thirties, feeling more at home in my own self than I ever have before, I realize I was mentally seating myself on the other side of the table, across from Miller. As a 14-year-old, I didn't even fully recognize how Christianity had hurt me. Now I feel it—I've been hurt, both personally and structurally; I've been wronged as a woman, as a queer person, in specific circumstances, and in the suffused air of patriarchy and homophobia and misogyny that permeates churches everywhere.

And what would I think if a young Christian apologized to me for . . . the Crusades?

In the margin, I wrote, *Well, fuck you.*

I don't mean to take out my anger on Miller, who is just one man, tripping along, trying to do his best—trying to be a good Christian and trying to write like Holden Caulfield. But I found the paucity of his remorse painful; the smugness of how he reported this story infuriating.

The church certainly has a lot to apologize for—including genocides much more recent than the Crusades—and you could argue that its hate toward queer people is only one item on an ever-extending checklist; that it's on my mind particularly because of my personal experience, and because of what's happening today, decades after *Blue Like Jazz* was written. But I couldn't help but feel that Miller's elision of this particular sin was somehow intentional. Was it a hot potato he didn't want to touch? Did he think the church had nothing to apologize for in that regard?

To make matters worse, the chapter about this is titled with (and makes repeated use of throughout) the metaphor of he and his friends "coming out" as Christian.

Only twice in the book does he explicitly mention gay people,* in asides about the necessity, as a Christian, of loving everyone, "loving people just because they exist," as Miller puts it. But I don't want to be loved for existing, I want to be understood.

I could watch Brad Stine and groan and roll my eyes, but *Blue Like Jazz* seemed worse, stuck with me more, a burr under the skin. It was like comedy, I realized; how it affected you had a lot to do with what community you counted yourself a part of, where you aligned yourself and your beliefs. That book had, in some small way, been a part of me, and extricating that part hurt like a vivisection.

5. The kids are alt-right

> **Brad Stine:** "I'm the government and I will raise your kids for you!" But who's in the government now? Pagans! We've got a pagan government. See, we used to be a Judeo-Christian nation and we had personal responsibility. Not now!

---

* Okay, there's a third time, where he briefly wonders if he is gay, which is really just there as a joke. Ha ha.

After watching Chonda Pierce's 2000s stand-up special, I entered her name into the YouTube search bar and discovered she is still performing. Her more recent clips (from 2023) are from former Republican Arkansas governor Mike Huckabee's talk show, *Huckabee*, which airs on TBN—the Trinity Broadcasting Network, which began its life as televangelists Paul and Jan Crouch's TV station in the late '70s and is now apparently "America's most-watched faith channel."

On *Huckabee*, Pierce takes the stage in leggings and a velour tunic, a long lariat necklace swinging from her neck. Her blond hair—cropped in a short, flippy style in the 2000s—is now long and piled atop her head. Her voice still has its cutesy Southern squeak, though now there's a hard edge hiding underneath.*

Bemoaning the tendency for women to put risqué pictures on social media, she swerves a joke about making a dating profile into an extended bit that plays on favourite right-wing conspiracy theories about "Hillary Clinton's emails" and "Hunter Biden's laptop." In another video, she gifts Huckabee a red yarmulke embroidered with Donald Trump's "Make America Great Again" campaign slogan, a neat visual embodiment of the unholy marriage of Christian Zionism and Trumpism. The occasion for the gift is an upcoming trip to Israel that Pierce and Huckabee are taking together. "They like us a lot [more] there than in America right now," says Pierce.

It's not that Pierce's 2002 material was completely apolitical (if such a thing could exist) but nowadays her jokes seem entirely topical, often focused on politics. There's also a clear shift in positioning; while her 2002 special had jokes about her patriotism ("I go to the airport and there's those little guys—little G.I. Joes—I just go up and hug 'em!"), they were delivered in a tone of gentle, *aw-shucks* faux-self-deprecation. Now the joke is on

---

* In the intervening years, according to *The Tennessean*, Pierce has faced some intense loss, including the deaths of her two sisters and her husband. She is also estranged from her daughter.

someone else, delivered with a sneering contempt for sensitive "snowflakes" and Bernie Sanders supporters.

I can't help but feel that in becoming more conservative, more moralistic, something in Pierce's comedy has hardened. It becomes difficult to watch. In the 2002 cooking segment, Pierce invites her son, Zach, onstage to help her make a dessert out of snack foods pulled from his backpack. The sweet, red-headed 12-year-old is game to help out, mugging for the audience and confidently delivering a few lines. Pierce seems genuinely distracted by her affection for him, giggling and pulling him toward her for a hug.

In a 2023 *Huckabee* appearance, she says, "My liberal snowflake son moved home," rolling her eyes and leaning on the words *liberal snowflake* with a sneer of contempt. "Every time I fix him lunch, I cut 30 percent out of his food and eat it myself."

Chonda Pierce: I'm just like my grandmother. She was so patriotic. I mean if the president was on the radio or on the television, the world stopped. "Stop, hush up, the president's on TV!" And I'm like, "Last month, before elections, you hated the guy." "Well, he's our president now, so you just hush up!"

Like Chonda Pierce, it seems to me that Christian comedy has, since the 2000s, moved even further to the right politically, and in many cases taken a dark turn.

The Christian media landscape has not been immune to the changes that affected the secular one in the 20 years since Brad Stine screamed *put a helmet on* from the stage of Jerry Falwell's church. Book publishing and record labels are not the behemoth industries they once were, and media has fractured and splintered into subcategories and fandoms catered to specific online communities. Which means that if you are not currently a conservative evangelical Christian, you may not have heard of The Babylon Bee, even though it boasts 3.5 million followers on X (née Twitter) and 1.5 million subscribers on YouTube.

Originally a direct rip-off of satirical news site The Onion, The Babylon Bee started its life in 2016 as a site publishing joke news articles generally focused on Christian beliefs and culture. Originally, the site had a fairly small-c-catholic approach to poking fun—Christians of more conservative or progressive views were both targeted, and some of its most viral headlines were jokes criticizing televangelist Joel Osteen and then-presidential candidate Donald Trump. But in 2018, the site's founder sold The Bee to a fan named Seth Dillon, who took the site in a decidedly more conservative direction. By 2020, the site was being *retweeted* by Donald Trump, and the targets of its mockery were almost exclusively left-wing and liberal figures, democratic politicians, members of the 2SLGBTQIA+ community, and basically anything that would fit under the nebulous right-wing definition of *woke*. In March 2022, the site's X account was banned for sharing a transphobic headline—they were reinstated when Elon Musk bought the social media platform. Today, the site has expanded with video content, a non-satirical podcast, a social media site called Bee Social, and a sister site Not the Bee, which features *real* news stories that "seem like they should be satire, but aren't"—which I suppose is one way of saying *news presented through such a warped prism that it comes out the other side basically fake.*

The trajectory of the site seems well summed-up by the difference between the property's first published print book, *How to Be a Perfect Christian: Your Comprehensive Guide to Flawless Spiritual Living* (2018), which satirized the Christian self-help publishing industry, and its most recent entries: *The Babylon Bee Guide to Wokeness* (2021), *The Babylon Bee Guide to Democracy* (2022), and *The Babylon Bee Guide to Gender* (2023).

The pretense of "humour" here seems to me, once again, a smokescreen to pass bigoted and widely discredited information and views into mainstream culture under the guise that "it's just a joke." But these things have more power than simple jokes.

While writing this chapter, I followed the news of Nex Benedict, a two-spirit/non-binary student in Oklahoma who died of an overdose the day after being beaten up by three classmates in a school washroom. The medical examiner's office ruled the teen's death a suicide and emphasized that the death was not a result of physical injury, as if to refute any relation between the violence Benedict had experienced the day before. However, Benedict had been bullied at school for months over their non-binary identity, their family said. The story seemed to indicate not just a diffuse transphobia at work but fit all too neatly with the coordinated attack on gender-nonconforming children the state of Oklahoma had been waging.* *Washington Post* reporter Taylor Lorenz quickly pointed out that the state had recently made a strange appointment to the Oklahoma Library Media Advisory Committee: Chaya Raichik, better known by her social media handle, @LibsofTikTok. Despite living in California and Florida (as of Lorenz's February 2024 article, Raichik had visited Oklahoma once), Raichik had been appointed to the position by Republican superintendent Ryan Walters, and had, in the first month of her appointment, already sought to pull books teaching sex education or depicting gay and transgender people from public school libraries. Along with spreading intensely transphobic rhetoric and policies, Raichik attended the January 6, 2021, Capitol Riot and has spread COVID-19 and child sex trafficking conspiracy theories and election denialism via her popular social media account.

At the start of its life, the @LibsofTikTok account actually received funding from Babylon Bee owner Seth Dillon. Both sites

---

* In fact, a federal investigation made public in November 2024 found that the Oklahoma school district of which Benedict's high school was a part "repeatedly failed to protect its students from discrimination and harassment." (*USA Today*, 13 November 2024)

are extremely active in politics; unlike The Onion or other similar parody sites, which are happy to comment on news and culture, The Babylon Bee has made it a mission to try and change that culture according to its own whims, participating in "free speech" litigation, threatening legal action against real news sites, and prompting action from lawmakers based on its satirical headlines. The Babylon Bee is "one of the most popular conservative sites after Fox News," *The Economist* reported in 2022.

@LibsofTikTok exists in that murky right-wing area where irony collapses and words like *joke*, *parody*, and *satire* begin to lose all meaning. As is clear from her baffling foray into school board advisory, Raichik is absolutely serious. But there is something undeniably internet-jokester about the tenor of the account. Before @LibsofTikTok took off in November 2020, Raichik tried out multiple usernames under which to peddle her conspiracy-laden screeds, including @houseplantpotus, a parody account that tweeted from the perspective of one of Joe Biden's houseplants. Most of the account's posts feature innocent educators that Raichik deems too woke—for appearing in a post, they may be subjected to weeks of harassment and death threats by Raichik's followers. But the tenor of the posts is a mix of overwrought fearmongering and the kind of troll-y humour endemic to the internet. Raichik went so far as to show up to an in-person interview with Lorenz wearing a homemade shirt with Lorenz's crying face screen-printed on it.

Somehow, this random former real estate salesperson has drawn fame and attention by marginalizing innocent children and vilifying hardworking educators, helping to create a cruel, heteronormative atmosphere where harassment, beatings, even suicides were simply a matter of time. This is all very depressing. How did we get here from comedy?

The Babylon Bee: "Biden Condemns Jesus for Rising Again on Trans Day of Visibility"

Unfortunately, looking away from this kind of comedy can be dangerous, Nick Marx and Matt Sienkiewicz argue in their book *That's Not Funny: How the Right Makes Comedy Work for Them*. "Matt and I started in the academic realm, and we noticed fellow researchers miscategorizing what was pretty clearly stuff meant to make you laugh," says Marx in an interview. "They would call it something else—'outrage programming' or 'new infotainment.' This in turn gets picked up by mainstream publications that run headlines like 'Why Don't Conservatives Like to Laugh?' and 'Why Is There No Conservative Jon Stewart?' It's the kind of self-perpetuating thing that's like sticking your fingers in your ears going, 'La, la, la, I'm going to pretend it's not there.'" The two argue that progressives shouldn't exclude conservative humour from the category of "comedy" just because it doesn't make *them* laugh—to do so misunderstands this media's function and prevents people from recognizing both the rise of potentially dangerous programming and the ability to "read" what is actually going on in there and why it connects with right-wing audiences.

Similarly, in his article "The Comedy Industry Has a Big Alt-Right Problem," Seth Simons traces the path of major white nationalist figures, like Gavin McInnes, through their start in comedy spaces and notes the way the alt-right overlaps with mainstream comedy—and breeds its own comedy shows like podcasts *Legion of Skanks* and *The Anthony Cumia Show*. "The credo of 'owning the libs' reads a lot like the traditional comedian's defense of his right to insult and offend," Simons writes. On YouTube, comedy is the gateway for people (statistically, mostly young, white men who feel emotionally disconnected or socially useless) into darker influences—the algorithm leads from comedy to conservative comedy to "prominent right-wing and white nationalist influencers like [Ben] Shapiro, Jordan Peterson, Steven Crowder, Michael Malice, Gavin McInnes, and Nick Fuentes," writes Jesse David Fox. (He adds, "It happened to me while researching.") Algorithmic suggestions, retweets and social media plugs, cross-promotion on podcasts, all push online users down the pathway from "more banal right-wing humor to the truly evil stuff, up to and including actual neo-Nazi comedy spaces." Comedy can be used here to slick the track, allowing a nearly frictionless slide through deeper successive layers, sometimes the difference between ironic and sincere blurring the line between what is really a joke.

In *Put a Helmet On!*, Stine tells us that the problem in the good ol' U.S. of A. these days is a lack of personal responsibility. "If you're fat, let's not blame you, let's sue McDonald's," he yells, parroting a common 2000s moral panic (a double moral panic if you count both the panic over perceived over-litigiousness among consumers and the obesity "epidemic"). Legal restrictions, he argues, just don't work. "First of all, when did banning anything ever work? We banned liquor once in this country. Ooh, that worked like a charm, didn't it folks? Why stop there? I know, let's not ban guns. Let's ban . . . crime!" This is his big laugh line.

This routine seems to me like the fertile soil in which the current right-wing and alt-right comedy, the weird alliance and overlap of libertarians and Christian nationalists, has flourished. I can see how we got from here to Chonda Pierce screaming about Hillary's emails on *Huckabee*. Today, right-wing commentators—including those whose shows could be filed under "comedy"—are whipping up a furor around the (big scare quotes here) "indoctrination" of children, pulling out homophobic arguments from the 1970s to try and convince lawmakers that drag queens are "grooming" children and queer teachers are somehow forcing children to transition their gender. The track easily runs from Brad Stine's "pagan government" to cries of "indoctrination," and the right-wing media is responding accordingly. During the writing of this chapter I heard the announcement both of a new kids' TV series launched by noted Christmas-warrior Kirk Cameron and an explicitly "anti-woke" streaming service for children's programming run by hyper-conservative media company The Daily Wire. (Just a moment of silence for the irony here of crying indoctrination and then building one's own special streaming service to teach kids the values you want. Okay.)

Stine is, in theory, doing some of the things that make jokes work—heightening, using energy and irony. But all of this is built on the shaky foundation of a faulty premise—a conception of reality that doesn't actually reflect what's going on in the world. Stine's jokes obviously don't stand up to a fact check; no one has ever sued McDonald's over their weight gain, countries that impose legal restrictions on firearms have significantly lower rates of gun violence, et cetera, et cetera. To find the joke funny, you have to buy into the set-up, and to buy into the set-up, you have to live in the same narrow, pessimistic worldview in which Stine lives: This world of no complexity, where everyone but you is whiny and stupid, and morality is black and white.

6. Hire me for your corporate event

> **Chonda Pierce:** I'm getting old, I'm cranky. I'm not funny anymore, I'm just bitter. But then you laugh, so you're sick.

Today, you won't find musings about Christian spirituality on Donald Miller's Instagram page or in his books. His blog has been scrubbed from existence. Happily, you won't find retweets from The Babylon Bee or jokes about liberal snowflakes, either. Instead, you'll find a clean, template-made website with a contact form to book Miller to speak at your business conference. You can look at his offerings on StoryBrand.com, where he offers steps to "Launch a StoryBrand Sales Funnel" by "clarify[ing] your message and build[ing] a marketing plan that works." Here, he is a clean-cut man in a business suit with tightly shorn hair. He doesn't look like the kind of person who would motorcycle up a mountain and sit there contemplating the universe with a pipe clenched between his teeth, but then again, maybe he is who this kind of person grows into. It seems like this is the current path for those who capitalized on the economic boom of Christian pop culture in the 2000s: Leverage those same marketing skills that helped you find a niche in evangelical pop culture to find a different gap to fill. For Christian comedians, it used to be clean or family-friendly comedy. Now, it's right-wing Christian nationalist media. For Miller, it was the Christian market for humour-laced memoir writing. But now he's churning out business books at an almost alarming rate (*Building a StoryBrand, Marketing Made Simple, Business Made Simple, How to Grow Your Small Business*).

Does this mean that Christian humourists are all sort of cynical figures? You might argue comedy is more entertainment than art, but I still feel that the best comedians are the ones who bring something genuine to the stage, who bare their soul, in a way—achieve that catharsis of laughter by reaching into the deepest or darkest or most uncomfortable parts of themselves. Despite Christian comedians trying to present their conservative views as "edgy" in a coddled, oversensitive world, they risk nothing, show no vulnerability, and are only attempting to expose others for *their* perceived vulnerabilities, what it is that makes them "snowflakes." Perhaps this entire category suffers from inauthenticity—a curse, maybe, passed down from its pioneer, Mike Warnke, whose entire life was a lie.

Donald Miller's 2022 book *Hero on a Mission: A Path to a Meaningful Life* is all about "playing a character." To get ahead, he writes, we must carefully choose which persona to take on:

> There are four characters in every story. The victim, the villain, the hero, and the guide. These four characters live inside us. If we play the victim, we're doomed to fail. If we play the villain, we will not create genuine bonds. But if we play the hero or guide, our lives will flourish. The hard part is being self-aware enough to know which character we are playing.

While I'm arguing a certain amount of cynicism on the part of these comedians, I also can see Miller's point about *which* character you choose to play. After all, on stage or on the page, anyone presenting themselves takes on a persona. And his points stand, somewhat: Brad Stine, yelling about being victimized by an oversensitive culture, failed spectacularly at making me laugh. I couldn't connect meaningfully with Donald Miller, portraying himself as a villain and taking on Christianity's "sins."

But what does it mean to "play the hero"?

It occurs to me that memoirs and comedy sets both offer a fair amount of cover for anyone attempting to make claims about things like religion, politics, how the world should be, or what's wrong with kids these days. If you like what the writer or comedian is saying, it's prophetic, revelatory. If you don't? Calm down, it's just a joke, it's just personal experience.

Brad Stine: Why is joking about people important? Well, how else are we going to tell you we're better than they are?

If there is a common thread between the seemingly-progressive-but-secretly-restrictive ideals presented by Donald Miller and the explicitly conservative, full-throated shouting of Brad Stine, I think it is the kind of joyless, tight humour that is only accessible to those who have already bought into the deeper message. As much as we might like to think there's something objective about humour—funny is funny is funny—it really does matter who's telling the joke and who's listening. Stine's most well-constructed, good-on-paper jokes just make me feel depressed, and Miller's flights of literary levity only irritate me.

What I understand now is that when, as a kid, I worried that Christians weren't funny, I was really worried about fitting in. It was me who didn't connect with the jokes, not the fault of the Christian improv troupes. And it turns out that whether something is funny or not is not the same as whether it's good, or true, or valuable, or hurtful, or destructive. Humour has a strange double-edged power to soften one's message and make it more accessible or to shut everyone out definitively. Miller's humour brought me in; those other Christian comedians shut me out.

In his book *Comedy Book*, Fox, interestingly, uses a religious allegory to portray the way comedy can feel like a community, likening comedy to a church in the wake of declining religious participation in North America. "Church isn't a place," he writes, "it's a people." There is something spiritual in a really good joke, something in its alchemy of being more than the sum of its parts, and drawing laughter, a semi-involuntary reaction, from you. Holy laughter has been a part of religions and spiritual communities throughout time for this magic, this transportive and bond-strengthening feeling. But for this warm feeling to exist, there has to be a genuine sense of joy.

I went home for Christmas recently. While sitting at my parents' kitchen table, playing a game with them and my partner, I did an actual spit-take, something that's never happened to me before. I can't remember what my dad said that I found so funny, just that suddenly—embarrassingly—a spray of IPA was rocketing out of my mouth and over their placemats. Maybe I don't want to remember the joke. It probably wasn't even that funny on its own. It's more about that warmth, being in a place where you feel safe, safe to laugh until you cry, until you spit your beer over the table.

CHAPTER NINE

ARMAGEDDON OUTTA HERE

ON LIVING IN THE END TIMES

> "I loved church. It was my life, my culture. I thought I believed everything there was to believe in the Bible. The Bible says that if you believe in Christ you have eternal life, so I assumed I was covered.... I thought I had a great life. I even went to Bible college. In church and at school, I said the right things and prayed in public and even encouraged people in their Christian lives. But I was still a sinner."
> *Left Behind,* p. 142

I exited the school bathroom and walked back down the empty hallway to class, my sneaker-squeak echoing on the tile floor. It was silent in the hall, and as I reached the classroom, still silent. I came level with the door and looked through the window: There were the lines of desks, the teacher's in the corner, and the whiteboard still full of the day's lesson—but no one inside. I looked down the hallway; rows of outdoor shoes lined up along the baseboard, under matching coat hooks hung with spring jackets, everything neatly in place. I could feel my pulse speeding up. Gingerly, I pulled open the classroom door. Unlocked. There was no sound, no movement inside, only the buzz of fluorescent light above, the sight of clouds silently moving across the sky out the classroom window. Not knowing what else to do, I returned to my desk, stood next to it. Loose pencils, open notebooks and stacks of binders dotted the desks around me, emitting an eerie feeling of absence. *Where had everyone gone?*

Just when panic started shooting into my bloodstream, the door cracked open, and my teacher appeared.

"There you are! The bell rang, everyone else is in music class."

Did anyone else experience panic attacks over the rapture? Someone asks on Reddit. There are hundreds of similar queries on the site, in r/exchristian and r/christianity alike. Particularly about the fear that the Rapture has happened, and you've been "left behind."

It's not a huge mystery where this idea comes from, considering its the title of the book series so closely identified with it.

Co-written by pastor and evangelical politico Tim LaHaye and Christian author Jerry B. Jenkins, the *Left Behind* book series was a smash hit for the Christian publishing industry upon its release in 1995, even cracking the *New York Times* bestsellers list—unheard of for Christian fiction. In the second-hand copy of the series' first book that I own—a 1998 reprint—the front and back pages are stuffed with quoted "praise" from secular outlets that read more like baffled journalists grappling with the fact of the book's success. "Tim LaHaye and Jerry B. Jenkins . . . are doing for Christian fiction what John Grisham did for courtroom thrillers," the *Time* pull quote reads; *USA Today* calls it a "wildly popular—and highly controversial—series of apocalyptic thrillers." The *Publishers Weekly* quote is simply a statement—"This is the most successful Christian-fiction series ever"—while the *Entertainment Weekly* one reads: "Christian thriller prophecy-based fiction. Juiced-up morality tale. Call it what you like, the

Left Behind series . . . now has a label its creators could never have predicted: Blockbuster success."

They're not wrong. Researcher Kristin Kobes Du Mez estimates that the book series has sold more than 65 million copies and cites a survey estimating that one in five Americans has read at least one of the books.

Such proliferation shows how easy it was to absorb LaHaye and Jenkins's vision of the apocalypse as a kid growing up Christian at the turn of the millennium. I never read the books as a kid, even though my school library was stocked with the colourful spines of *Left Behind: The Kids*, a young adult fiction adaptation that followed four adolescents through the Tribulation. I didn't have to read the books: I was already afraid. I somehow had absorbed the content inside anyway. I knew about the Rapture, the Good Christians being yanked suddenly up to heaven and leaving everyone else on Earth for seven years of terror and Tribulation. I knew about the Antichrist rising to power and taking over the world and stamping everyone with the Mark of the Beast. I knew it all had something to do with biblical prophecies and the Middle East, and I knew there were freaky signs involved—earthquakes and war and destruction and pestilence. I wasn't clear on the details, but I knew it was scary. And I knew about perhaps *Left Behind*'s biggest and best narrative innovation, which was the visualization of the Rapture: Christians disappearing and leaving in their wake every item of clothing on their body, streets and homes and beds littered with complete sets of empty clothes laid out neatly. Shoes leading into pants, crumpled under a buttoned shirt. Activities from a moment ago left frozen in time: water from the tap still running, coffee burning on the percolator. As a writer, I wonder if the authors of *Left Behind* can't credit a huge portion of their book's success to this eerie image.

In retrospect, the Rapture seems almost purpose built to scare children. The belief that suddenly all the good people will disappear in the blink of an eye, leaving the world careening into chaos? Terrifying.

I had my fair share of fears about being left behind—I knew, deep down, this was highly unlikely, but the possibility did cross my mind on occasion, when I came home to an empty house or misplaced my friends in a crowd. What *really* scared me was the possibility that I *wouldn't* be left behind—that the Rapture would happen and my life on Earth would be unceremoniously cut short.

Another Reddit post from March 2024 shows I was not alone—and, in fact, kids are still worrying about this.

Reasonable_Can6771 posted:

> *I'm scared the rapture will happen before I have a chance to live life.*
>
> I'm 17 and I see the world falling apart more and more by the day. The climate getting worse, the wars going on, the people in Hollywood being exposed. It scares me. I'm afraid the second coming will happen before I get the chance to go to college, meet a beautiful girl who can be my wife, get to be a father, accomplish my dreams. It's like life has no meaning because I'm so sure it's gonna end soon anyway.

As a teenager, I found the blog *Stuff Christians Like*, a blatant rip-off of the then-popular *Stuff White People Like* that sought to apply the same sense of humour to Christianity (with mixed results). The post I remember immediately connecting to, the one that made me laugh—and one of the first things to make me realize I wasn't alone in thinking this subculture I'd found myself in was so strange—was #64:

Fearing the rapture would come before you lost your virginity.

When I was in the 9th grade I had three fears that defined my life:

A. Zits.
B. Having Knights of the Round Table shirts instead of Polo.
C. That the rapture would come before I lost my virginity.

If I'm being honest on this site, that was a serious concern for me when I was a teenager. I just kept thinking about how mad I would be at God if the rapture came before I had sex. But really what would I say to him? Can you imagine me getting up to heaven and being like, "Really, today? You just had to rapture us today? I'm in college. I'm like 2 or 3 years away from getting married. What's the rush?"

Laying aside the inherent regressive views (and serious expectations about college dating—I guess he must have been going to Bible school) inherent to the post, I can still recall the feeling I got reading it the first time. It was kind of like absolution. *So, I'm not the only one who has worried about this,* I remember thinking.

I also remember a moment when I was younger—maybe 11 or so—spilling with the crowd of other kids onto the field where we had our recesses. It was a nice day, the kind of day that makes you remember you're alive. Warm sun, blue sky, healthy grass, puffy clouds. In the prairies, the sky looks so wide and flat, like it's pressing down on you. I remember being struck in that moment by a horrible fear that God would come back and rapture everyone within my lifetime—specifically, I was convinced He would come take us all to heaven before I became an adult, before I got the chance to grow up. I wasn't the biggest fan of being a kid. I really couldn't wait to just grow up and be an adult already. But what if I never got the chance? All the things I might not be able to do before the Rapture flicked through my head—have sex, yes, graduate high school and university, fall in love, publish a book. (Hey, I guess God can take me now!)

Even at the time, I felt embarrassed by this rush of feeling. It was silly, I knew that. At least, I thought I knew that. But then again . . . All I remember is the fear that gripped me so hard and sudden that I felt the need to stare up into the sky and pray, very fervently, to God not to come back until I was an old woman.[*]

♥ † ♥

> "I'm not going to push you into something you're not ready for, but just let me encourage you that if God impresses upon you that this is true, don't put it off. What would be worse than finally finding God and then dying without him because you waited too long?"
>
> *Left Behind*, p. 148

Scaring kids into Christianity by threatening the apocalypse isn't exactly new. My mother had her own experience with the 1970s iteration, a movie called *Thief in the Night* that stressed that Jesus could come at any hour. My father's great-aunt wouldn't allow her great-nephews and -nieces to go to movie theatres because "if Jesus comes back, he's not going to go in there to get you!"

In 2005, Harold Camping, an evangelical radio broadcaster, made a bold prediction: The Second Coming of Christ would take place on May 21, 2011.

---

[*] That way he could also spare me from dying, which was also a terrifying idea.

This was actually his third revision of his timeline. Originally, Judgment Day was supposed to be September 6, 1994, no wait, September 29, no wait, October 2. Of course, none of those guesses proved true, so he went back to the drawing board to come up with the 2011 date.

All of these predictions were based on some kind of biblical numerology calculations spelled out in his books, like *1994?* and the chillingly titled *We Are Almost There!* Reportedly, Camping brought in donations numbering in the millions after widely publicizing his Rapture prediction campaign. (On May 23, 2011, asked if he would return any of the donations, Camping replied, "Why would we return it?")

That publicity stretched from California all the way to the Canadian prairies, where a big billboard propped up next to Pembina Highway announced:

JUDGMENT DAY MAY 21
. . . Cry mightily unto God

And in the corner, in the little star-shaped word bubble typically slapped on sale flyers and "new and improved" formulas of cleaning supplies:

The Bible Guarantees It

According to a *Winnipeg Free Press* article from 2011, this billboard was one of a thousand that Camping's radio station, Family Radio, had paid to erect across the U.S. and Canada, with another two thousand overseas. In the article, Family Radio spokesperson Gunther von Harringa explains that the world has "been around for 13,023 years," but "God has exhausted his patience with the world. That's just the reality." Judgment Day would, supposedly, begin with a series of devastating earthquakes, starting in New Zealand ("We'll be able to see the chosen rise to heaven" because of the time difference, he notes), and slowly over the course of 153 days, the world will be destroyed. "'Then God will destroy the entire universe. Nothing will remain of planet Earth or its inhabitants,' Harringa said. 'Then God will create the universe all over again.'"

I would certainly not suggest that most evangelicals would have been on board with Camping's predictions. After all, there's always that old fallback, the verse that says no one will know "the day or the hour" of Christ's return, always available to quote to prove that the latest doomsday-sayer is a vaguely blasphemous fraud. No matter how carefully he's done the math.

But somehow that billboard, which went up the year I began university, represented to me the childhood fears that had held me in their grip for so long at Christian school.

Weirdly, the billboard was raised right at the intersection where I would have turned right while driving to school just over a year earlier. Now that I was going to university, I would bypass the turn and continue straight. It felt significant.

♥ † ♥

> "Up to a certain age, which is probably different for each individual, we believe God will not hold a child accountable for a decision that must be made with heart and mind, fully cognizant of the ramifications. You may also find that unborn children have disappeared from their mothers' wombs. I can only imagine the pain and heartache of a world without precious children, and the deep despair of parents who will miss them so."
> *Left Behind*, p. 153

Some sins weigh heavier on your conscience than others. I once told a lie that haunted me for years. It was during a classroom game of Never Have I Ever in junior high, on a day right before some holiday break where we were allowed to just play games rather than learn. Since it was a teacher-supervised version of the game, there was no drinking involved, just some kind of modified musical-chairs game mechanic where a person who didn't find a seat would be out. Also because of the teacher supervision, the *I have never*s were quite tame.

"Never have I ever," someone said, "read the whole Bible."

As a young, evangelical tween whose main hobby was reading, I had of course attempted to read the whole Bible. My teen study Bible, in fact, had a little breakdown in the back that showed what to read each day in order to read through the whole Bible in a year. I'd taken it as a personal challenge and a slightly guilt-motivated one—I'd read the whole *Harry Potter* series about ten times, so shouldn't I have read the entirety of the scriptures my religion was based on?

It was, unfortunately, not as gripping as *Harry Potter*. But I'd stuck it out, dazedly scanning through the columns of Leviticus and Numbers, flipping those tissue-thin pages of the Old Testament minor prophets, understanding nothing. I'd also been hoping that reading the whole Bible would help with the anxiety I felt around Christianity, the fundamental difficulties I had with the whole set-up of belief and some of the hypocrisies I saw around me. But I didn't find much of modern-day Christianity in the Bible. I didn't even find some of the stories that were in my little illustrated children's Bible (where was this whole business of the Devil being kicked out of heaven?) but I did find a whole lot of confusing stuff, like the cruelties Job suffered, or the destruction of Sodom and Gomorrah, the strange poetics of Song of Songs, and questionable instruction from the apostle Paul.

Still, I had suffered through and persevered. I had sunk hours of my life into reading that tome. So, when I heard that "never have I ever," I gritted my teeth and jumped up.

Only I and one other girl rose from our seats and quickly swapped chairs.

"Wow," said our teacher appreciatively. "Good for you."

Guilt bubbled in my stomach.

Because, actually, I hadn't read the whole Bible. After suffering through ancient poetry and endless genealogies and graphic stories of God smiting entire towns full of people, I'd reached the last book in the Bible: Revelation.

And there, I could go no further.

I tried. But I was instantly overwhelmed, gripped with fear. I knew what this book had in store for me. Stories of trials and tribulations and the end of the world—and even worse, on some level, descriptions of what happened *after* that.

I know many people who grew up in Christian spaces were terrified of hell, but I wonder if others were, like me, equally terrified of heaven. The horrors of damnation were a little too abstract for me to picture and thus didn't seem quite as pressingly awful. But anytime I tried to think, as I was often encouraged by preachers and teachers to do, about what it would be like to live forever in eternal glory, I felt my hands clam with sweat and my heart start palpitating.

What do you mean "forever"?

An elementary school teacher once told my class that heaven would be like this: "Imagine your favourite ice cream flavour, and how much you love eating that. Now multiply that by one hundred. That's the feeling you'll have in heaven, forever and ever."

Even that supposedly idyllic promise was horrifying. Forever and ever? I imagined myself bathed, entombed, in an endless river of bubblegum and tiger tiger.

Biblical imagery of heaven holds little of interest to a 2000s kid: streets of gold, angels circling and singing hymns for all of eternity. Not exactly a utopia crafted to intrigue a generation who just wanted to get home and log into their Neopets accounts in their family basements. The scope of it seemed both far too expansive—that terrifying existential spiral of trying to quantify eternity—and far too narrow. How could you possibly not imagine boredom, distaste? On Earth, the good things seem good because we have constant reminders to the contrary. How would it be to freeze all of life in a happy moment? Where, then, does meaning go? Isn't it only in struggle that we are able to construct our lives into something recognizable and satisfying?

These were the kinds of questions that would spiral through my mind whenever I cracked open the book of Revelation and attempted to be a Bible-reading completionist. For some reason, I couldn't even start reading. I told myself what I found there wouldn't be as bad as what I was imagining, but I just couldn't get over the fear.

♥ † ♥

Another book I couldn't read was *The Last Battle* by C.S. Lewis. It was the seventh and final book in the *Chronicles of Narnia* series and stood in, I gathered, for the apocalyptic narratives of Revelation the way *The Lion, the Witch, and the Wardrobe* allegorized Jesus and the Gospels.

The book opens with a story of an ape finding a lion's skin and dressing up his friend, the donkey, in it, preaching and gaining followers on the basis of this lion-ness, while really being a deceitful ape and donkey in disguise. I assumed this was supposed to be some kind of metaphor for the Antichrist, a figure I knew little about but also found—surprise, surprise—deeply frightening.

There was something about this ape story that scared me inordinately. It was unlike the fear from a horror movie; more like the fear that strikes alongside the uncanny, in the Freudian sense. It reminded me of the things that had scared me as a child, fears that my parents told me about as funny stories. I was scared of the *Barney* episode where the kids go camping. I was scared of *Scooby-Doo* and would watch it from around the corner, peeking just my eyes out from the kitchen to see the living room TV. I was so scared during the Mr. Bean movie, *Bean*, that I made my dad leave the theatre. These fears were not like being scared of the dark or of the evil witch in *Snow White* or of monsters coming to get you. These felt irrational and like deeper reactions than the simple surface stimuli—I felt there was some darkness lurking underneath the purportedly innocent children's entertainment. I dreaded the tenuousness of everything: What I'd been taught could happen, would happen, and destroy the world as I knew it.

I flipped to the last page of *The Last Battle*:

> And for us this is the end of all the stories, and we can most truly say that they all lived happily ever after. But for them it was only the beginning of the real story. All their life in this world and all their adventures in Narnia had only been the cover and the title page: now at last they were beginning Chapter One of the Great Story which no one on earth has read: which goes on forever: in which every chapter is better than the one before.

Dead, they were dead. Panic darted through my guts. I snapped the book shut and piled it under a stack of other books behind my bed. Eventually, I took it back downstairs and slipped it into the corresponding set on the family bookshelf. I never opened it again.

> "Strange as this may sound to you, this is God's final effort to get the attention of every person who has ignored or rejected him. He is allowing now a vast period of trial and tribulation to come to those who remain. He has removed his church from a corrupt world that seeks its own way, its own pleasures, its own ends."
>
> *Left Behind*, p. 154

These ideas about what Earth's end of days will look like are a relatively new ideological strain in Christianity.

The Rapture—this disappearance of Christians that frightened so many evangelical kids—was first expressed in the 1800s by Puritan theologians and refers to the idea that believers would be taken up to heaven before Jesus's second coming and judgment on Earth. There is no clear biblical basis for this concept, but the verse typically cited is 1 Thessalonians 4:17: "After that, we who are still alive and are left will be caught up together with them in the clouds to meet the Lord in the air. And so we will be with the Lord forever."

In the modern era, these ideas were popularized perhaps most widely by a man named Hal Lindsey. The author of several fearmongering books, including the Satanic Panic–spawning *Satan Is Alive and Well on Planet Earth*, he is perhaps most well-known for his 1970 book, *The Late Great Planet Earth*. Lindsey's book rested on the premise that the apocalypse was coming sooner than anyone might think, and his main evidence for this conjecture was his reading of certain verses in the Bible—the book of Revelation, yes, as well as certain Old Testament prophets—as predictions that were quickly coming true in the modern day.

In the 1979 made-for-television documentary special of the same name, Lindsey appears in '70s glory—denim jumpsuit, visible chest hair, moustache, and an extremely large gold Star of David medallion—to warn the world about the tribulations of the coming years. The film proclaims, "70 percent of the Bible's prophecies have already come true."[*] Over distressing stock footage, Lindsey lays out his reasoning for why everything from the 1973 oil crisis to famines in Africa and India are actually signs predicted in the Bible, pointing toward Jesus's hastening return. "I believe that we're racing on a countdown to the end of history," he declares.

---

[*] The narrator of this film is, for some reason, Orson Welles.

"Lindsey's version of the end times reflected the rampant pessimism of the younger generation and utilized the vernacular of the Jesus generation to engage his readers," Sara Moslener writes in *Virgin Nation*. "He helped college-age students make sense of global and local events and trends fraught with violence and confusion."

From today's vantage point, it's hard to understand why anyone would have sought out such a bleak offering, but in the crushing anxiety of the Cold War, I think I can understand the need to find meaning in geopolitical events and forces that seem so far beyond one's control. The book was popular in evangelical culture, as was the music of Larry Norman, a Lindsey devotee and hugely popular Christian rocker, who "had long been concerned with the end times and whose songs chronicled a culture in decline and anticipated large-scale destruction," Moslener writes.

Most famous was Norman's song, "I Wish We'd All Been Ready," which was sung in youth groups, played on Christian radio, and appeared in the end credits of *The Thief in the Night*, the film that tormented my mom. In the song, Norman paints vivid scenes of pairs of people—a husband and wife together in bed, two friends walking together—who are suddenly disrupted: In the flash of a moment, one is gone and the other is left behind. At the end of each verse, the haunting titular refrain, "I wish we'd all been ready."

"Though crafted to elicit fear and despair, the apocalyptic message shared by Lindsey and Norman situated the signs of a world in decline as part of a divine plan," Moslener asserts. "Just as Cold War fundamentalism offered prophetic explanations for the rise of the Soviet Union, Lindsey offered young evangelicals a way to cope with the violence and disruption of the 1970s. . . . In a new age of spiritual seekers, [Lindsey] popularized the idea of the Rapture by giving people a way to comprehend an incomprehensible future."

In 1972, Norman played this song to cap off an eight-hour-long Christian rock concert at Campus Crusade for Christ's Expo '72, in front of 100,000 people. Evangelical pop culture had fully embraced the Rapture and the horrors that went along with it—and would only continue to do so.

♥ † ♥

Hal Lindsey is still holding on, currently 94 years old. His website is still extremely active, constantly reposting old videos of sermons and his weekly show, *The Hal Lindsey Report*, where he compares current events to the ancient prophecies (and surprise, surprise, tends to find connections).

No one who listens to Lindsey's teachings seems to mind that none of his predictions have come true. In *The Late Great Planet Earth* TV special, he suggests that the 1980s might be the world's last decade; in a section talking about the pressures of a growing population (Paul Ehrlich of *The Population Bomb* fame is interviewed), the narration tells us, "It is well known that the Earth will be put out of resources by the year 2000."

While Lindsey's innovation was to link end times prophecies with the current-day threats of the Cold War, his perspective was merely a repackaging of a 19th century idea.

The Rapture as an idea gained traction primarily thanks to a theologian named John Nelson Darby and its inclusion in popular reference Bibles. Darby basically founded what is called *dispensationalism*, a school of Christian thought that divides history into eras (called *dispensations*) that mark shifts in how God interacts with his Chosen People. It is this strain of Christian thought that you can find at the root of Larry Norman's songs,

Hal Lindsey's books, and the *Left Behind* series. As Wikipedia neatly summarizes:

> Dispensationalists use a literal interpretation of the Bible and believe that divine revelation unfolds throughout the Bible. They believe that there is a distinction between Israel and the Church, and that Christians are not bound by Mosaic law. They maintain beliefs in premillennialism, Christian Zionism, and a rapture of the Church that will come before the Second Coming of Christ, generally seen as happening before a period of tribulation.

Dispensationalism is not a sect or denomination of Christianity but rather a way of believing that many Christians participate in, cutting across different denominations. With acceptance from the wider conservative evangelical segment of Christianity, it's become a popular (and sometimes singular) view in many Protestant churches, sometimes without even being named. I certainly didn't realize that I was being taught "dispensationalist theology" in school.

Perhaps that's why scratching at these belief systems makes my head spin; I was taught these things by the most literal interpreters of the Bible I've ever known, people who professed that being a Christian was just a matter of reading the Bible and following and believing exactly what it said, that it was all there in plain black and white, in absolute truth. And yet, here was this idea that had wound its way into the teaching I received that, beyond being only a couple hundred years old, was not really in the Bible at all.

In her book *The Armageddon Factor: The Rise of Christian Nationalism in Canada,* Marci McDonald relays her experience visiting Jerry Falwell's church in the mid-1980s, an "introduction to a scriptural scenario I'd never heard back in Ontario's mainline

Protestant pews." Falwell's "thunderous baritone" washed over the massive sanctuary "as he related his version of the Rapture—that mythic moment when some born-again Christians expect to be snatched up to salvation before the Battle of Armageddon."

Where does this idea come from? "Only a single verse in St. Paul's first epistle to the Thessalonians hints at that apocalyptic plotline, but Falwell had no hesitation about fleshing it out in vivid, updated detail," McDonald notes. The Moral Majority leader spun a vivid tale about believers blinking out of corporeal existence at any moment, even while driving their cars on the freeway.

> As it turned out, I wasn't the only one captivated by his imagery. More than a decade later, San Diego pastor Timothy LaHaye and his writing partner, Jerry Jenkins, released *Left Behind*, the first of their best-selling potboilers depicting life on earth in the wake of the Rapture, which opens with exactly that scene of global traffic mayhem. A longtime pal of Falwell's, LaHaye had been one of the Republican strategists who devised the notion of tapping into evangelical discontent to expand the party's base, and then christened the resulting constituency the Moral Majority. But it was later in his *Left Behind* novels that he provided the rationale for the Christian right's sense of urgency about effecting political change—the conviction that, with Armageddon looming, the faithful have not a moment to lose in preparing the way for the Second Coming of Christ.

Beyond writing these bestsellers, LaHaye was an active part of American politics, helping found the Moral Majority and serving on its board of directors. He helped both Ronald Reagan and George W. Bush get elected and served as Mike Huckabee's spiritual advisor in 2007. He also founded the anti-2SLBGTQIA+

American Coalition for Traditional Values and the Pre-Trib[ulation] Research Centre, explicitly focused on promoting his end-of-days theological views. While I knew him only as a name on the cover of these books that stocked the shelves at Christian bookstores and Costco alike, LaHaye had a heavy thumb on the scale of American politics as early as the 1970s.

All of this doomsaying was good business. As historian Paul Boyer points out to PBS *Frontline*:

> Apocalyptic belief has become big business. It's become an industry. It's a subset of the publishing industry... And books that become successful literally sell millions of copies. And what we're seeing is a kind of synergistic process where a successful televangelist will publish a book which is successful, which will then spin off into videotapes and movies and sometimes prophecy magazines, and even we have bumper stickers and wristwatches and other kinds of material, all of which reinforce popular belief and interest in Bible prophecy.

If Lindsey pioneered this capitalization, LaHaye and Jenkins perfected it. *Left Behind* became a 16-book series and spawned a three-film series in the early 2000s, a young adult series (*Left Behind: The Kids*) with over 40 entries, a spinoff book series, a graphic novel adaptation, a video game series, a soundtrack album, and, most recently, a 2014 film adaptation of the first book, starring Nicolas Cage as pilot Rayford Steele.

The plot of the series is a fairly straightforward rundown of "pre-tribulation" theology, laying out what LaHaye and Jenkins believe will happen during the promised Second Coming of Christ: First, the Rapture, when all the Christians disappear from Earth and are taken up to heaven; then, Tribulation, a seven-year period in which all hell breaks loose on Earth (no pun intended), and a shadowy figure called the Antichrist rises to power; then, finally, Judgment Day, when Jesus returns to sort everybody neatly into heaven or hell for the rest of eternity. The books follow four poor souls who chose not to follow Jesus and were thus *left behind*—pilot Rayford Steele and his daughter Chloe, straight-shooting journalist prodigy Buck Williams, and formerly insincere Pastor Bruce Barnes—as they become Christians and form the Tribulation Force, determined to spend the next seven years saving souls and kicking the butts of God's enemies.

The beats are cribbed neatly from '80s and '90s thriller-action flicks, complete with assembling a team and some tacked-on romantic plotlines. All of this in service, I suppose, of introducing the secular public to the terrors they will face if they don't turn to Jesus—and quick.

♥ † ♥

> "I believe the Bible teaches that the Rapture of the church ushers in a seven-year period of trial and tribulation, during which terrible things will happen. If you have not received Christ as your Savior, your soul is in jeopardy. And because of the cataclysmic events that will take place during this period, your very life is in danger. If you turn to Christ, you may still have to die as a martyr."
> *Left Behind*, p. 155

As a kid, I felt like a bad Christian for being so scared of the Rapture. After all, wasn't that supposed to be what we were all waiting for—a time when we would be whisked off into heaven?

In actuality, I now see pop culture products like the *Left Behind* series as part of a very intentional method of Christian programming—attempts to scare kids into religion, to put it bluntly. Or in the more academic language of researcher Jason Bivins, to connect "fears of damnation to a carefully identified range of sociopolitical practices and beliefs." Picking up the language and purposes of earlier movements like the Moral Majority and the Save the Children campaign, but leaving behind overt political messaging, "the narratives of evangelical popular culture position children or adolescents as victims of the nation's failure to observe biblical prohibitions."

I saw this clearly at play when I cracked the spine of *Left Behind: The Kids* (book one, *The Vanishings*). I'd steered clear of these books in my school library, put off equally by the end times content and the graphic design—black covers popping with bands of neon colours, signalling a young adult version of the fast-paced John le Carré- and Grisham-style thrillers they were supposed to be. But I'd always been a bit curious what those kids were up to in the apocalypse.

The answer is basically the same thing the adults are up to in the regular *Left Behind* books. The first books in each series cover the same events (the Rapture and formation of a Tribulation Force of demonic-power-fighting heroes), and the kid characters are all tangentially connected to the adults from the main series: Judd Thompson Jr. is on pilot Rayford Steele's flight when the Rapture strikes; Vicki Byrne and Lionel Washington are connected to the Chicago church at which the Tribulation Force forms; and Ryan Daley is friends with Rayford's son. In all but Ryan's case, the kids lose their entire families to the Rapture, which makes the repetition of each of their stories pretty obnoxious; Ryan alone has non-Christian parents, but they are quickly disposed of when they die in auto and plane accidents caused by the disappearance of random drivers and pilots. (One difficulty I have morally with this conception of the end times is that it feels like God wouldn't want to be responsible for so many auto deaths—but, whatever.) Despite being for kids, the subject matter and content seemed nearly identical—the adult version was so unbelievably chaste and milquetoast that the kids' version actually seemed slightly more intense. And though there was less overt violence depicted in *The Kids*, I was surprised at how many references to suicide it retained. Also, as cringey as the narrative voices sometimes sounded in *Left Behind*—the voices of two right-wing evangelical authors trying and failing to sound like secular humanists—this problem was even worse in *The Kids*; now it was two right-wing evangelical men trying to sound like secular *teenagers*. You can't help but feel the narration is fighting constantly against snapping back into a parental perspective.

"[Judd's] mother picked that day to ask him to bring in the mail. . . . Judd sighed loudly at his mother's request. She said he acted like any small chore or favor was the biggest burden in the world. That was exactly how he felt. He didn't want to be told to do anything."

I was surprised at how familiar the story seemed, how much had seeped into my consciousness without me ever reading it. Not only about the details of the Rapture and the Tribulation but the specific language that accompanied discussions of the nuances of what it meant to be saved.

Vicki, who is introduced as *the rebel*, witnesses her parents immediately change all their ways when they become Christians at a revival service in their trailer park. They give up drinking and smoking and swearing and start going to church every Sunday, and suddenly they also decide to stop being racist. Vicki seems to represent the wayward soul who's never heard the Good News. Ryan, by contrast, is labelled *the skeptic* and is supposed to be the one who relies too much on science and reason to accept Jesus into his heart. Judd and Lionel are both ostensibly Christian but not "real Christians"—neither good enough to get taken up to heaven. Judd's main problem seems to be that he "cops an attitude," as the book puts it. Lionel, however, looks like the perfect Christian boy but secretly doesn't believe.

The "types" represented by each of the teens seem like shorthand for the demographics the writers are hoping to reach: skeptics, rebels, and teens raised Christian but starting to explore other options. But the *Left Behind: The Kids* characters also show how difficult it is to fit into the narrow definition of someone worthy of heaven, in LaHaye and Jenkins's estimation. The only way to ensure passage to heaven, it seems, is to not only be a cheerful and obedient kid who never does anything bad but also to be perfectly doubt-free and inordinately confident in your faith at all times.

Slowly over the course of the book, each kid discovers that they are home alone and finds the evidence of their parents being whisked up to heaven, their clothes and dental fillings left strewn on the spot where they sat or lay at the moment of the Rapture. It seems calculated to play on a pressing childhood anxiety—to be left alone, completely alone, orphaned; your entire family victim of something beyond your control. Abandonment, really.

If you were a child growing up in an evangelical community in the 2000s, there was plenty on offer to scare you. You might be invited to a Halloween Hell House, the Christian antidote to a haunted house, where rather than ghouls and vampires you'd be treated to tableaus of the horrors that would befall you if you didn't redeem your soul and were taken by the Devil. You might be subjected to interpretive theatrical productions set to music—sometimes called *Drime* (an amalgamation of drama and mime) or *human videos*—that offered creepy morality plays. Maybe the "Lifehouse Everything Skit," where a teenager is offered an increasingly intense series of temptations (drinking, sex, drugs!) before being shielded from an onslaught of his demons by another teen playing Jesus, arms outstretched, to the emotional swell of the background accompanying music. Or you might read a book by Ted Dekker or Frank Peretti featuring supernatural hauntings or a mystery that turned out, *Scooby-Doo*-like, to always have been perpetrated by the Devil.*

---

* Peretti's novels are quite dark, even for this genre. Famously (or maybe infamously), one featured protagonist is an abortion doctor being haunted by the fetuses he's terminated. One year, a teacher read from Peretti's *The Hangman's Curse* to our class, a novel that includes descriptions of a teen boy hanging himself from a school stairwell.

Now that I'm an adult, I find all this a little baffling. Why would you intentionally want to scare children, especially if your goal was to get them on your side?

I suppose the point was to impress upon us the urgency of the situation. In *Left Behind*, Rayford Steele becomes born-again in the wake of his wife's rapture and tries continually to convince his university-age daughter, Chloe, to accept Christ as well. She keeps telling him she's not quite ready, which sends him into a panic. The world has become dangerous, now that a chunk of the population has disappeared, and he obsesses over the possibility that she might die before she has become born-again.

Throughout, it seems the authors are trying to imply that this is not so different from the situation in which Christians currently live. I've heard something to this effect before, when it comes to proselytizing: *If someone you loved was in a building that was on fire, wouldn't you tell them to get out and try to save them?* Anyone could die at any moment and end up in hell but for one little prayer, the logic follows. So why wouldn't you use any means necessary to make them pray that prayer?

> "If Bruce Barnes was right, the disappearance of God's people was only the beginning of the most cataclysmic period in the history of the world. *And here I am*, Rayford thought, *worried about offending people. I'm liable to not offend my own daughter right into hell.*"
>
> *Left Behind*, p. 250

Something else comes to mind when I think about urgency and the end of the world.

I was shown *An Inconvenient Truth* in high school by a teacher who, when pressed, told us that it was his personal belief that we had nothing to worry about—climate change was merely part of a natural process in Earth's orbit where the planet moved closer and further away from the sun, and over time, everything would self-correct. This did not sit well with me.

By my teenage years, I had fairly effectively quashed my worries about the end of the world by simply trying never to think about it and tuning out whenever someone started referencing Revelation or the Rapture. Just in time, a new and much more pressing anxiety arrived to take its place. I didn't have to worry about the potential end of the world, it seemed, because the world appeared to be ending right before my very eyes.

Despite the fact that I hadn't yet developed the best sense of political and social consciousness, I could still see the changes in the world around me, on the news and in the air. What do I remember from that time? Natural disasters: the massive tsunami that hit Thailand in 2004, Hurricane Katrina in 2005; news of the ice caps melting; fears about acid rain and the ozone layer (all the hair products switching away from aerosolized cans). I remember the jokes in so-called "Winterpeg" about global warming—*We could use a little of that!*—but also the adults around me marvelling at the shifts in weather patterns in their own lifetimes: later winters, hotter summers, more volatile weather patterns. *Highest flood on record, hottest summer on record, coldest day on record, first tornado in southern Manitoba*—I remember those kinds of superlatives lacing the nightly news.

At the same time, Al Gore and his documentary were at the forefront of a push in the late 2000s to get popular sentiment on board with environmentalism. I could see this playing out in my media consumption in real time. All my favourite NBC sitcoms suddenly adopted "green week" once a year. There were youth-focused pushes on MTV and MuchMusic. I remember watching a televised benefit called *Flick Off* that was ostensibly promoting—between pop music performances—the idea of turning off the lights when you left a room to save electricity. There was some kind of hope in it, I suppose—this was a moment in time when I was still under the misapprehension that all of this climate damage was reversible, and more widespread cultural recognition meant that we were surely going to *do something about it*—but mostly I felt overwhelmed by the paucity of response to such a large issue. The facts I'd learned about the quick retreat of the glaciers in the Arctic and the massive swell of the Pacific Garbage Patch seemed wildly out of step in scale to committing to turn off the lights in my bedroom and unplug my laptop charger when it wasn't in use.

And then, another crushing blow: In 2008, the economy collapsed. I was 16, and I didn't know economies *could* collapse. Yet another globally significant event, taking place on my television screen, shaking the things I had unconsciously thought of as unfailingly stable.

For some end times preachers, the 2008 financial crisis was yet another fatalistic sign. For me, it was just a sign that capitalism was fucked. But I was particularly haunted by the news coverage that told me about American voters quickly shifting priorities in the run-up to the presidential election. I remember watching a graphic that showed climate change diving down to the bottom of the list, replaced by "the economy." It made sense, of course, but I felt a mournful pang. Any flicker of hope I'd felt seeing the popular push toward climate action was squashed out. And I still had no idea what to do about it.

It was never a foregone conclusion that evangelicalism would end up being so closely associated with climate change denialism. But that fate played out, you guessed it, in the early 2000s.

In his book *The Jesus Machine*, Dan Gilgoff recounts the saga of Richard Cizik, a prominent evangelical voice who attempted to push climate change—or rather, climate *care*—as a central evangelical issue with the creation of the Evangelical Climate Initiative campaign. In 2006, the group put out its petition, "Climate Change: An Evangelical Call to Action," signed by 86 evangelical leaders and pastors and presidents of 39 evangelical colleges; the total signatories would eventually grow to 220 by 2011. The "Call to Action" promoted itself with television spots and full-page ads in the *New York Times* and *Christianity Today*.

Logically, this position seems to make sense—for a group trying to brand themselves as pro-life, what could be more life-affirming than protecting the very source of life on Earth? In some strains of Christianity, like the tradition I grew up going to church in, nature is positioned as God's "creation" and therefore next to holy—it is the prerogative of God's people to protect and nurture it. Christians will often talk of "stewardship" when it comes to the natural environment, a positioning premised on the belief that God has charged humanity with looking after His creation.

This very well might have been the official position of the National Association of Evangelicals in the United States if Cizik had had his way, but instead, it was opposed by the Interfaith Stewardship Alliance. Signatories included prominent evangelical speaker (and former Nixon "hatchet man") Chuck Colson and Focus on the Family founder James Dobson.

Gilgoff writes:

> In the eyes of Dobson and other Christian Right leaders . . . the Evangelical Climate Initiative was not only a concession to its liberal enemies, but a threat to the movement's core agenda: fighting same-sex marriage, abortion, and the removal of religion from the public square. America's cultural crisis was too dire for the evangelical movement to be distracted by a bunch of Christian tree huggers.

The initiative failed to make a splash with conservative evangelical heavy-hitters, and though the NAE's more liberal contingent signed on, environmentalism also didn't seem to gain traction in the wider evangelical movement. Instead, there was general backlash and attacks from other prominent evangelicals, like Republican Senator James Inhofe, who denounced environmentalism as "an attack on the very heart of evangelical faith."

Nearly 20 years later, evangelical Christianity at large has all but abandoned the environmentalist cause. "Polls show that white American evangelicals are the only major religious group to largely disbelieve climate science and to oppose action on climate change," Josiah Neufeld writes in *The Temple at the End of the Universe*. "Surveys that control for factors such as political loyalties, education levels, and media exposure reveal that a commitment to evangelical Christianity is the trait most consistently associated with climate skepticism."

♥ † ♥

> "Something had happened in the disappearances of loved ones all over the globe. Journalism might never be the same. Oh, there would be skeptics and those who worshiped objectivity. But what had happened to brotherly love? What had become of depending on one another? What had happened to the brotherhood of men and nations?"
>
> *Left Behind*, pp. 178–79

If it hasn't become clear already, a lot of these so-called predictions in the Bible have to do with Israel.

I really didn't plan on writing about Christian Zionism, but it turns out it's completely unavoidable. As Marci McDonald argues in *The Armageddon Factor*, the mainstream adoption of this dispensationalist theology is a major driver of Christian Zionism, and right-wing Zionist policies, in North America.

In brief, Christian Zionism is the belief that Jewish sovereignty in modern-day Israel is both God-ordained and necessary to fulfill biblical prophecies. (The founding of the state of Israel in 1948 is seen as an explicit fulfillment of Old Testament prophecies.) Specifically, the "gathering of Israel," referred to in the book of Deuteronomy, is meant to take place before the return of Christ. Since Christian Zionists are not Jewish, they also tend to believe that this return to a Jewish homeland will be accompanied by a mass conversion of Jewish people to Christianity, which puts them in the strange position of supporting Israel but completely invalidating Judaism as a religion. Over the past century or two, Christian Zionism has become completely enmeshed with general evangelical belief; tens of millions of evangelical churches in the U.S. "strongly support Israel for religious reasons," and the organization Christians United for Israel boasts ten million members. A Pew Research Center survey in 2003 found that 60 percent of evangelical Christians in the U.S. "agreed that the existence of Israel fulfilled biblical prophecy," and a similar poll in 2017 by LifeWay placed that number at 80 percent of evangelicals. When President Donald Trump moved the US Embassy from Tel Aviv to Jerusalem in 2017, he was "met with rapturous gladness by his evangelical supporters as the fulfillment of a biblical propecy," Jewish researcher Talia Levin writes.

In Canada, in 2003, while I was probably being subjected to some preacher in a school assembly telling us how the Antichrist is going to try to implant microchips under our skin,[*] Stephen Harper was giving a speech in which he "called for a foreign policy based on morality," McDonald writes. "A criterion that he equated with unflinching support for Israel." She attributes this as part of a way to ensure the Jewish and Christian Zionist vote for the

---

[*] This is unfortunately a real sermon that I remember.

Conservatives, and I would venture to guess it was also a sincere part of Harper's own belief system.

The strange thing about Christian Zionism, is that its proponents seem both intensely Zionist and antisemitic. Perhaps because at the heart of it, they are trying to hasten Israel's control over Jerusalem *so that* everyone can be destroyed by another global power. There is, of course, no care for the Palestinians being displaced, but neither is there concern over the entire city that will, in their predictions, be completely wiped out in the course of the Tribulation. As Talia Levin puts it in her book *Wild Faith*: "Christian Zionists love Jews like a hungry man loves a chicken wing; it's an interest born out of need whose end is total consumption."

Left Behind walks this same line, belying a completely unquestioning support of Israel politically while still making constant use of antisemitic stereotypes—Jewish characters are shady, power-hungry power brokers operating in the shadows.

In *The Late Great Planet Earth* documentary, we get a brief historic interlude on the founding of the state of Israel, all in the passive voice. Palestinians "who had dwelt there for centuries," *were displaced*, the narration explains, as though it just happened one day. All political agency is again removed, these actions once again portrayed as almost natural happenings in fulfillment of ancient prophecies, not the outcome of a complex series of geopolitical choices and actions.

In the film, this section is accompanied by stock footage taken in contemporary Israel, in the middle of a bustling, modern city. When the narration begins to reference the displacement of Palestinians, the film suddenly cuts to footage of a lone older man, a shepherd it seems, walking through a scrubby field next to a couple of sheep.

When I heard these end times predictions as a child, I was ignorant of any history. *The Holy Land*, as the doomsdayer preachers I heard speak would call this area of the world, was an abstraction to me, a place I knew only as it had existed a few thousand years ago, a place I had only read about in the Bible. I was more preoccupied with the visions of terrifying angels and dragons and horsemen in the Revelation story and didn't absorb the political implications. Returning to the subject now was shocking and difficult. Not least because, as I write this, an ongoing genocide rages in Palestine. The Israel Defense Forces forces have killed more than 50,000 people. Daily, I see horrifying news of death and destruction, in refugee camps that are meant to be safe; the shelled-out hollows of hospitals and schools; the horrific images of violence that can't be unseen. It is a kind of apocalypse.

And I can see, in real time, evangelical Christians choosing to ignore the violence or even support it. Immediately after Hamas's October 7 attack, an "Evangelical statement in support of Israel" was released, signed by more than two thousand evangelical leaders who said they "fully support Israel's right and duty to defend itself against further attack." That support continued as attacks raged on, bloodier and bloodier; Christians United for Israel had raised and disbursed more than $3 million to Israel by March 2024, and the *Associated Press* reported a wave of evangelical "volunteerism," with young Americans flying across the ocean to support the IDF.

As countless Jewish activist groups have expressed to be Jewish—in religion or culture—does not mean to be Zionist; just as to be opposed to the actions of the Israeli government is not inherently antisemitic. It appears that many Christian Zionists are incapable of making this distinction, and they offer only blind support. But of course, only in service of hastening their own vision of the end of the world. They don't seem to care about the way the world ends for hundreds of thousands of people—the victims of the violence, the famines, the earthquakes, the wars that they see as portents of biblical truth. These human lives turn into pieces of *evidence*, abstracted like non-player characters in a video game.

♥ † ♥

> "It doesn't make any difference, at this point, why you're still on earth. You may have been too selfish or prideful or busy, or perhaps you simply didn't take the time to examine the claims of Christ for yourself. The point now is, you have another chance. Don't miss it."
> *Left Behind*, p. 156

After taking in everyone else's interpretation of the book of Revelation, I decided I should finally read this thing that had haunted me so much in my childhood.

Reading Revelation is kind of like reading about someone else's fever dream or listening to someone who's tripping on salvia describe what they're seeing.

Most of the book is the writer, identified as John—but apparently not the one from the Gospel or the three epistles—relaying a very complicated vision he's had while on the remote island of Patmos. It's hard to parse. Strange creatures keep popping up—a dragon waiting to devour a woman's baby as soon as she births it; a beast with ten horns and seven heads that looks like a leopard with bear's feet and a lion's mouth but is coming out of the sea; the beast that comes out of the earth that "had two horns like a lamb, but it spoke like a dragon." (Whatever that means.) It's not surprising to me that there was a pretty conflicted historical debate about whether to include this book in the Bible. Even as late as the Protestant Reformation, this weird book was barely hanging onto its place in the canon by the skin of its teeth; Martin Luther included it in his 1522 edition of the New Testament but said that he thought there were better books that could be kept in the Bible instead, since no one could figure out what this one meant.

Traditionally, theologians have fallen into four main schools of thought about how to read Revelation. There are the *historicists*, who see the book as an allegorical reading of history that has already passed; the *preterists*, who also view the events of Revelation as happening in the past, though usually, in their case, entirely in the first century or in the time of the Roman Empire; the *idealists*, who don't think the events laid out in the book will or have happened at all but are merely allegories for a struggle between forces of good and evil; and the *futurists*, who believe the events of Revelation will happen in a time yet to come.

It's kind of strange to me that in my evangelical school and the evangelical pop culture I encountered, the futurist (also called millennialist) view was presented so completely and without asterisks that I didn't even realize there *could* be other views.

My fear of Revelation might have driven me right out of Christianity, except that, as an adult, I discovered *leftist liberation theology*.* Writers from this school of thought see the book as a fable about how the churches John was writing to could live in the world without succumbing to, or assimilating into, oppressive systems. It's not much of a stretch to read the evils represented by beasts and evil sexy ladies in the text as standing in for imperialism or nationalism or even capitalism and the righteous imagery as working toward an ideal of peace and justice. I'd even heard the assertion that some of the wacky language in the text was meant as a sort of code to evade censors of John's messages (he was in government-imposed exile, after all). Again, the imagery and language are elastic enough to really make any interpretation fit.

But I still never read it until I began writing this book. I had felt safer thinking that this was not, after all, the portent of the Tribulation to come. But something still freaked me out about it.

---

* Liberation theology arose out of Latin American Catholicism but has been adapted by theologians and thinkers from marginalized and oppressed cultures around the globe. It sees the ultimate Christian project as liberation of the oppressed and is associated with left-wing politics, pacifism, and social justice activism.

Even reading Revelation with no context, it seems clear that unless you want to discount all of it as the ramblings of someone who's been alone on an island staring at the sun for too long, you're going to have to take most of it as symbolism or metaphor.

The problem is, of course, agreeing on what the symbols represent. And when it comes to the dispensationalist version of the end times, another pertinent question seems to be: Why are some elements from Revelation taken as symbols and others as literal? While the beasts rising from the oceans and the earth are seen as metaphors for human leaders rising up, are the earthquakes and fire that will rain down on Earth supposed to be just earthquakes and fire?

If you start looking for signs, you can easily find them.

As I finally read through the book of Revelation, I began to understand something else. The mind wants to look for patterns; we want to make sense of things as we read them. As far as I know, as a layperson reading this ancient text in translation via a free website, the text might as well have been written by ChatGPT. But as I read, I could feel my brain trying to make connections. I kept having thoughts like *this beast sounds like capitalism,* or *these plagues sound like current-day climate change.* I could feel the symbols sucking me in, feel myself trying to assemble them into some kind of cosmology that makes sense with my own viewpoint on the world, the way reality is currently arrayed around me. Suddenly, I could understand Hal Lindsey in some small way. It's satisfying, the feeling of flicking a light switch like you've made a connection—the way people feel when they get sucked into a conspiracy theory or finish a Sudoku puzzle.

♥ † ♥

"I've been convinced," she said, "but I'm still fighting. I'm supposed to be an intellectual. I have

critical friends to answer to. Who's going to believe this? Who's going to think I haven't lost my mind?"
Left Behind, p. 293

In an essay for the National Endowment of the Humanities' magazine, religion scholar Timothy Beal points out that the *Left Behind* books and films represent "the changing face of evangelical apocalyptic culture." Compared with *The Late Great Planet Earth* and movies like *A Thief in the Night*, the series made a clear shift "away from horror and toward thrill," he writes. "In them, apocalyptic dread has become apocalyptic anticipation."

He continues:

> In *A Thief in the Night*, being left behind really was a living nightmare, abandoned in a creepily dull, God-forsaken Iowa wasteland.... In the *Left Behind* movies, on the other hand, as in the novels and video game, the postrapture [sic] world is where all the action is. Here we have an apocalyptic thriller, as our heroes, the "tribulation saints," lead the ultimate resistance movement against the ultimate bad guy: the Antichrist, Nicolae Carpathia, whose name and Bela Lugosi–like accent suggest a sort of evil descendant of Bram Stoker's original invader from the Carpathian Mountains. In these movies, unlike in *Thief*, we almost feel bad for the ones who got raptured. They are missing out on all the excitement.

"But to be frank, I no longer have time for the pleasantries and small talk that used to characterize my work. We live in perilous times. I have a message

> and an answer for people genuinely seeking. I tell everyone in advance that I have quit apologizing for what I'm going to say. If that's a ground rule you can live with, I have all the time you need."
>
> *Left Behind*, p. 306

This shift into thriller territory might go deeper than a change in media trends.

Writing about the rise of Christian nationalism in Canada, journalist Marci McDonald notes: "What drives that growing Christian nationalist movement is its adherents' conviction that the end times foretold in the book of Revelation are at hand. Braced for an impending apocalypse, they feel impelled to ensure that Canada assumes a unique, scripturally ordained role in the final days before the Second Coming—and little else."

This tunnel vision might explain why hundreds of young Christians could be mobilized for causes such as abstinence and anti-abortion, while "ignoring the perils of global warming," and why the Christian right has birthed a powerful Christian Zionist lobby, "convinced that the end times of biblical prophecy will only materialize after the Jewish homeland has been restored to its Old Testament might."

While *The Late Great Planet Earth* seemed almost laughably staunch in its attempt at apoliticism—showing footage of Democratic and Republican presidents alike over a voiceover about the power of a potential Antichrist—*Left Behind* seems to be on the other end of the spectrum. By the end of the first novel, protagonist Buck Williams finds himself in a high-powered, revolutionary meeting of the UN, mere feet away from the seat of power, as the Antichrist declares himself ruler of a one-world government. Though the group of characters at the centre of the story are ostensibly "normal" people, it's clear from the jump that they will be where the action is throughout the Tribulation, playing out a Christian action-hero fantasy where they will save lives and souls.

Likewise, the book's authors, and those who subscribe to their version of apocalyptic foretelling, are not content to sit back and look for signs of the end of the world.

"Aggressive and insistent, [Christian nationalists] are driven by a fierce imperative to reconstruct Canada in a biblical mold," McDonald writes. Their agenda "is ultimately exclusionary," she says: "In their idealized Christian nation, non-believers—aethesists [sic], non-Christians and even Christian secularists—have no place, and those in violation of biblical law, notably homosexuals and adulterers, would merit severe punishment and the sort of shunning that once characterized a society where suspected witches were burned. Theirs is a dark and dangerous vision, one that brooks no dissent and requires the dismantling of key democratic institutions."

The United States offers a "preview," she adds, of "decades of religious-right triumphs" that have "left a nation bitterly splintered along lines of faith and ideology, trapped in the hysteria of overcharged rhetoric and resentment."

McDonald's warnings are strongly worded, but unlike end times predictions, hers seem to be coming true. If the United States was "bitterly splintered" and "trapped in the hysteria of overcharged rhetoric" in 2010, when McDonald's book was published, how much more so is it today? The meteoric rise of the alt-right, the ascendancy of Donald Trump, the festering of harmful conspiracies, a global pandemic that particularly decimated the U.S., the rollback of abortion rights, and constant attacks on 2SLGBTQIA+ rights jump immediately to mind. These strains are alive and well in Canada, too—and though not exclusive to right-wing evangelicals and Christian nationalists, all are enabled and backed by their hands

In all, I begin to understand more clearly where the end times soothsayers and doomsday hopefuls are coming from as they look for signs of the end. It all makes me feel quite doomy. And it's hard to keep going in the face of that feeling. How nice would it be to find some external locus on which to hang all of that horror? Some source of hope.

How nice would it be to think that none of this mattered because you are among the privileged few who will be saved? How nice would it be to see a pattern in the madness? To think that we would soon wipe the slate and be made good and new—a new Earth, new bodies, no more conflict, only joy. How nice would it be to know that you're above it all?

♥ † ♥

> "They moved through the terminal toward the parking garage, striding four abreast, arms around each other's shoulders, knit with a common purpose. Rayford Steele, Chloe Steele, Buck Williams, and Bruce Barnes faced the gravest dangers anyone could face, and they knew their mission.
>
> The task of the Tribulation Force was clear and their goal nothing less than to stand and fight the enemies of God during the seven most chaotic years the planet would ever see."
>
> *Left Behind*, p. 339

And yet.

The Bible itself, especially Jesus's story, is about humility and suffering.

I could never really give myself over to a way of belief that required hard-heartedness, a willingness to leave people to certain destruction. I couldn't do it then, and I can't do it now.

"What do you know about freedom?" asks the duplicitous ape in C.S. Lewis's *The Last Battle*.

"You think freedom means doing what you like. Well, you're wrong. That isn't true freedom. Freedom means doing what I tell you."

For ten years at Christian school, my childhood and adolescence, I tried to find freedom that way. I thought that when things seemed uncomfortable or strange or even painful, it was a fault of my own, not the systems and environment around me. I thought if I could just do what I was told, think the way I was taught to, I could find some kind of freedom. I could live with the comfort and confidence that the adults around me said would come along with these kinds of beliefs. But it never worked.

When I finally read *The Last Battle*, I no longer felt afraid. But I did feel sad. The promise at the end—the characters' journey into eternal life in the glowing City on the Hill—used to feel too much, too big, overwhelming in its eternity, enough to inspire fear in me. Now, it was the opposite; what was offered seemed too small. It was an anticlimax: a view of perfection that offered nothing but descriptions of beauty. Nothing like the grip of emotion and conflict offered by the "real" world. It's the shortness, the precariousness, of life that makes our daily lives interesting. That feeling of a beautiful too-small-ness was hollow. Is that all there is?

Writing this book has been a process of coming closer to, and further from, faith, prompting shifts in my understanding that make me rethink what has shaped me before I knew better, before I understood that I was young and moldable. "For now we see through a glass, darkly," the apostle Paul wrote, "but then face to face. Now I know in part; but then shall I know even as also I am known."

Maybe the real promise of heaven isn't about its goodness at all. The real promise of heaven is the promise of certainty. To finally *know*, entirely, what this life had all been about.

"I have come home at last!" Lewis's unicorn says, as he leaps through the grass in Narnia's version of heaven. "This is my real country! I belong here. This is the land I have been looking for all my life, though I never knew it till now. The reason why we love the old Narnia is that it sometimes looked a little like this."

What could heaven be if it were not a place above the clouds? Coming home at last: the thing that feels right, that you honestly never want to end. The metaphors for heaven, the light and sweetness and streets paved with gold, are unmoving because they are too rooted in the quotidian, but Lewis's unicorn says we only pick those associations because they reflect a tiny sliver of heaven.

We could take that feeling of homecoming, or rootedness, safety, security, wonder, joy, and cut out the tribulations and raptures that make up the metaphorical middle. That could be heaven. The comfort of a loving hand grasping yours; that feeling just after you finish a really good cry; a perfectly ripe peach; the comfortable silence between you and your closest friend; laughter; the coolness of a breeze; standing with your feet in the ocean; your dog's little warm head on your lap; your favourite song. That would mean we'd need to recognize heaven when it's right in front of our eyes. If only we'd really look.

SOURCES

INTRODUCTION

Klein, Linda Kay. *Pure: Inside the Evangelical Movement That Shamed a Generation of Young Women and How I Broke Free* (Atria Books, 2018).

Kobes Du Mez, Kristin. *Jesus and John Wayne: How White Evangelicals Corrupted a Faith and Fractured a Nation* (Liveright, 2020).

NIV Bible. Matthew 28:19. BibleGateway.com.

Radosh, Daniel. *Rapture Ready! Adventures in the Parallel Universe of Christian Pop Culture* (Scribner, 2008).

Statistics Canada. "Census Profile, 2021 Census of Population." Revised November 15, 2023. https://www12.statcan.gc.ca/census-recensement/2021/dp-pd/prof/index.cfm?Lang=E.

Vaca, Daniel. *Evangelicals Incorporated: Books and the Business of Religion in America* (Harvard University Press, 2019).

Wheaton College, Institute for the Study of American Evangelicals. "How Many Evangelicals Are There?" Revised 2012. https://web.archive.org/web/20160130062242/http://www.wheaton.edu/ISAE/Defining-Evangelicalism/How-Many-Are-There.

CHAPTER ONE

GMA Dove Awards. "Superchick - 'Barlow Girls' (33rd Dove Awards)." PAX TV, airdate April 25, 2002. https://www.youtube.com/watch?v=hMkHYqrXYl4.

Jump5. "Spinnin' Around." Music video, 2002. https://www.youtube.com/watch?v=pB8Nb5iuIK0.

Know Your Meme. "Nu Thang." Accessed August 29, 2024. https://knowyourmeme.com/memes/nu-thang.

Rice, Chris. "Cartoons (Live)." *Short Term Memories*, track 17. Rocketown Records, 2004. https://www.youtube.com/watch?v=sZObQuoaEQc.

Superchick. "Barlow Girls." Song lyrics. *Karaoke Superstars*, track 1, 2001. https://songmeanings.com/songs/view/102100/.

CHAPTER TWO

Amazon. "*Revolve: The Complete New Testament* (Biblezines)." Accessed September 18, 2023. https://www.amazon.com/Revolve-Complete-New-Testament-Biblezines/dp/B003E7F1BE.

BarlowGirl. "Clothes." Self-titled album, track 8. Fervent Records, 2004. https://www.youtube.com/watch?v=mFQsOo8blEc.

BarlowGirl. "Clothes." Song lyrics, 2004. https://genius.com/Barlowgirl-clothes-lyrics.

Cameron, Sue. "The Bare Facts." *Brio*, July 2006. https://web.archive.org/web/20080729043046/http://www.briomag.com/briomagazine/healthandbeauty/a0006816.html.

Cosper, Mike, host. *The Rise and Fall of Mars Hill* (podcast), episodes 4 and 5.

Edwards, Stassa. "The Return of *Brio*, the Christian Teen Magazine I Hated to Read." Jezebel, July 13, 2017. https://

jezebel.com/the-return-of-brio-the-christian-teen-magazine
-i-hated-1796677818.

Family.org. "*Secret Keeper: The Delicate Power of Modesty* by Dannah Gresh." Sales page. Archived October 23, 2006. https://web.archive.org/web/20061023082610/https://www.family.org/resources/itempg.cfm?itemid=5674.

Gilgoff, Dan. *The Jesus Machine: How James Dobson, Focus on the Family, and Evangelical America Are Winning the Culture War* (St. Martin's Press, 2007).

Google Books. "NIV, Boys Bible." Book overview. Accessed August 30, 2024. https://www.google.ca/books/edition/NIV_Boys_Bible/TFZ48IyaKcEC?hl=en&gbpv=0.

Gresh, Dannah. "What Advertisers Know About Your Body!" *Brio*, 2002. https://web.archive.org/web/20040415035250/http://www.briomag.com/briomagazine/healthandbeauty/a0004123.html.

Hollinger, Herb. "Biblical Manhood, Womanhood Conference Makes Note of Southern Baptists' Stance." *Baptist Press*, March 23, 2000. https://www.baptistpress.com/resource-library/news/biblical-manhood-womanhood-conference-makes-note-of-southern-baptists-stance/.

Johnson, Jessica. *Biblical Porn: Affect, Labour, and Pastor Mark Driscoll's Evangelical Empire* (Duke University Press, 2018).

Kasza, Marty. "Modelling Modesty." *Brio*, 2004. https://web.archive.org/web/20050420030532/http://www.briomag.com/briomagazine/healthandbeauty/a0005126.html.

Klein, Linda Kay. *Pure: Inside the Evangelical Movement That Shamed a Generation of Young Women and How I Broke Free* (Atria Books, 2018).

Kobes Du Mez, Kristin. *Jesus and John Wayne: How White Evangelicals Corrupted a Faith and Fractured a Nation* (Liveright, 2020).

Moslener, Sara. *Virgin Nation: Sexual Purity and American Adolescence* (Oxford University Press, 2015).

New Life Ministries. "Bounce Your Eyes." Accessed August 30, 2024. https://newlife.com/bounce-your-eyes/.

NIV Bible. Ecclesiastes 1:9. BibleGateway.com.

NIV Bible. Matthew 5:27–29. BibleGateway.com.

NIV Bible. Romans 14:13–15. BibleGateway.com.

O'Connor, Anahad. "In Sex, Brain Studies Show, 'la Différence' Still Holds." *The New York Times*, March 16, 2004. https://www.nytimes.com/2004/03/16/health/in-sex-brain-studies-show-la-difference-still-holds.html.

Partin, Rory. "Straight from a Guy." *Brio*, 2001. https://web.archive.org/web/20041028104723/http://briomag.com/briomagazine/relationships/a0004406.html.

Radke, Heather. *Butts: A Backstory* (Simon & Schuster, 2022).

Reddit. "Blushing Bride or Miss Piggy?" Photo of an old *Brio* article. Accessed August 30, 2024. https://www.reddit.com/media?url=https%3A%2F%2Fpreview.redd.it%2Fupdate-brio-magazine-project-v0-mpazr48vz42c1.jpg%3Fwidth%3D3024%26format%3Dpjpg%26auto%3Dwebp%26s%3D7755bf40c5bac08b44aff863a2cc6e24076e0469.

Reddit. Photos of an old *Brio* issue, posted by FebFaith03 in 2022. https://www.reddit.com/r/FundieSnarkUncensored/comments/vcn8xk/has_anyone_ever_heard_of_these_they_are_called/#lightbox.

Wikipedia. "Council on Biblical Manhood and Womanhood." Accessed August 30, 2024. https://en.wikipedia.org/wiki/Council_on_Biblical_Manhood_and_Womanhood.

Wikipedia. "Mars Hill Church." Accessed August 30, 2024. https://en.wikipedia.org/wiki/Mars_Hill_Church.

Willingham, Emily. "Universal Desire: Men and Women Respond Identically to Erotic Images." *Scientific American*, July 18, 2019. https://www.scientificamerican.com/article/universal-desire-men-and-women-respond-identically-to-erotic-images/.

CHAPTER THREE

Aaron, Charlene. "Kendrick Bros Taking Their Films Beyond Sherwood." CBN.com. Accessed September 5, 2024. https://www2.cbn.com/news/us/kendrick-bros-taking-their-films-beyond-sherwood.

ABC News. "'*Fireproof*' Shows Christian Movies Sell." October 2, 2008. https://abcnews.go.com/Entertainment/story?id=5941016.

Bernard, Jami. "Gore's the Crime of '*Passion*': Over-the-Top Brutality Saps Movie's Power." *New York Daily News*, February 24, 2004. https://web.archive.org/web/20240209154127/https://www.nydailynews.com/2004/02/24/gores-the-crime-of-passion-over-the-top-brutality-saps-movies-power/.

Bernard, Jami. "Week of Real Hatred: News Film Critic Jami Bernard Suffers Backlash to *'Passion'* Review." *New York Daily News*, February 29, 2004. https://www.nydailynews.com/2004/02/29/week-of-real-hatred-news-film-critic-jami-bernard-suffers-backlash-to-passion-review/.

Bond, Paul. "Box Office Shocker: How Moviemaking Georgia Church Behind '*Courageous*' Outperforms Hollywood." *The Hollywood Reporter*, October 13, 2011. https://www.hollywoodreporter.com/news/general-news/sherwood-pictures-courageous-248204/.

Catholic League for Religious and Civil Rights. "*The Passion of the Christ*." Organizational responses, 2004. https://www.catholicleague.org/the-passion-of-the-christ/.

Chattaway, Peter T. "Hollywood? No, SHER-wood!" *Christianity Today*, September 23, 2008. https://www.christianitytoday.com/2008/09/fireproof-a/.

Chattaway, Peter T., with Mark Moring. "'*Fireproof*' Is Hot." *Christianity Today*, December 2008. https://www.christianitytoday.com/2008/11/fireproof-is-hot/.

Chilton, Louis. "The Blood, the Outrage and *The Passion of the Christ*: Mel Gibson's Biblical Firestorm, 15 Years On." *The Independent*, February 25, 2019. https://www.independent.co.uk/arts-entertainment/films/features/passion-of-the-christ-15-years-mel-gibson-jim-cavieziel-movie-reaction-christianity-a8788381.html.

Ebert, Roger. "*The Passion of the Christ*." RogerEbert.com. February 24, 2004. https://www.rogerebert.com/reviews/the-passion-of-the-christ-2004.

Erwin, Andrew and Jon, dir. *October Baby*. Provident Films, Samuel Goldwyn Films, 2011.

Erwin Brothers Entertainment. "About." https://erwinbrothers.com/about/.

Eternal World Television Network. "Notes on the Correct Way to Present the Jews and Judaism in Preaching and Catechesis in the Roman Catholic Church." First published in *L'Osservatore Romano* (newspaper of the Holy See), July 1, 1985. https://www.ewtn.com/catholicism/library/notes-on-the-correct-way-to-present-the-jews-and-judaism-in-Preaching-and-catechesis-in-the-roman--catholic-church-2480.

Ewing, Heidi, and Rachel Grady, dir. *Jesus Camp*. Magnolia Pictures, A+E Networks, 2006.

Feddes, Morgan. "The Problem with '*October Baby*,' a Christian Film About Abortion." *Christianity Today*, March 21, 2012. https://www.christianitytoday.com/2012/03/christian filmmaking/.

Foust, Michael. "'*Fireproof*' Has Made Millions, But It's Split Multiple Ways." *Baptist Press*, November 14, 2008. https://www.baptistpress.com/resource-library/news/fireproof-has-made-millions-but-its-split-multiple-ways/.

Gamerman, Ellen. "Candace Cameron Bure Wants to Put Christianity Back in Christmas Movies." *The Wall Street Journal*, November 14, 2022. https://www.wsj.com/articles/candace-cameron-bure-great-american-family-11668205295.

Great American Pure Flix (streaming service). https://www.pureflix.com.

IMDb. "*The Passion of the Christ: Resurrection.*" Accessed September 5, 2024. https://www.imdb.com/title/tt5795232/.

Johnson, Lucas L. "2 Bible Belt Filmmakers Expand Box Office Horizons." Associated Press via *The Tennessean*, August 3, 2014. https://www.tennessean.com/story/news/local/2014/08/03/bible-belt-filmmakers-expand-box-office-horizons/13544983/.

Lawton, Kim. "Church Movies Keep Coming." *Christianity Today*, April 20, 2011. https://www.christianitytoday.com/2011/04/churchmoviescoming/.

Longeretta, Emily. "Great American Family's TV Rise: CEO Bill Abbott on Candace Cameron Bure Backlash and Why His Network Is 'For All People.'" *Variety*, October 25, 2023. https://variety.com/2023/tv/news/great-american-family-ceo-candace-cameron-bure-backlash-1235763798/.

Moring, Mark. "Facing the Critics." *Christianity Today*, September 26, 2008. https://www.christianitytoday.com/2006/09/alexkendrick/.

Newcomb, Tim. "Faith-Based Filmmaking: The Sherwood Pictures Crusade." *TIME*, August 25, 2011. https://web.archive.org/web/20110905173549/http://www.time.com/time/arts/article/0,8599,2090429-2,00.html.

Porter, Kevin T., and Caroline Ely, hosts. "*Blue Like Jazz* (with James Austin Johnson)." *Good Christian Fun* (podcast), April 21, 2021. https://podcasts.apple.com/gb/podcast/blue-like-jazz-with-james-austin-johnson/id1276704640?i=1000518018555.

Pringle, Gil. "*The Nativity Story*: There's Something About Mary." *The Independent*, December 1, 2006. https://www.independent.co.uk/arts-entertainment/films/features/the-nativity-story-there-s-something-about-mary-426445.html.

Sanneh, Kelefa. "How Christian Is Christian Nationalism?" *The New Yorker*, March 27, 2023. https://www.newyorker.com/magazine/2023/04/03/how-christian-is-christian-nationalism.

Sherwood Baptist Church. "About Us." Accessed February 8, 2023. https://old.sherwoodbaptist.net/about-us/.

Sherwood Baptist Church. "Sherwood Pictures." Accessed February 8, 2023. https://old.sherwoodbaptist.net/ministries/sherwood-pictures/.

Storm, Alison, host. "Before Making Movies the Kendrick Brothers Starred in Chickfila Training Videos." *My Pleasure: The Unofficial Chick-fil-A Podcast*, December 1, 2021. https://numberonecombo.com/before-making-movies-the-kendrick-brothers-starred-in-chickfila-training-videos/.

Susman, Gary. "Charged Performance." *Entertainment Weekly*, October 24, 2003. https://web.archive.org/web/20130525182358/http://www.ew.com/ew/article/0,,525927,00.html.

Susman, Gary. "Gibson Cuts Controversial Scene from '*Passion*.'" *Entertainment Weekly*, February 4, 2004. https://ew.com/article/2004/02/04/gibson-cuts-controversial-scene-passion.

United States Conference of Catholic Bishops. "Guidelines for Catholic-Jewish Relations." Revised 1985. https://www.usccb.org/prayer-and-worship/liturgical-year/lent/guidelines-for-catholic-jewish-relations.

Vogler, Christopher. *The Writers Journey: Mythic Structure for Writers*. First edition, 1992 (Michael Wiese Productions, 2020).

Wikipedia. "Christian Zionism." Accessed September 5, 2024. https://en.wikipedia.org/wiki/Christian_Zionism.

Wikipedia. "Great American Media." Accessed September 5, 2024. https://en.wikipedia.org/wiki/Great_American_Media.

Wikipedia. "Hero's Journey." Accessed September 5, 2024. https://en.wikipedia.org/wiki/Hero%27s_journey.

Wikipedia. "Installation Abortion." https://en.wikipedia.org/wiki/Instillation_abortion.

Wikipedia. "*Jesus* (1979 Film)." Accessed September 5, 2024. https://en.wikipedia.org/wiki/Jesus_(1979_film).

Wikipedia. "*Sound of Freedom* (Film)." Accessed September 5, 2024. https://en.wikipedia.org/wiki/Sound_of_Freedom_(film).

CHAPTER FOUR

Beahm, Anna. "Josh Harris, a Key Purity Culture Figure, Created a Course on Losing Your Faith. A Firestorm Ensued." Reckon News, August 19, 2021. https://www.reckon.news/honey/2021/08/josh-harris-a-key-purity-culture-figure-created-a-course-on-losing-your-faith-a-firestorm-ensued.html.

Cills, Hazel. "The Rise and Fall of the Pop Star Purity Ring." Jezebel, January 25, 2018. https://jezebel.com/the-rise-and-fall-of-the-pop-star-purity-ring-1822170318.

Ethridge, Shannon, and Arterburn M. Stephen. *Every Young Woman's Battle: Guarding Your Mind, Heart, and Body in a Sex-Saturated World* (Multnomah Books, 2004).

Graham, Ruth. "Hello *Goodbye*." *Slate*, August 23, 2016. https://slate.com/human-interest/2016/08/i-kissed-dating-goodbye-author-is-maybe-kind-of-sorry.html.

Goins-Phillips, Tré. "Film Distributor Drops Joshua Harris' Documentary After Being Blindsided by Author Saying He's No Longer Christian." Faithwire, August 29, 2019. https://www.faithwire.com/2019/08/29/film-distributor-drops-joshua-harris-documentary-after-being-blindsided-by-author-saying-hes-no-longer-christian/.

Harris, Joshua. *I Kissed Dating Goodbye: A New Attitude Toward Relationships and Romance* (Multnomah Books, 1997).

"Jordin Sparks Is Amazing." MTV VMAs, airdate September 7, 2008. YouTube video posted September 8, 2008, by amylvsjb. https://www.youtube.com/watch?v=qYQ8IKxrnDM.

"Katy Perry - Like a Virgin (Live MTV Music Video Awards) HD." MTV VMAs, airdate September 7, 2008. YouTube video posted August 12, 2012, by Stamonline. https://www.youtube.com/watch?v=PLhHqqpo8LA&t=3s.

Klein, Linda Kay. *Pure: Inside the Evangelical Movement That Shamed a Generation of Young Women and How I Broke Free* (Atria Books, 2018).

Klett, Leah MarieAnn. "Joshua Harris Says '*I Kissed Dating Goodbye*' Will Be Discontinued, Apologizes for 'Flaws.'" *Christian Post*, October 23, 2018. https://www.christianpost.com/news/joshua-harris-says-i-kissed-dating-goodbye-will-be-discontinued-apologizes-for-flaws.html.

Kobes Du Mez, Kristin. *Jesus and John Wayne: How White Evangelicals Corrupted a Faith and Fractured a Nation* (Liveright, 2020).

Lenz, Lyz. "Recovering from *I Kissed Dating Goodbye*: A Roundtable." *The Toast*, June 8, 2016. https://the-toast.net/2016/06/08/recovering-from-i-kissed-dating-goodbye-a-roundtable/.

Moslener, Sara. *Virgin Nation: Sexual Purity and American Adolescence* (Oxford University Press, 2015).

No Shame Movement (platform). Accessed September 6, 2024. https://noshamemovement.tumblr.com/.

Payne, Ed. "Group Apologizes to Gay Community, Shuts Down 'Cure' Ministry." CNN, July 8, 2013. https://www.cnn.com/2013/06/20/us/exodus-international-shutdown/index.html.

Sessions Stepp, Laura. "Study Casts Doubt on Abstinence-Only Programs." *The Washington Post*, April 14, 2007. https://www.washingtonpost.com/wp-dyn/content/article/2007/04/13/AR2007041301003.html.

Unaltered Ministries (online store). "UN Lifestyle Ring." https://www.lifeunaltered.com/collections/featured-products/products/un-lifestyle-ring.

Unaltered Ministries. https://www.unaltered.org/.

CHAPTER FIVE

Andrew-Gee, Eric. "Conservatives Vow to Establish 'Barbaric Cultural Practices' Tip Line." *The Globe and Mail*, October 2, 2015. https://www.theglobeandmail.com/news/politics/conservatives-vow-to-establish-barbaric-cultural-practices-tip-line/article26640072/.

Catalini, Mike, Julie Carr Smyth, and Bruce Shipkowski. "Trump Campaign Falsely Accuses Immigrants in Ohio of Abducting and Eating Pets." *Associated Press*, September 11, 2024. https://apnews.com/article/haitian-immigrants-vance-trump-ohio-6e4a47c52b23ae2c802d216369512ca5.

CBS News. "CIA Chief: No 'Imminent Threat.'" February 24, 2004. https://www.cbsnews.com/news/cia-chief-no-imminent-threat/.

Denvir, Daniel. "A Short History of the War on Christmas." *Politico*, December 16, 2013. https://www.politico.com/magazine/story/2013/12/war-on-christmas-short-history-101222/.

Evangelical Council for Financial Accountability. "The Voice of the Martyrs." Accessed September 19, 2024. https://www.ecfa.org/MemberProfile.aspx?ID=12238.

Giesbrecht, Libby. "Balloons Launched into North Korea Banned by South Korea." CHVN, December 19, 2020. https://chvnradio.com/articles/balloons-launched-into-north-korea-banned-by-south-korea.

Gilgoff, Dan. *The Jesus Machine: How James Dobson, Focus on the Family, and Evangelical America Are Winning the Culture War* (St. Martin's Press, 2007), p. 194.

KJV Bible. Matthew 5:11–12. BibleGateway.com.

Kobes Du Mez, Kristin. *Jesus and John Wayne: How White Evangelicals Corrupted a Faith and Fractured a Nation* (Liveright, 2020).

Levin, Talia. *Wild Faith: How the Christian Right is Taking Over America* (Legacy Lit, 2024).

Moss, Candida. *The Myth of Persecution: How Early Christians Invented a Story of Martyrdom* (HarperCollins, 2013).

Murray, Lorraine. "Murder Most Horrid: The Grisliest Deaths of Roman Catholic Saints." *Encyclopaedia Brittanica*. Accessed September 19, 2024. https://www.britannica.com/list/murder-most-horrid-the-grisliest-deaths-of-roman-catholic-saints.

NIV Bible. Luke 6:29. BibleGateway.com.

NIV Bible. Philippians 3:7–14. BibleGateway.com.

O'Reilly, Bill. "Christmas Under Siege: The Big Picture." Fox News, December 24, 2004. https://www.foxnews.com/story/christmas-under-siege-the-big-picture.

Riedel, Samantha. "Trump Vows to Create a Task Force That Combats 'Anti-Christian Bias' if Reelected." *Them*, September 12, 2024. https://www.them.us/story/trump-vows-to-create-a-task-force-that-combats-anti-christian-bias-if-reelected.

Sibley, Robert. "Harper Breaks the Great Political Taboo — Again." *Ottawa Citizen*, October 15, 2008. https://ottawacitizen.com/opinion/harper-breaks-the-great-political-taboo-again.

Smith, Michael W. "This Is Your Time." Music video, 2000. https://www.youtube.com/watch?app=desktop&v=lgXotghvz4A.

The Voice of the Martyrs and DC Talk. *Jesus Freaks* (Albury Publishing, 1999).

The Voice of the Martyrs. "Our Founders." Accessed September 19, 2024. https://www.persecution.com/founders/.

Wikipedia. "Foxe's *Book of Martyrs*." Accessed September 19, 2024. https://en.wikipedia.org/wiki/Foxe%27s_Book_of_Martyrs.

Wikipedia. "King James Version." Accessed September 19, 2024. https://en.wikipedia.org/wiki/King_James_Version.

Wikipedia. "*Saving Christmas*." Accessed September 19, 2024. https://en.wikipedia.org/wiki/Saving_Christmas.

Williams, Roger Ross, dir. *God Loves Uganda*, 2013.

Wilkinson, Alissa. "After Columbine, Martyrdom Became a Powerful Fantasy for Christian Teenagers." *Vox*, April 17, 2019. https://www.vox.com/culture/2017/4/20/15369442/columbine-anniversary-cassie-bernall-rachel-scott-martyrdom.

Zafar, Walid. "Ergun Caner, Ex-Muslim Evangelical Leader, Exposed as Fake." *The Huffington Post*, May 19, 2010. https://www.huffpost.com/entry/ex-muslim-evangelical-exp_b_582225.

CHAPTER SIX

Badlands Amphitheatre. "Badlands Passion Play." Accessed September 19, 2024. https://badlandsamp.com/badlands-passion-play/.

Big Valley Creation Science Museum. "Welcome." Accessed September 19, 2024. https://bvcsm.com/.

Bishop, G., R. Thomas, J. Wood, and M. Gwon. "Americans' Scientific Knowledge and Beliefs about Human Evolution in the Year of Darwin." *Reports of the National Center for Science Education* 30, no. 3 (May–June 2010): pp. 16–18.

Discovery Institute. "What Is Intelligent Design?" Accessed September 19, 2024. https://intelligentdesign.org/whatisid/.

Dobbin, Murray. "The Man Who Walks with Dinosaurs." *The Tyee*, December 1, 2004. https://thetyee.ca/Views/2004/12/01/TheManwhoWalkswithDinosaurs/.

Evans, Robert, host. "Part One: Kent Hovind: Fake Dinosaur Scholar and Accidental Child Killer." *Behind the Bastards* (podcast), May 28, 2024. https://podcasts.apple.com/nz/podcast/part-one-kent-hovind-fake-dinosaur-scholar-and/id1373812661?i=1000657009354.

Ewing, Heidi, and Rachel Grady, dir. *Jesus Camp*. Magnolia Pictures, A+E Networks, 2006.

Ham, Ken. *How Could a Loving God . . . ? Powerful Answers on Suffering and Loss* (New Leaf Publishing Group, 2007).

KJV Bible. Genesis 1:27–28. BibleGateway.com.

McDonald, Marci. *The Armageddon Factor: The Rise of Christian Nationalism in Canada* (Random House, 2010), p. 182.

McDowell, Josh, and Bob Hostetler. *Don't Check Your Brains at the Door: A Book of Christian Evidences* (Word Publishing, 1992).

Mortenson, Terry. "Young-Earth Creationist View Summarized and Defended." Answers in Genesis. Accessed September 19, 2024. https://answersingenesis.org/creationism/young-earth/young-earth-creationist-view-summarized-and-defended/.

NIV Bible. Acts 17:11. BibleGateway.com.

NIV Bible. Genesis 1:1. BibleGateway.com.

Rosenhouse, Jason. *Among the Creationists: Dispatches from the Anti-Evolutionist Front Line* (Oxford University Press, 2012).

Thomas, Antony, dir. *Questioning Darwin*. HBO documentary, 2014.

Town of Drumheller (civic website). Accessed September 19, 2024. https://www.drumheller.ca/.

Wikipedia. "Curse of Ham." Accessed September 19, 2024. https://en.wikipedia.org/wiki/Curse_of_Ham.

Wikipedia. "Intelligent Design." Accessed September 19, 2024. https://en.wikipedia.org/wiki/Intelligent_design.

Wikipedia. "Kent Hovind." Accessed September 19, 2024. https://en.wikipedia.org/wiki/Kent_Hovind.

Wikipedia. "Michael Farris (Lawyer)." Accessed September 19, 2024. https://en.wikipedia.org/wiki/Michael_Farris_(lawyer).

Wikipedia. "Scopes Trial." Accessed September 19, 2024. https://en.wikipedia.org/wiki/Scopes_trial.

Wikipedia. "Stockwell Day." Accessed September 19, 2024. https://en.wikipedia.org/wiki/Stockwell_Day.

Wikipedia. "Young Earth Creationism." Accessed September 19, 2024. https://en.wikipedia.org/wiki/Young_Earth_creationism.

CHAPTER SEVEN

30 Rock (TV show). "Chain Reaction of Mental Anguish." Season 5, episode 9. NBC, airdate December 2, 2010.

Amazon. "Easy Read, Good Writing Style." Review of *Under the Overpass* by Travel Light, April 1, 2022. https://www.amazon.ca/product-reviews/1590524020/ref=cm_cr_unknown?ie=UTF8&filterByStar=three_star&reviewerType=all_reviews&pageNumber=1#reviews-filter-bar.

Andrade, Chittaranjan. "Prayer and Healing: A Medical and Scientific Perspective on Randomized Control Trials." *Indian Journal of Psychiatry* 51, no. 4 (Oct–Dec 2009): 247–53. https://www.ncbi.nlm.nih.gov/pmc/articles/PMC2802370/.

Andrade, Gabriel. "The Ethics of Positive Thinking in Healthcare." *Journal of Medical Ethics and History of Medicine* (December 21, 2019): 247–53. https://www.ncbi.nlm.nih.gov/pmc/articles/PMC7166246/.

Bowler, Kate. *Blessed: A History of the American Prosperity Gospel* (Oxford University Press, 2013).

Claiborne, Shane. *The Irresistible Revolution: Living as an Ordinary Radical* (Zondervan, 2006).

Changing Your World Bookstore. "Frankincense Anointing Oil." Creflo Dollar Ministries, product listing. Accessed September 24, 2024. https://cywestore.com/products/frankincense-anointing-oil.

Changing Your World Bookstore. "Trust, Relax, and Rest Candle — Novelty." Creflo Dollar Ministries, product listing. Accessed September 24, 2024. https://cywestore.com/products/trust-relax-and-rest-candle-novelty.

Gjelten, Tom. "How Positive Thinking, Prosperity Gospel Define Donald Trump's Faith Outlook." *All Things Considered*, NPR, August 3, 2016. https://www.npr.org/2016/08/03/488513585/how-positive-thinking-prosperity-gospel-define-donald-trumps-faith-outlook.

Goodstein, Laurie. "He's a Superstar Pastor. She Worked for Him and Says He Groped Her Repeatedly." *The New York Times*, August 5, 2018. https://www.nytimes.com/2018/08/05/us/bill-hybels-willow-creek-pat-baranowski.html.

Hinch, Jim. "How the Pandemic Radicalized Evangelicals." *Los Angeles Review of Books*, August 15, 2021. https://lareviewofbooks.org/article/how-the-pandemic-radicalized-evangelicals/.

Joel Osteen Ministries. "Store: Gifts." Accessed September 24, 2024. https://www.joelosteen.com/store/gifts.

Kenneth Copeland Ministries. "Question of the Day: How Much Is a Hundredfold Return?" Accessed September 24, 2024. https://www.kcm.org/read/question-of-the-day/how-much-hundredfold-return?language_content_entity=en-US.

KJV Bible. 1 Timothy 6:10. BibleGateway.com.

Longhurst, John. "Early Cancer Death of Prosperity Gospel Preacher Leon Fontaine Raises Questions for His Followers." *Faith Today*, January 16, 2023. https://www.faithtoday.ca/Magazines/2023-Jan-Feb/Early-cancer-death-of-prosperity-gospel-preacher-L.

McDonald, Marci. *The Armageddon Factor: The Rise of Christian Nationalism in Canada* (Random House Canada, 2010), p. 260.

Miracle Channel. "Fontaine Family Statement." November 24, 2022. https://www.miraclechannel.ca/leonfontaine.

Moll, Rob. "The New Monasticism." *Christianity Today*. September 2005. https://www.christianitytoday.com/2005/09/new-monasticism/.

Neufeld, Josiah. *The Temple at the End of the Universe: A Search for Spirituality in the Anthropocene* (House of Anansi, 2023), p. 48.

NIV Bible. Matthew 7:7. BibleGateway.com.

NIV Bible. Matthew 19:24. BibleGateway.com.

Roys, Julie. "Willow Creek Community Church Announces Closure of Chicago Campus." *The Roys Report*, February 5,

2024. https://julieroys.com/willow-creek-community-church-announces-closure-of-chicago-campus/.

The Simple Way. "Our Story." Accessed September 24, 2024. https://thesimpleway.org/about/#our-story.

Springs Church. "Our Senior Pastor." Accessed September 24, 2024. https://springschurch.com/our-senior-pastor/.

Stringer, Sam. "Minister Creflo Dollar Asks for $60 Million In Donations for a New Jet." CNN, March 16, 2015. https://www.cnn.com/2015/03/13/living/creflo-dollar-jet-feat/index.html.

Vaca, Daniel. *Evangelicals Incorporated: Books and the Business of Religion in America* (Harvard University Press, 2019), p. 3.

Van Biema, David, and Jeff Chu. "Does God Want You to Be Rich?" *TIME*, September 10, 2006. https://time.com/archive/6596739/does-god-want-you-to-be-rich/.

Wikipedia. "Christ Cathedral (Garden Grove, California)." Accessed September 24, 2024. https://en.wikipedia.org/wiki/Christ_Cathedral_(Garden_Grove,_California).

Wikipedia. "Creflo Dollar." Accessed September 24, 2024. https://en.wikipedia.org/wiki/Creflo_Dollar.

Wikipedia. "Kenneth Copeland." Accessed September 24, 2024. https://en.wikipedia.org/wiki/Kenneth_Copeland.

Wikipedia. "Law of Attraction (New Thought)." Accessed September 24, 2024. https://en.wikipedia.org/wiki/Law_of_attraction_(New_Thought).

Wikipedia. "*The Secret* (Byrne Book)." Accessed September 24, 2024. https://en.wikipedia.org/wiki/The_Secret_(Byrne_book).

Wikipedia. "The Simple Way." Accessed September 24, 2024. https://en.wikipedia.org/wiki/The_Simple_Way.

Yankowski, Mike. *Under the Overpass* (Multnomah Books, 2005), pp. 142–44.

Yoffe, Emily. "I've Got the Secret: What Happened When I Followed the Best-Selling Book's Advice for Two Months."

Slate, May 7, 2007. Accessed September 24, 2024. https://slate
.com/human-interest/2007/05/what-happened-when-i
-followed-the-secrets-advice-for-two-months.html.

CHAPTER EIGHT

The Babylon Bee. "Biden Condemns Jesus for Rising Again on Trans Day of Visibility." March 30, 2024. https://babylonbee.com/news/biden-condemns-jesus-for-rising-again-on-trans-day-of-visibility.

The Babylon Bee. Profile on X (formerly known as Twitter). https://twitter.com/TheBabylonBee.

Bach, Parker J. "Can the Right Make Good Satire Without Collapsing Due to Fake News?" *Slate*, June 22, 2021. https://slate.com/news-and-politics/2021/06/babylon-bee-satire-from-right.html.

Challies, Tim. "The Bestsellers: *Blue Like Jazz*." The Bestsellers (blog series), April 27, 2014. https://www.challies.com/bestsellers/the-bestsellers-blue-like-jazz/.

Cunningham, Vinson, Naomi Fry, and Alexandra Schwartz, hosts. "What Is the Comic For?" *Critics at Large* (podcast), January 25, 2024. https://www.newyorker.com/podcast/critics-at-large/what-is-the-comic-for.

Dickson, Ej. "What Is the Babylon Bee? Trump Retweeted the Satirical Website." *Rolling Stone*, October 16, 2020. https://www.rollingstone.com/culture/culture-news/babylon-bee-satire-news-trump-tweet-1076701/.

The Economist. "No, American Schools Are Not Encouraging Pupils to Identify as Cats." October 20, 2022. https://www.economist.com/united-states/2022/10/20/no-american-schools-are-not-encouraging-pupils-to-identify-as-cats.

Ford, Adam. "Welcome to Not the Bee, A Brand New Site from the Creators of The Babylon Bee and Disrn." Not the

Bee, August 31, 2020. https://notthebee.com/article/welcome-to-not-the-bee.

Fox, Jesse David. *Comedy Book: How Comedy Conquered Culture—and the Magic That Makes it Work* (Farrar, Strauss and Giroux, 2023), p. 205.

Fox, Jesse David, host. "Joe Rogan Is Just the Start of It." *Good One* (podcast), May 15, 2022. https://www.vulture.com/article/conservative-comedy-matt-sienkiewicz-nick-marx-good-one-podcast.html.

Green, Adam. "Standup for the Lord." *The New Yorker*, August 1, 2004. https://www.newyorker.com/magazine/2004/08/09/standup-for-the-lord.

Hertenstein, Mike, and Jon Trott. *Selling Satan: The Tragic History of Mike Warnke* (Cornerstone, 1993).

Huckabee (TV show). "How Chonda Pierce Shuts Up Millennials." Trinity Broadcasting Network, airdate unknown. YouTube video posted February 1, 2020. https://www.youtube.com/watch?v=Ei9RkAmWLik.

Jones, Timothy W. "Calling Drag Queens 'Groomers' and 'Pedophiles' Is the Latest in a Long History of Weaponizing Those Terms Against the LGBTIQA Community." *The Conversation*, May 16, 2023. https://theconversation.com/calling-drag-queens-groomers-and-pedophiles-is-the-latest-in-a-long-history-of-weaponising-those-terms-against-the-lgbtiqa-community-205648.

Kois, Dan. "I Watched All of the Daily Wire's New Children's Shows So You Don't Have To." *Slate*, October 24, 2024. https://slate.com/culture/2023/10/daily-wire-bentkey-disney-snow-white-bluey-chip-chilla.html.

Lorenz, Taylor. "How Libs of TikTok Became a Powerful Presence in Oklahoma Schools." *The Washington Post*, February 24, 2024. https://www.washingtonpost.com/technology/2024/02/24/libs-tiktok-oklahoma-nonbinary-teen-death/.

Lorenz, Taylor. "Meet the Woman Behind Libs of TikTok, Secretly Fueling the Right's Outrage Machine." *The Washington Post*, April 19, 2022. https://www.washingtonpost.com/technology/2022/04/19/libs-of-tiktok-right-wing-media/.

Mandler, C. "What Happened to Nex Benedict?" NPR, March 22, 2024. https://www.npr.org/2024/03/15/1238780699/nex-benedict-nonbinary-oklahoma-death-bullying.

Marshall, Sarah, host. "Summer Book Club: 'The Satan Seller' (The Debunking!)." *You're Wrong About* (podcast), August 9, 2021. https://www.buzzsprout.com/1112270/8994639-summer-book-club-the-satan-seller-the-debunking.

Miller, Donald. *Blue Like Jazz: Non-Religious Thoughts on Christian Spirituality* (Thomas Nelson, 2003).

Miller, Donald. *Hero on a Mission: A Path to a Meaningful Life* (HarperCollins Leadership, 2022).

Miller, Donald. *Searching for God Knows What* (Thomas Nelson, 2004).

O'Connor, Roisin. "*Joker* Director Todd Phillips Says 'Woke Culture' Has Ruined Comedy." *The Independent*, October 2, 2019. https://www.independent.co.uk/arts-entertainment/films/news/joker-film-joaquin-phoenix-todd-phillips-woke-culture-comedy-a9129166.html.

Pierce, Chonda. *Be Afraid . . . Be Very Afraid*. Comedy special. Integrity Media, 2002. https://www.youtube.com/watch?v=gwBinJRRjhU.

Roose, Kevin. "How The Babylon Bee, a Right-Wing Satire Site, Capitalizes on Confusion." *The New York Times*, October 16, 2020. https://www.nytimes.com/2020/10/16/technology/babylon-bee.html.

Ross, Tamie. "Laughs Stopped for Christian Comic Mike Warnke Offers Fans New Outlook After Ministry's Crash." *The Oklahoman*, September 30, 2000. https://www.oklahoman.com/story/news/2000/09/30/laughs-stopped-for-christian

-comic-mike-warnke-offers-fans-new-outlook-after-ministrys-crash/62178378007/.

Schermele, Zachary, Dale Denwalt and Kayla Jimenez. "Nex Benedict's School District Failed to Protect Students, Investigation Finds." *USA Today*, November 13, 2024. https://www.usatoday.com/story/news/education/2024/11/13/nex-benedict-discrimination-investigation/76263888007/

Schmitt, Brad. "Comic Chonda Pierce Watched Her Husband Drink Himself to Death." *The Tennessean*, March 28, 2016. https://www.tennessean.com/story/life/2016/03/28/comic-chonda-pierce-watched-husband-drink-himself-death/81855846/.

Simons, Seth. "The Comedy Industry Has a Big Alt-Right Problem." *The New Republic*, February 9, 2021. https://newrepublic.com/article/161200/alt-right-comedy-gavin-mcinnes-problem.

StoryBrand. Accessed November 29, 2024. https://storybrand.com/.

Stine, Brad. *Brad Stine: Put a Helmet On!* Comedy stand-up film. Right Minded Productions, 2004.

Stine, Brad. "Brad Stine: Put a Helmet On (FULL SPECIAL)." YouTube video posted August 21, 2023. See the comment posted by @lhkraut. https://www.youtube.com/watch?v=yki-gNzyotE&lc=UgyrbY5b2LydfEnz5_l4AaABAg.

Stine, Brad. "Dear People Who Can't Take a JOKE!" *Brad Stine Has Issues* (podcast show). YouTube video posted December 15, 2020. https://www.youtube.com/watch?v=gldNIKumwYo&t=14s.

Thorkelson, Erika. "The Comedy Culture War." *The Walrus*, June 18, 2020. https://thewalrus.ca/the-comedy-culture-war/.

Trinity Broadcasting Network. "About." Accessed September 27, 2024. https://www.tbn.org/about.

Warnke, Mike, David Balsiger, and Les Jones. *The Satan Seller* (Logos International, 1972).

Warnke, Mike. *Alive!* Comedy album. Myrrh, 1975.
Warnke, Mike. "Many Hats." Comedy bit from his special, *Do You Hear Me?* Zoe Corporation, 1989. https://www.youtube.com/watch?v=tZPBAp3c_xc&t=14s.
Warnke, Mike. *Stuff Happens.* Comedy album. Dayspring, 1985.

CHAPTER NINE

Acuff, Jon. "#64: Fearing the Rapture Would Come Before You Lost Your Virginity." *Stuff Christians Like* (blog), March 5, 2008. https://web.archive.org/web/20120104230112/http://www.jonacuff.com/stuffchristianslike/2008/03/64-fearing-the-rapture-would-come-before-you-lost-your-virginity/.
Amram, Robert, and Rolf Forsberg, dir. *The Late Great Planet Earth.* Trinity Home Entertainment, 1979. DVD.
Beal, Timothy. "The Rise of Rapture Horror Culture." *Humanities: The Magazine of the National Endowment for the Humanities* 43, no. 4 (Fall 2022). https://www.neh.gov/article/rise-rapture-horror-culture.
Boyer, Paul. "America's Doom Industry." Interview with *Frontline.* Accessed September 24, 2024. https://www.pbs.org/wgbh/pages/frontline/shows/apocalypse/explanation/doomindustry.html.
Gabbatt, Adam. "'This War Is Prophetically Significant': Why US Evangelical Christians Support Israel." *The Guardian,* October 30, 2023. https://www.theguardian.com/world/2023/oct/30/us-evangelical-christians-israel-hamas-war.
Gilgoff, Dan. *The Jesus Machine: How James Dobson, Focus on the Family, and Evangelical America Are Winning the Culture War* (St. Martin's Press, 2007).
Kobes Du Mez, Kristin. *Jesus and John Wayne: How White Evangelicals Corrupted a Faith and Fractured a Nation* (Liveright, 2020), p. 89.

LaHaye, Tim, and Jerry B. Jenkins. *Left Behind* (Tyndale House, 1995).

LaHaye, Tim, and Jerry B. Jenkins. *The Vanishing (Left Behind: The Kids #1)* (Tyndale House Publishers, 1998).

Levin, Talia. *Wild Faith: How the Christian Right is Taking Over America* (Legacy Lit, 2024).

Lewis, C.S. *The Last Battle* (The Bodley Head, 1956). Scholastic Inc. edition, 1995.

Lidman, Melanie. "Evangelical Christians Are Fierce Israel Supporters. Now They Are Visiting as War-Time Volunteers." Associated Press, March 13, 2024. https://apnews.com/article/evangelical-christians-israel-volunteer-trips-462329e04459191fd6ae061e722cae30.

McDonald, Marci. *The Armageddon Factor: The Rise of Christian Nationalism in Canada* (Random House 2010).

Moslener, Sara. *Virgin Nation: Sexual Purity and American Adolescence* (Oxford University Press, 2015).

Neufeld, Josiah. *The Temple at the End of the Universe: A Search for Spirituality in the Anthropocene* (House of Anansi, 2023), p. 38.

NIV Bible. 1 Thessalonians 4:17. BibleGateway.com.

NIV Bible. 1 Corinthians 13:12. BibleGateway.com.

NIV Bible. Matthew 24:26. BibleGateway.com.

NIV Bible. Revelation 13:11. BibleGateway.com.

Norman, Larry. "I Wish We'd All Been Ready." *Upon This Rock*, LP side 2, track 4. Capitol, 1969.

Reddit. "Did Anyone Else Experience Panic Attacks Over the Rapture?" Thread posted by r/exchristian, 2019. https://www.reddit.com/r/exchristian/comments/dqpwin/did_anyone_else_experience_panic_attacks_over_the/.

Reddit. "I'm Scared the Rapture Will Happen Before I Have a Chance to Live Life." Thread posted by Reasonable_Can6771, March 2024. https://www.reddit.com/r/Christianity/comments/1bklho4/im_scared_the_rapture_will_happen_before_i_have_a/.

Santin, Aldo. "Pray Judgment Day Predictor's Calculations Are Wrong Again." *Winnipeg Free Press*, May 11, 2011. https://www.winnipegfreepress.com/breakingnews/2011/05/11/pray-judgment-day-predictors-calculations-are-wrong-again.

Wikipedia. "Book of Revelation." Accessed September 24, 2024. https://en.wikipedia.org/wiki/Book_of_Revelation.

Wikipedia. "Christian Zionism." Accessed September 24, 2024. https://en.wikipedia.org/wiki/Christian_Zionism.

Wikipedia. "Dispensationalism." Accessed September 24, 2024. https://en.wikipedia.org/wiki/Dispensationalism.

Wikipedia. "Evangelical Climate Initiative." Accessed September 24, 2024. https://en.wikipedia.org/wiki/Evangelical_Climate_Initiative.

Wikipedia. "Gathering of Israel." Accessed September 24, 2024. https://en.wikipedia.org/wiki/Gathering_of_Israel.

Wikipedia. "Harold Camping." Accessed September 24, 2024. https://en.wikipedia.org/wiki/Harold_Camping.

Wikipedia. "Rapture." Accessed September 24, 2024. https://en.wikipedia.org/wiki/Rapture.

Wikipedia. "Tim LaHaye." Accessed September 24, 2024. https://en.wikipedia.org/wiki/Tim_LaHaye.

ACKNOWLEDGEMENTS

It's been thrilling to be able to write the book that feels like it's been working its way out of my brain for almost my whole life. I'm so grateful for many, many people who supported the process of creating this book!

Thank you, first and foremost, to Jen Sookfong Lee, the most spectacular editor, for seeing a spark in this idea and thoughtfully guiding me to the best version of what I was trying to say. My thanks, too, to the entire ECW Press team.

I gratefully acknowledge the support of the Ontario Arts Council, Toronto Arts Council, and Access Copyright Foundation. The grant funding I received allowed me the time I needed to make this book a reality.

I want to extend my deepest thanks to the friends and acquaintances who generously shared their experiences and thoughts on growing up in purity culture for the chapter "Pledges and Purity Rings": Alanna Schwartz, Carla Ginter Dyck, Carly, Courtney K, Dorien, Hannah Foulger, Josh Bergmann, KR Byggdin, Marie Raynard, Rachel Twigg, Rebecca, Sara M, Tim Cruickshank, and those who wished to remain anonymous. Shout-out to Dorien for letting me crash at her house and making me an excellent latte while we talked.

I'm also incredibly grateful for my wonderful writing communities, the people who read scraps of these essays and even reassured me by laughing at the funny parts. Firefly Creative Writing and the Wonderpens: Ailsa, Chris, Courtney, Jess, Mikaela, Myriad, Rebecca, and Saroo, thank you for the most nourishing encouragement. (Next year in writing-castle!) Thank you times one million to my amazing MFA cohort at the University of Guelph and to Kyo Maclear, in whose class I wrote the first words of what would become this book. Yabba-dabba-loo-yah, I am so grateful for all of you.

Special thanks to Michael Melgaard for encouraging and reading through multiple drafts of a book proposal, Hannah Foulger for always supplying good memes (and the vintage BarlowGirl CD), Courtney for the weekly coworking sessions that truly, truly kept me going, and Alanna and Lee for being up for watching terrible movies and making research fun. Amanda Proctor, my writing kindred spirit, thank you for cheering me on the whole way. True friendship is being able to invite yourself over to watch a 1970s conspiracy theory doc on DVD.

I also want to thank my wonderful parents, who are endlessly encouraging and supportive and both extremely adept at finding typos. The safety and love you provided and the critical thinking skills you taught me are why I am the person (and writer) I am. I'm so lucky to have you, Mom and Dad!

I'm also the most lucky to have found the love of my life, Jon, so early . . . I'm so glad to have grown together with you for the last decade. Thank you for the long walks and long talks that helped clarify this book for me. You're my soulmate, even though we don't believe in those.

JOELLE KIDD is a writer, award-winning journalist, and editor who lives in a book-filled basement apartment in Tkaronto/Toronto. Her work has appeared in outlets such as *The Walrus, This Magazine, Literary Hub, The Rumpus,* and *Xtra Magazine.* She holds an MFA in creative writing from the University of Guelph. *Jesusland* is her first book.

Entertainment. Writing. Culture. ─────────

ECW is a proudly independent, Canadian-owned book publisher. We know great writing can improve people's lives, and we're passionate about sharing original, exciting, and insightful writing across genres.

──────────────────── **Thanks for reading along!**

We want our books not just to sustain our imaginations, but to help construct a healthier, more just world, and so we've become a certified B Corporation, meaning we meet a high standard of social and environmental responsibility — and we're going to keep aiming higher. We believe books can drive change, but the way we make them can too.

Certified Corporation

Being a B Corp means that the act of publishing this book should be a force for good — for the planet, for our communities, and for the people that worked to make this book. For example, everyone who worked on this book was paid at least a living wage. You can learn more at the Ontario Living Wage Network.

This book is also available as a Global Certified Accessible™ (GCA) ebook. ECW Press's ebooks are screen reader friendly and are built to meet the needs of those who are unable to read standard print due to blindness, low vision, dyslexia, or a physical disability.

This book is printed on FSC®-certified paper. It contains recycled materials, and other controlled sources, is processed chlorine free, and is manufactured using biogas energy.

FSC
www.fsc.org
MIX
Paper | Supporting responsible forestry
FSC® C103567

ECW's office is situated on land that was the traditional territory of many nations, including the Wendat, the Anishinaabeg, Haudenosaunee, Chippewa, Métis, and current treaty holders the Mississaugas of the Credit. In the 1880s, the land was developed as part of a growing community around St. Matthew's Anglican and other churches. Starting in the 1950s, our neighbourhood was transformed by immigrants fleeing the Vietnam War and Chinese Canadians dispossessed by the building of Nathan Phillips Square and the subsequent rise in real estate value in other Chinatowns. We are grateful to those who cared for the land before us and are proud to be working amidst this mix of cultures.

ecwpress.com